Truly thy friend
John G. Whittier.

Truly thy friend
John G. Whittier.

POEMS

BY

JOHN G. WHITTIER

ILLUSTRATED BY H. BILLINGS.

———————— "WAS IT RIGHT,
While my unnumbered brethren toiled and bled,
That I should dream away th' entrusted hours
On rose leaf beds, pampering the coward heart
With feelings all too delicate for use?"

S. T. COLERIDGE.

BOSTON:
BENJAMIN B. MUSSEY & CO.
1850.

STEREOTYPED BY S. N. DICKINSON, BOSTON

PROEM.

I LOVE the old melodious lays
Which softly melt the ages through,
The songs of Spenser's golden days,
Arcadian Sidney's silvery phrase,
Sprinkling our noon of time with freshest morning dew.

Yet, vainly in my quiet hours
To breathe their marvellous notes I try;
I feel them, as the leaves and flowers
In silence feel the dewy showers,
And drink with glad still lips the blessing of the sky.

The rigor of a frozen clime,
The harshness of an untaught ear,
The jarring words of one whose rhyme
Beat often Labor's hurried time,
Or Duty's rugged march through storm and strife, are here.

Of mystic beauty, dreamy grace,
No rounded art the lack supplies;
Unskilled the subtle lines to trace
Or softer shades of Nature's face,
I view her common forms with unanointed eyes.

Nor mine the seer-like power to show
The secrets of the heart and mind;
To drop the plummet-line below
Our common world of joy and woe,
A more intense despair or brighter hope to find.

Yet here at least an earnest sense
Of human right and weal is shown;
A hate of tyranny intense,
And hearty in its vehemence,
As if my brother's pain and sorrow were my own.

Oh Freedom! if to me belong
Nor mighty Milton's gift divine,
Nor Marvel's wit and graceful song,
Still with a love as deep and strong
As theirs, I lay, like them, my best gifts on thy shrine!

AMESBURY, 11th mo., 1847.

CONTENTS.

POEMS.

LEGENDARY.

VOICES OF FREEDOM.

MISCELLANEOUS.

MEMORIALS.

APPENDIX.

ILLUSTRATIONS,

DESIGNED BY H. BILLINGS.

PORTRAIT OF THE AUTHOR,

FROM A PAINTING BY A. G. HOIT.

ENGRAVED BY A. C. WARREN.

Title Page.

THE NORSEMEN,

ENGRAVED BY J. ANDREWS AND J. DUTHIE.

"Onward they glide—and now I view
Their iron-armed and stalwart crew."

Page 80.

BRIDAL OF PENNACOOK,

ENGRAVED BY A. C. WARREN.

"On that strong turbid water, a small boat
Guided by one weak hand was seen to float."

Page 29.

THE PENITENT,

ENGRAVED BY D. L. GLOVER.

"Two forms are now in that chapel dim,
The Jesuit, silent and sad and pale,
Anxiously heeding some fearful tale,
Which a stranger is telling him."

Mogg Megone, Page 55.

MOGG MEGONE,

ENGRAVED BY J. ANDREWS AND J. DUTHIE.

"I only saw that victim's smile—
The still, green places where we met—"

Page 62.

VOICES OF FREEDOM,

ENGRAVED BY A. C. WARREN.

" The blast which Freedom's Angel blew
O'er her green Islands, echoes through
Each valley of our forest land."

Page 121.

ANGELS OF BUENA VISTA,

ENGRAVED BY J. ANDREWS AND J. DUTHIE.

"But, as tenderly before him, the lorn Ximena knelt,
She saw the Northern eagle shining on his pistol belt."

Page 310.

BARCLAY OF URY,

ENGRAVED BY D. L. GLOVER.

"Nay, I do not need thy sword,
Comrade mine," said Ury's lord;
"Put it up I pray thee."

Page 314.

SLAVES OF MARTINIQUE,

ENGRAVED BY D. L. GLOVER.

From a Daguerreotype of a French Print.

"Beams of noon like burning lances, through the tree-tops flash and glisten,
As she stands before her lover, with raised face to look and listen."

Page 385.

THE STAR OF BETHLEHEM.

ENGRAVED BY A. C. WARREN.

Each Moslem, Tomb, and Cypress old,
Looked holy through the sunset air.

Page 239.

THE BRIDAL OF PENNACOOK.*

We had been wandering for many days
Through the rough northern country. We had seen
The sunset, with its bars of purple cloud,
Like a new heaven, shine upward from the lake
Of Winnepiseogee; and had felt
The sunrise breezes, midst the leafy isles
Which stoop their summer beauty to the lips
Of the bright waters. We had checked our steeds,
Silent with wonder, where the mountain wall
Is piled to heaven; and, through the narrow rift
Of the vast rocks, against whose rugged feet
Beats the mad torrent with perpetual roar,
Where noonday is as twilight, and the wind
Comes burdened with the everlasting moan
Of forests and of far-off water-falls,
We had looked upward where the summer sky,
Tasseled with clouds light-woven by the sun,

* Winnepurkit, otherwise called George, Sachem of Saugus, married a daughter of Passaconaway, the great Pennacook chieftain, in 1662. The wedding took place at Pennacook (now Concord, N. H.), and the ceremonies closed with a great feast. According to the usages of the chiefs, Passaconaway ordered a select number of his men to accompany the newly-married couple to the dwelling of the husband, where in turn there was another great feast. Some time after, the wife of Winnepurkit expressing a desire to visit her father's house, was permitted to go accompanied by a brave escort of her husband's chief men. But when she wished to return, her father sent a messenger to Saugus, informing her husband, and asking him to come and take her away. He returned for answer that he had escorted his wife to her father's house in a style that became a chief, and that now if she wished to return, her father must send her back in the same way. This Passaconaway refused to do, and it is said that here terminated the connection of his daughter with the Saugus chief. — *Vide Morton's New Canaan.*

Sprung its blue arch above the abutting crags
O'er-roofing the vast portal of the land
Beyond the wall of mountains. We had passed
The high source of the Saco; and, bewildered
In the dwarf spruce-belts of the Crystal Hills
Had heard above us, like a voice in the cloud,
The horn of Fabyan sounding; and atop
Of old Agioochook had seen the mountains
Piled to the northward, shagged with wood, and thick
As meadow mole hills — the far sea of Casco,
A white gleam on the horizon of the east;
Fair lakes, embosomed in the woods and hills;
Moosehillock's mountain range, and Kearsarge
Lifting his Titan forehead to the sun!

And we had rested underneath the oaks
Shadowing the bank, whose grassy spires are shaken
By the perpetual beating of the falls
Of the wild Ammonoosuc. We had tracked
The winding Pemigewasset, overhung
By beechen shadows, whitening down its rocks,
Or lazily gliding through its intervals,
From waving rye-fields sending up the gleam
Of sunlit waters. We had seen the moon
Rising behind Umbagog's eastern pines
Like a great Indian camp-fire; and its beams
At midnight spanning with a bridge of silver
The Merrimac by Uncanoonuc's falls.

There were five souls of us whom travel's chance
Had thrown together in these wild north hills: —
A city lawyer, for a month escaping
From his dull office, where the weary eye
Saw only hot brick walls and close thronged streets —
Briefless as yet, but with an eye to see
Life's sunniest side, and with a heart to take
Its chances all as God-sends; and his brother,
Pale from long pulpit studies, yet retaining
The warmth and freshness of a genial heart,

Whose mirror of the beautiful and true,
In Man and Nature, was as yet undimmed
By dust of theologic strife, or breath
Of sect, or cobwebs of scholastic lore;
Like a clear crystal calm of water, taking
The hue and image of o'erleaning flowers,
Sweet human faces, white clouds of the noon,
Slant starlight glimpses through the dewy leaves,
And tenderest moonrise. 'Twas, in truth, a study,
To mark his spirit, alternating between
A decent and professional gravity
And an irreverent mirthfulness, which often
Laughed in the face of his divinity,
Plucked off the sacred ephod, quite unshrined
The oracle, and for the pattern priest
Left us the man. A shrewd, sagacious merchant,
To whom the soiled sheet found in Crawford's inn,
Giving the latest news of city stocks
And sales of cotton had a deeper meaning
Than the great presence of the awful mountains
Glorified by the sunset; — and his daughter,
A delicate flower on whom had blown too long
Those evil winds, which, sweeping from the ice
And winnowing the fogs of Labrador,
Shed their cold blight round Massachusetts' bay,
With the same breath which stirs Spring's opening leaves
And lifts her half-formed flower-bell on its stem,
Poisoning our sea-side atmosphere.

It chanced
That as we turned upon our homeward way,
A drear north-eastern storm came howling up
The valley of the Saco; and that girl
Who had stood with us upon Mount Washington,
Her brown locks ruffled by the wind which whirled
In gusts around its sharp cold pinnacle,
Who had joined our gay trout-fishing in the streams
Which lave that giant's feet; whose laugh was heard
Like a bird's carol on the sunrise breeze

Which swelled our sail amidst the lake's green islands,
Shrank from its harsh, chill breath, and visibly drooped
Like a flower in the frost. So, in that quiet inn
Which looks from Conway on the mountains piled
Heavily against the horizon of the north,
Like summer thunder-clouds, we made our home:
And while the mist hung over dripping hills,
And the cold wind-driven rain-drops, all day long
Beat their sad music upon roof and pane,
We strove to cheer our gentle invalid.

The lawyer in the pauses of the storm
Went angling down the Saco, and, returning,
Recounted his adventures and mishaps;
Gave us the history of his scaly clients,
Mingling with ludicrous yet apt citations
Of barbarous law Latin, passages
From Izaak Walton's Angler, sweet and fresh
As the flower-skirted streams of Staffordshire
Where, under aged trees, the south-west wind
Of soft June mornings fanned the thin, white hair
Of the sage fisher. And, if truth be told,
Our youthful candidate forsook his sermons,
His commentaries, articles and creeds
For the fair page of human loveliness —
The missal of young hearts, whose sacred text
Is music, its illumining sweet smiles.
He sang the songs she loved; and in his low,
Deep earnest voice, recited many a page
Of poetry — the holiest, tenderest lines
Of the sad bard of Olney — the sweet songs,
Simple and beautiful as Truth and Nature,
Of him whose whitened locks on Rydal Mount
Are lifted yet by morning breezes blowing
From the green hills, immortal in his lays.
And for myself, obedient to her wish,
I searched our landlord's proffered library:
A well-thumbed Bunyan, with its nice wood pictures
Of scaly fiends and angels not unlike them —

Watts' unmelodious psalms — Astrology's
Last home, a musty file of Almanacs,
And an old chronicle of border wars
And Indian history. And, as I read
A story of the marriage of the Chief
Of Saugus to the dusky Weetamoo,
Daughter of Passaconaway, who dwelt
In the old time upon Merrimack,
Our fair one, in the playful exercise
Of her prerogative — the right divine
Of youth and beauty, — bade us versify
The legend, and with ready pencil sketched
Its plan and outlines, laughingly assigning
To each his part, and barring our excuses
With absolute will. So, like the cavaliers
Whose voices still are heard in the Romance
Of silver-tongued Boccacio, on the banks
Of Arno, with soft tales of love beguiling
The ear of languid beauty, plague-exiled
From stately Florence, we rehearsed our rhymes
To their fair auditor, and shared by turns
Her kind approval and her playful censure.

It may be that these fragments owe alone
To the fair setting of their circumstances —
The associations of time, scene and audience —
Their place amid the pictures which fill up
The chambers of my memory. Yet I trust
That some, who sigh, while wandering in thought,
Pilgrims of Romance o'er the olden world,
That our broad land — our sea-like lakes, and mountains
Piled to the clouds, — our rivers overhung
By forests which have known no other change
For ages, than the budding and the fall
Of leaves — our valleys lovelier than those
Which the old poets sang of — should but figure
On the apocryphal chart of speculation
As pastures, wood-lots, mill-sites, with the privileges,
Rights and appurtenances, which make up

A Yankee Paradise — unsung, unknown,
To beautiful tradition; even their names,
Whose melody yet lingers like the last
Vibration of the red man's requiem,
Exchanged for syllables significant
Of cotton-mill and rail-car, — will look kindly
Upon this effort to call up the ghost
Of our dim Past, and listen with pleased ear
To the responses of the questioned Shade:

I. — THE MERRIMACK.

Oh, child of that white-crested mountain whose springs
Gush forth in the shade of the cliff-eagle's wings,
Down whose slopes to the lowlands thy wild waters shine,
Leaping grey walls of rock, flashing through the dwarf pine.

From that cloud-curtained cradle so cold and so lone,
From the arms of that wintry-locked mother of stone,
By hills hung with forests, through vales wide and free,
Thy mountain-born brightness glanced down to the sea!

No bridge arched thy waters save that where the trees
Stretched their long arms above thee and kissed in the breeze:
No sound save the lapse of the waves on thy shores,
The plunging of otters, the light dip of oars.

Green-tufted, oak-shaded, by Amoskeag's fall
Thy twin Uncanoonucs rose stately and tall,
Thy Nashua meadows lay green and unshorn,
And the hills of Pentucket were tasseled with corn.

But thy Pennacook valley was fairer than these,
And greener its grasses and taller its trees,
Ere the sound of an axe in the forest had rung,
Or the mower his scythe in the meadows had swung.

In their sheltered repose looking out from the wood
The bark-builded wigwams of Pennacook stood,
There glided the corn-dance — the Council fire shone,
And against the red war-post the hatchet was thrown.

There the old smoked in silence their pipes, and the young
To the pike and the white perch their baited lines flung;
There the boy shaped his arrows, and there the shy maid
Wove her many-hued baskets and bright wampum braid.

Oh, Stream of the Mountains! if answer of thine
Could rise from thy waters to question of mine,
Methinks through the din of thy thronged banks a moan
Of sorrow would swell for the days which have gone.

Not for thee the dull jar of the loom and the wheel,
The gliding of shuttles, the ringing of steel;
But that old voice of waters, of bird and of breeze,
The dip of the wild-fowl, the rustling of trees!

II. — THE BASHABA. *

Lift we the twilight curtains of the Past,
And turning from familiar sight and sound
Sadly and full of reverence let us cast
A glance upon Tradition's shadowy ground,
Led by the few pale lights, which glimmering round,
That dim, strange land of Eld, seem dying fast;
And that which history gives not to the eye,
The faded coloring of Time's tapestry,
Let Fancy, with her dream-dipped brush supply.

Roof of bark and walls of pine,
Through whose chinks the sunbeams shine,

* This was the name which the Indians of New England gave to two or three of their principal chiefs, to whom all their inferior sagamores acknowledged allegiance. Passaconaway seems to have been one of these chiefs. His residence was at Pennacook.—*Mass. Hist. Coll.*, vol. iii., pp. 21, 22. "He was regarded," says Hubbard, "as a great sorcerer, and his fame was widely spread. It was said of him that he could cause a green leaf to grow in winter, trees to dance, water to burn, &c. He was, undoubtedly, one of those shrewd and powerful men whose achievements are always regarded by a barbarous people as the result of supernatural aid. The Indians gave to such the names of Powahs or Panisees."

"The Panisees are men of great courage and wisdom, and to these the Devill appeareth more familiarly than to others."—*Winslow's Relation.*

Tracing many a golden line
  On the ample floor within;
Where upon that earth-floor stark,
Lay the gaudy mats of bark,
With the bear's hide, rough and dark,
  And the red-deer's skin.

Window-tracery, small and slight,
Woven of the willow white,
Lent a dimly-chequered light,
  And the night-stars glimmered down,
Where the lodge-fire's heavy smoke,
Slowly through an opening broke,
In the low roof, ribbed with oak,
  Sheathed with hemlock brown.

Gloomed behind the changeless shade,
By the solemn pine-wood made;
Through the rugged palisade,
  In the open fore-ground planted,
Glimpses came of rowers rowing,
Stir of leaves and wild flowers blowing,
Steel-like gleams of water flowing,
  In the sun-light slanted.

Here the mighty Bashaba,
Held his long-unquestioned sway,
From the White Hills, far away,
  To the great sea's sounding shore;
Chief of chiefs, his regal word
All the river Sachems heard,
At his call the war-dance stirred,
  Or was still once more.

There his spoils of chase and war,
Jaw of wolf and black bear's paw,
Panther's skin and eagle's claw,
  Lay beside his axe and bow;
And, adown the roof-pole hung,
Loosely on a snake-skin strung,

In the smoke his scalp-locks swung
  Grimly to and fro.

Nightly down the river going,
Swifter was the hunter's rowing,
When he saw that lodge-fire glowing
  O'er the waters still and red;
And the squaw's dark eye burned brighter,
And she drew her blanket tighter,
As, with quicker step and lighter,
  From that door she fled.

For that chief had magic skill,
And a Panisee's dark will,
Over powers of good and ill,
  Powers which bless and powers which ban —
Wizard lord of Pennacook,
Chiefs upon their war-path shook,
When they met the steady look
  Of that wise dark man.

Tales of him the grey squaw told,
When the winter night-wind cold
Pierced her blanket's thickest fold,
  And the fire burned low and small,
Till the very child a-bed,
Drew its bear-skin over head,
Shrinking from the pale lights shed
  On the trembling wall.

All the subtle spirits hiding
Under earth or wave, abiding
In the caverned rock, or riding
  Misty clouds or morning breeze;
Every dark intelligence,
Secret soul, and influence
Of all things which outward sense
  Feels, or hears or sees, —

These the wizard's skill confessed,
At his bidding banned or blessed,

Stormful woke or lulled to rest
  Wind and cloud, and fire and flood;
Burned for him the drifted snow,
Bade through ice fresh lillies blow,
And the leaves of summer grow
  Over winter's wood!

Not untrue that tale of old!
Now, as then, the wise and bold
All the powers of Nature hold
  Subject to their kingly will;
From the wondering crowds ashore,
Treading life's wild waters o'er,
As upon a marble floor,
  Moves the strong man still

Still, to such, life's elements
With their sterner laws dispense,
And the chain of consequence
  Broken in their pathway lies;
Time and change their vassals making,
Flowers from icy pillows waking,
Tresses of the sunrise shaking
  Over midnight skies.

Still, to earnest souls, the sun
Rests on towered Gibeon,
And the moon of Ajalon
  Lights the battle-grounds of life;
To his aid the strong reverses
Hidden powers and giant forces,
And the high stars in their courses
  Mingle in his strife!

III. — THE DAUGHTER.

THE soot-black brows of men — the yell
  Of women thronging round the bed —
The tinkling charm of ring and shell —
  The Powah whispering o'er the dead! —

All these the Sachem's home had known,
When, on her journey long and wild
To the dim World of Souls, alone,
In her young beauty passed the mother of his child.

Three bow-shots from the Sachem's dwelling
They laid her in the walnut shade,
Where a green hillock gently swelling
Her fitting mound of burial made.
There trailed the vine in Summer hours —
The tree-perched squirrel dropped his shell —
On velvet moss and pale-hued flowers,
Woven with leaf and spray, the softened sunshine fell!

The Indian's heart is hard and cold —
It closes darkly o'er its care,
And, formed in Nature's sternest mould,
Is slow to feel, and strong to bear.
The war-paint on the Sachem's face,
Unwet with tears, shone fierce and red,
And, still in battle or in chase,
Dry leaf and snow-rime crisped beneath his foremost tread.

Yet, when her name was heard no more,
And when the robe her mother gave,
And small, light mocasin she wore,
Had slowly wasted on her grave,
Unmarked of him the dark maids sped
Their sunset dance and moon-lit play;
No other shared his lonely bed,
No other fair young head upon his bosom lay.

A lone, stern man. Yet, as sometimes
The tempest-smitten tree receives
From one small root the sap which climbs
Its topmost spray and crowning leaves,
So from his child the Sachem drew
A life of Love and Hope, and felt
His cold and rugged nature through
The softness and the warmth of her young being melt.

A laugh which in the woodland rang
  Bemocking April's gladdest bird —
A light and graceful form which sprang
  To meet him when his step was heard —
Eyes by his lodge-fire flashing dark,
  Small fingers stringing bead and shell
Or weaving mats of bright-hued bark, —
With these the household-god* had graced his wigwam well.

Child of the forest! — strong and free,
  Slight-robed, with loosely flowing hair,
She swam the lake or climbed the tree,
  Or struck the flying bird in air.
O'er the heaped drifts of Winter's moon
  Her snow-shoes tracked the hunter's way;
And dazzling in the Summer noon
The blade of her light oar threw off its shower of spray!

Unknown to her the rigid rule,
  The dull restraint, the chiding frown,
The weary torture of the school,
  The taming of wild nature down.
Her only lore, the legends told
  Around the hunter's fire at night;
Stars rose and set, and seasons rolled,
Flowers bloomed and snow-flakes fell, unquestioned in her sight.

Unknown to her the subtle skill
  With which the artist-eye can trace
In rock and tree and lake and hill
  The outlines of divinest grace;
Unknown the fine soul's keen unrest
  Which sees, admires, yet yearns alway;
Too closely on her mother's breast
To note her smiles of love the child of Nature lay!

It is enough for such to be
  Of common, natural things a part,

* "The Indians," says Roger Williams, "have a god whom they call Wetuomanit, who presides over the household."

To feel with bird and stream and tree
  The pulses of the same great heart;
But we, from Nature long exiled
  In our cold homes of Art and Thought,
Grieve like the stranger-tended child,
Which seeks its mother's arms, and sees but feels them not.

The garden rose may richly bloom
  In cultured soil and genial air,
To cloud the light of Fashion's room
  Or droop in Beauty's midnight hair,
In lonelier grace, to sun and dew
  The sweet-briar on the hill-side shows
Its single leaf and fainter hue,
Untrained and wildly free, yet still a sister rose!

Thus o'er the heart of Weetamoo
  Their mingling shades of joy and ill
The instincts of her nature threw, —
  The savage was a woman still.
Midst outlines dim of maiden schemes,
  Heart-colored prophecies of life,
Rose on the ground of her young dreams
The light of a new home — the lover and the wife!

IV. — THE WEDDING.

Cool and dark fell the Autumn night,
But the Bashaba's wigwam glowed with light,
For down from its roof by green withes hung
Flaring and smoking the pine-knots swung.

And along the river great wood fires
Shot into the night their long red spires,
Showing behind the tall, dark wood
Flashing before on the sweeping flood.

In the changeful wind, with shimmer and shade,
Now high, now low, that fire-light played,
On tree-leaves wet with evening dews,
On gliding water and still canoes.

The trapper, that night on Turee's brook
And the weary fisher on Contoocook
Saw over the marshes and through the pine,
And down on the river the dance-lights shine.

For the Saugus Sachem had come to woo
The Bashaba's daughter Weetamoo,
And laid at her father's feet that night
His softest furs and wampum white.

From the Crystal Hills to the far South East
The river Sagamores came to the feast;
And chiefs whose homes the sea-winds shook,
Sat down on the mats of Pennacook.

They came from Sunapee's shore of rock,
From the snowy sources of Snooganock,
And from rough Coös whose thick woods shake
Their pine-cones in Umbagog lake.

From Ammonoosuck's mountain pass
Wild as his home came Chepewass;
And the Keenomps of the hills which throw
Their shade on the Smile of Manito.

With pipes of peace and bows unstrung,
Glowing with paint came old and young,
In wampum and furs and feathers arrayed
To the dance and feast the Bashaba made.

Bird of the air and beast of the field,
All which the woods and waters yield
On dishes of birch and hemlock piled
Garnished and graced that banquet wild.

Steaks of the brown bear fat and large
From the rocky slopes of the Kearsarge;
Delicate trout from Babboosuck brook,
And salmon spear'd in the Contoocook;

Squirrels which fed where nuts fell thick
In the gravelly bed of the Otternic,

And small wild hens in reed-snares caught
From the banks of Sondagardee brought;

Pike and perch from the Suncook taken,
Nuts from the trees of the Black Hills shaken,
Cranberries picked in the Squamscot bog,
And grapes from the vines of Piscataquog:

And, drawn from that great stone vase which stands
In the river scooped by a spirit's hands, *
Garnished with spoons of shell and horn,
Stood the birchen dishes of smoking corn.

Thus bird of the air and beast of the field,
All which the woods and the waters yield,
Furnished in that olden day
The bridal feast of the Bashaba.

And merrily when that feast was done
On the fire-lit green the dance begun,
With squaws' shrill stave, and deeper hum
Of old men beating the Indian drum.

Painted and plumed, with scalp locks flowing,
And red arms tossing and black eyes glowing,
Now in the light and now in the shade
Around the fires the dancers played.

The step was quicker, the song more shrill,
And the beat of the small drums louder still
Whenever within the circle drew
The Saugus Sachem and Weetamoo.

The moons of forty winters had shed
Their snow upon that chieftain's head,
And toil and care, and battle's chance
Had seamed his hard dark countenance.

* There are rocks in the River at the Falls of Amoskeag, in the cavities of which, tradition says the Indians formerly stored and concealed their corn.

A fawn beside the bison grim —
Why turns the bride's fond eye on him,
In whose cold look is naught beside
The triumph of a sullen pride?

Ask why the graceful grape entwines
The rough oak with her arm of vines;
And why the gray rock's rugged cheek
The soft lips of the mosses seek:

Why, with wise instinct, Nature seems
To harmonize her wide extremes,
Linking the stronger with the weak
The haughty with the soft and meek!

V. — THE NEW HOME.

A wild and broken landscape, spiked with firs,
  Roughening the bleak horizon's northern edge,
Steep, cavernous hill-side, where black hemlock spurs
  And sharp, grey splinters of the wind-swept ledge
Pierced the thin-glaz'd ice, or bristling rose,
Where the cold rim of the sky sunk down upon the snows.

And eastward cold, wide marshes stretched away,
  Dull, dreary flats without a bush or tree,
O'er-crossed by icy creeks, where twice a day
  Gurgled the waters of the moon-struck sea;
And faint with distance came the stifled roar,
The melancholy lapse of waves on that low shore.

No cheerful village with its mingling smokes,
  No laugh of children wrestling in the snow,
No camp-fire blazing through the hill-side oaks,
  No fishers kneeling on the ice below;
Yet midst all desolate things of sound and view,
Through the long winter moons smiled dark-eyed Weetamoo.

Her heart had found a home; and freshly all
  Its beautiful affections overgrew

Their rugged prop. As o'er some granite wall
  Soft vine leaves open to the moistening dew
And warm bright sun, the love of that young wife
Found on a hard cold breast the dew and warmth of life.

The steep bleak hills, the melancholy shore,
  The long dead level of the marsh between,
A coloring of unreal beauty wore
  Through the soft golden mist of young love seen,
For o'er those hills and from that dreary plain,
Nightly she welcomed home her hunter chief again.

No warmth of heart, no passionate burst of feeling
  Repaid her welcoming smile, and parting kiss,
No fond and playful dalliance half concealing,
  Under the guise of mirth, its tenderness ;
But, in their stead, the warrior's settled pride,
And vanity's pleased smile with homage satisfied.

Enough for Weetamoo, that she alone
  Sat on his mat and slumbered at his side ;
That he whose fame to her young ear had flown,
  Now looked upon her proudly as his bride ;
That he whose name the Mohawk trembling heard
Vouchsafed to her at times a kindly look or word.

For she had learned the maxims of her race,
  Which teach the woman to become a slave
And feel herself the pardonless disgrace
  Of love's fond weakness in the wise and brave —
The scandal and the shame which they incur,
Who give to woman all which man requires of her.

So passed the winter moons. The sun at last
  Broke link by link the frost chain of the rills,
And the warm breathings of the southwest passed
  Over the hoar rime of the Saugus hills,
The gray and desolate marsh grew green once more,
And the birch-tree's tremulous shade fell round the Sachem's door.

Then from far Pennacook swift runners came,
With gift and greeting for the Saugus chief;
Beseeching him in the great Sachem's name,
That, with the coming of the flower and leaf,
The song of birds, the warm breeze and the rain,
Young Weetamoo might greet her lonely sire again.

And Winnepurkit called his chiefs together,
And a grave council in his wigwam met,
Solemn and brief in words, considering whether
The rigid rules of forest etiquette
Permitted Weetamoo once more to look
Upon her father's face and green-banked Pennacook.

With interludes of pipe-smoke and strong water,
The forest sages pondered, and at length,
Concluded in a body to escort her
Up to her father's home of pride and strength,
Impressing thus on Pennacook a sense
Of Winnepurkit's power and regal consequence.

So through old woods which Aukeetamit's * hand,
A soft and many-shaded greenness lent,
Over high breezy hills, and meadow land
Yellow with flowers, the wild procession went,
Till rolling down its wooded banks between,
A broad, clear, mountain stream, the Merrimack was seen.

The hunter leaning on his bow undrawn —
The fisher lounging on the pebbled shores,
Squaws in the clearing dropping the seed-corn,
Young children peering through the wigwam doors,
Saw with delight, surrounded by her train
Of painted Saugus braves, their Weetamoo again.

VI. — AT PENNACOOK.

The hills are dearest which our childish feet
Have climbed the earliest; and the streams most sweet,

* The Spring God. — *See Roger Williams's Key*, &c.

Are ever those at which our young lips drank,
Stooped to their waters o'er the grassy bank:

Midst the cold dreary sea-watch, Home's hearth-light
Shines round the helmsman plunging through the night;
And still, with inward eye, the traveller sees
In close, dark, stranger streets his native trees.

The home-sick dreamer's brow is nightly fanned
By breezes whispering of his native land,
And, on the stranger's dim and dying eye
The soft, sweet pictures of his childhood lie!

Joy then for Weetamoo, to sit once more
A child upon her father's wigwam floor!
Once more with her old fondness to beguile
From his cold eye the strange light of a smile.

The long bright days of Summer swiftly passed,
The dry leaves whirled in Autumn's rising blast,
And evening cloud and whitening sunrise rime
Told of the coming of the winter time.

But vainly looked, the while, young Weetamoo,
Down the dark river for her chief's canoe;
No dusky messenger from Saugus brought,
The grateful tidings which the young wife sought.

At length a runner from her father sent,
To Winnepurkit's sea-cooled wigwam went:
"Eagle of Saugus, — in the woods the dove,
Mourns for the shelter of thy wings of love."

But the dark chief of Saugus turned aside
In the grim anger of hard-hearted pride;
"I bore her as became a chieftain's daughter,
Up to her home beside the gliding water.

"If now no more a mat for her is found
Of all which line her father's wigwam round,
Let Pennacook call out his warrior train
And send her back with wampum gifts again."

The baffled runner turned upon his track,
Bearing the words of Winnepurkit back,
"Dog of the Marsh," cried Pennacook, "no more
Shall child of mine sit on his wigwam floor.

"Go — let him seek some meaner squaw to spread
The stolen bear-skin of his beggar's bed:
Son of a fish-hawk! — let him dig his clams
For some vile daughter of the Agawams,

"Or coward Nipmucks! — may his scalp dry black
In Mohawk smoke, before I send her back."
He shook his clenched hand towards the ocean wave,
While hoarse assent his listening council gave.

Alas poor bride! — can thy grim sire impart
His iron hardness to thy woman's heart?
Or cold self-torturing pride like his atone
For love denied and life's warm beauty flown?

On Autumn's grey and mournful grave the snow
Hung its white wreaths; with stifled voice and low
The river crept, by one vast bridge o'ercrossed,
Built by the hoar-locked artisan of Frost.

And many a Moon in beauty newly born
Pierced the red sunset with her silver horn,
Or, from the east across her azure field
Rolled the wide brightness of her full-orbed shield.

Yet Winnepurkit came not — on the mat
Of the scorned wife her dusky rival sat,
And he, the while, in Western woods afar —
Urged the long chase, or trod the path of war.

Dry up thy tears, young daughter of a chief!
Waste not on him the sacredness of grief;
Be the fierce spirit of thy sire thine own,
His lips of scorning, and his heart of stone.

What heeds the warrior of a hundred fights,
The storm-worn watcher through long hunting nights,

H. Billings del. A. C. Warren Sc.

On that strong turbid water, a small boat
Guided by one weak hand was seen to float.

Page [illegible]

Cold, crafty, proud, of woman's weak distress,
Her home-bound grief and pining loneliness?

VII. — THE DEPARTURE.

The wild March rains had fallen fast and long
The snowy mountains of the North among,
Making each vale a water-course — each hill
Bright with the cascade of some new made rill.

Gnawed by the sunbeams, softened by the rain,
Heaved underneath by the swollen current's strain,
The ice-bridge yielded, and the Merrimack
Bore the huge ruin crashing down its track.

On that strong turbid water, a small boat
Guided by one weak hand was seen to float,
Evil the fate which loosed it from the shore,
Too early voyager with too frail an oar!

Down the vexed centre of that rushing tide,
The thick huge ice-blocks threatening either side,
The foam-white rocks of Amoskeag in view,
With arrowy swiftness sped that light canoe.

The trapper moistening his moose's meat
On the wet bank by Uncanoonuc's feet,
Saw the swift boat flash down the troubled stream —
Slept he, or waked he? — was it truth or dream?

The straining eye bent fearfully before,
The small hand clenching on the useless oar,
The bead-wrought blanket trailing o'er the water —
He knew them all — wo for the Sachem's daughter!

Sick and aweary of her lonely life,
Heedless of peril the still faithful wife
Had left her mother's grave, her father's door,
To seek the wigwam of her chief once more.

Down the white rapids like a sear leaf whirled,
On the sharp rocks and piled up ices hurled,

Empty and broken, circled the canoe
In the vexed pool below — but, where was Weetamoo?

VIII. — SONG OF INDIAN WOMEN.

The Dark eye has left us,
The Spring-bird has flown,
On the pathway of spirits
She wanders alone.
The song of the wood-dove has died on our shore
*Mat wonck kunna-monee!** — we hear it no more!

Oh, dark water Spirit!
We cast on thy wave
These furs which may never
Hang over her grave;
Bear down to the lost one the robes that she wore;
Mat wonck kunna-monee! — We see her no more!

Of the strange land she walks in
No Powah has told:
It may burn with the sunshine,
Or freeze with the cold.
Let us give to our lost one the robes that she wore,
Mat wonck kunna-monee! — We see her no more!

The path she is treading
Shall soon be our own;
Each gliding in shadow
Unseen and alone! —
In vain shall we call on the souls gone before —
Mat wonck kunna-monee! — They hear us no more!

Oh mighty Sowanna!†
Thy gateways unfold,
From thy wigwam of sunset
Lift curtains of gold!
Take home the poor Spirit whose journey is o'er —
Mat wonck kunna-monee! — We see her no more!

* "Mat wonck kunna-monee." We shall see thee or her no more. — *Vide Roger Williams's "Key to the Indian Language."*

† "The Great South West God." — *See Roger Williams's "Observations,"* &c.

So sang the Children of the Leaves beside
The broad, dark river's coldly-flowing tide,
Now low, now harsh, with sob-like pause and swell
On the high wind their voices rose and fell.
Nature's wild music — sounds of wind-swept trees,
The scream of birds, the wailing of the breeze,
The roar of waters, steady, deep and strong,
Mingled and murmured in that farewell song.

MOGG MEGONE.

PART I.

[THE story of MOGG MEGONE has been considered by the author only as a frame-work for sketches of the scenery of New England, and of its early inhabitants. In portraying the Indian character, he has followed, as closely as his story would admit, the rough but natural delineations of Church, Mayhew, Charlevoix, and Roger Williams; and in so doing he has necessarily discarded much of the romance which poets and novelists have thrown around the ill-fated red man.] — ED.

WHO stands on that cliff, like a figure of stone,
  Unmoving and tall in the light of the sky,
  Where the spray of the cataract sparkles on high,
Lonely and sternly, save Mogg Megone ? *
Close to the verge of the rock is he,
  While beneath him the Saco its work is doing,
Hurrying down to its grave, the sea,
  And slow through the rock its pathway hewing !
Far down, through the mist of the falling river,
Which rises up like an incense ever,
The splintered points of the crags are seen,
With water howling and vexed between,
While the scooping whirl of the pool beneath
Seems an open throat, with its granite teeth !

* MOGG MEGONE, or Hegone, was a leader among the Saco Indians, in the bloody war of 1677. He attacked and captured the garrison at Black Point, October 12th of that year; and cut off, at the same time, a party of Englishmen near Saco river. From a deed signed by this Indian in 1664, and from other circumstances, it seems that, previous to the war, he had mingled much with the colonists. On this account, he was probably selected by the principal sachems as their agent, in the treaty signed in November, 1676.

But Mogg Megone never trembled yet
Wherever his eye or his foot was set.
He is watchful : each form, in the moonlight dim,
Of rock or of tree, is seen of him :
He listens ; each sound from afar is caught,
The faintest shiver of leaf and limb :
But he sees not the waters, which foam and fret,
Whose moonlit spray has his moccasin wet —
And the roar of their rushing, he hears it not.

The moonlight, through the open bough
  Of the gnarl'd beech, whose naked root
  Coils like a serpent at his foot,
Falls, chequered, on the Indian's brow.
His head is bare, save only where
Waves in the wind one lock of hair,
  Reserved for him, whoe'er he be,
More mighty than Megone in strife,
  When breast to breast and knee to knee,
Above the fallen warrior's life
Gleams, quick and keen, the scalping-knife.

Megone hath his knife and hatchet and gun,
And his gaudy and tasseled blanket on :
His knife hath a handle with gold inlaid,
And magic words on its polished blade —
'T was the gift of Castine* to Mogg Megone,
For a scalp or twain from the Yengees torn :
His gun was the gift of the Tarrantine,
  And Modocawando's wives had strung
The brass and the beads, which tinkle and shine
On the polished breech, and broad bright line
  Of beaded wampum around it hung.

* Baron de St. Castine came to Canada in 1644. Leaving his civilized companions, he plunged into the great wilderness, and settled among the Penobscot Indians, near the mouth of their noble river. He here took for his wives the daughters of the great Modocawando — the most powerful sachem of the east. His castle was plundered by Governor Andros, during his reckless administration; and the enraged Baron is supposed to have excited the Indians into open hostility to the English.

What seeks Megone? His foes are near—
  Grey Jocelyn's * eye is never sleeping,
And the garrison lights are burning clear,
  Where Phillips' † men their watch are keeping.
Let him hie him away through the dank river fog,
  Never rustling the boughs nor displacing the rocks,
For the eyes and the ears which are watching for Mogg,
  Are keener than those of the wolf or the fox.

He starts—there's a rustle among the leaves:
  Another—the click of his gun is heard!—
A footstep—is it the step of Cleaves,
  With Indian blood on his English sword?
Steals Harmon ‡ down from the sands of York,
With hand of iron and foot of cork?
Has Scammon, versed in Indian wile,
For vengeance left his vine hung isle? §
Hark! at that whistle, soft and low,
  How lights the eye of Mogg Megone!

* The owner and commander of the garrison at Black Point, which Mogg attacked and plundered. He was an old man at the period to which the tale relates.

† Major Phillips, one of the principle men of the Colony. His garrison sustained a long and terrible siege by the savages. As a magistrate and a gentleman, he exacted of his plebeian neighbors a remarkable degree of deference. The Court Records of the settlement inform us that an individual was fined for the heinous offence of saying that "Major Phillips' mare was as lean as an Indian dog."

‡ Captain Harmon, of Georgeana, now York, was, for many years, the terror of the Eastern Indians. In one of his expeditions up the Kennebec river, at the head of a party of rangers, he discovered twenty of the savages asleep by a large fire. Cautiously creeping towards them, until he was certain of his aim, he ordered his men to single out their objects. The first discharge killed or mortally wounded the whole number of the unconscious sleepers.

§ Wood Island, near the mouth of the Saco. It was visited by the Sieur De Monts and Champlain, in 1603. The following extract, from the journal of the latter, relates to it. "Having left the Kennebec, we ran along the coast to the westward, and cast anchor under a small island, near the main-land, where we saw twenty or more natives. I here visited an island, beautifully clothed with a fine growth of forest trees, particularly of the oak and walnut; and over-spread with vines, that, in their season, produce excellent grapes. We named it the island of Bacchus."—*Les voyages de Sieur Champlain. Liv.* 2, *c.* 3.

A smile gleams o'er his dusky brow —
"Boon welcome, Johnny Bonython!"

Out steps, with cautious foot and slow,
And quick, keen glances to and fro,
The hunted outlaw, Bonython! *
A low, lean swarthy man is he,
With blanket-garb and buskined knee,
And nought of English fashion on;
For he hates the race from whence he sprung,
And he couches his words in the Indian tongue.

"Hush — let the Sachem's voice be weak;
The water-rat shall hear him speak —
The owl shall whoop in the white man's ear,
That Mogg Megone, with his scalps, is here!"
He pauses — dark, over cheek and brow,
A flush, as of shame, is stealing now:
"Sachem!" he says, "let me have the land,
Which stretches away upon either hand,

* John Bonython was the son of Richard Bonython, Gent., one of the most efficient and able magistrates of the Colony. John proved to be "a degenerate plant." In 1635, we find, by the Court Records, that, for some offence, he was fined 40s. In 1640, he was fined for abuse toward R. Gibson, the minister, and Mary, his wife. Soon after, he was fined for disorderly conduct in the house of his father. In 1645, the "Great and General Court" adjudged "John Bonython outlawed, and incapable of any of his majesty's laws, and proclaimed him a rebel." [Court Records of the Province, 1645.] In 1651, he bade defiance to the laws of Massachusetts, and was again outlawed. He acted independently of all law and authority; and hence, doubtless, his burlesque title of "The Sagamore of Saco," which has come down to the present generation in the following epitaph:

"Here lies Bonython; the Sagamore of Saco,
He lived a rogue, and died a knave, and went to Hobomoko."

By some means or other, he obtained a large estate. In this poem, I have taken some liberties with him, not strictly warranted by historical facts, although the conduct imputed to him is in keeping with his general character. Over the last years of his life lingers a deep obscurity. Even the manner of his death is uncertain. He was supposed to have been killed by the Indians; but this is doubted by the able and indefatigable author of the history of Saco and Biddeford. — *Part I. p.* 115.

As far about as my feet can stray
In the half of a gentle summer's day,
From the leaping brook* to the Saco river —
And the fair-haired girl, thou hast sought of me,
Shall sit in the Sachem's wigwam, and be
The wife of Mogg Megone forever."

There's a sudden light in the Indian's glance,
A moment's trace of powerful feeling —
Of love or triumph, or both perchance,
Over his proud, calm features stealing.
"The words of my father are very good;
He shall have the land, and water, and wood;
And he who harms the Sagamore John,
Shall feel the knife of Mogg Megone;
But the fawn of the Yengees shall sleep on my breast,
And the bird of the clearing shall sing in my nest."

"But father!" — and the Indian's hand
Falls gently on the white man's arm,
And with a smile as shrewdly bland
As the deep voice is slow and calm —
"Where is my father's singing-bird —
The sunny eye, and sunset hair?
I know I have my father's word,
And that his word is good and fair;
But, will my father tell me where
Megone shall go and look for his bride? —
For he sees her not by her father's side."

The dark, stern eye of Bonython
Flashes over the features of Mogg Megone,
In one of those glances which search within;
But the stolid calm of the Indian alone
Remains where the trace of emotion has been.
"Does the Sachem doubt? Let him go with me,
And the eyes of the Sachem his bride shall see."

* Foxwell's Brook flows from a marsh or bog, called the "Heath," in Saco, containing thirteen hundred acres. On this brook, and surrounded by wild and romantic scenery, is a beautiful waterfall, of more than sixty feet.

Cautious and slow, with pauses oft,
And watchful eyes and whispers soft,
The twain are stealing through the wood,
Leaving the downward-rushing flood,
Whose deep and solemn roar behind,
Grows fainter on the evening wind.

Hark ! — is that the angry howl
Of the wolf, the hills among ? —
Or the hooting of the owl,
On his leafy cradle swung ? —
Quickly glancing, to and fro,
Listening to each sound they go :
Round the columns of the pine,
Indistinct, in shadow, seeming
Like some old and pillared shrine ;
With the soft and white moonshine,
Round the foliage-tracery shed
Of each column's branching head,
For its lamps of worship gleaming !
And the sounds awakened there,
In the pine leaves fine and small,
Soft and sweetly musical,
By the fingers of the air,
For the anthem's dying fall
Lingering round some temple's wall ! —
Niche and cornice round and round
Wailing like the ghost of sound !
Is not Nature's worship thus
Ceaseless ever, going on ?
Hath it not a voice for us
In the thunder, or the tone
Of the leaf-harp faint and small,
Speaking to the unsealed ear
Words of blended love and fear,
Of the mighty Soul of all ?

Nought had the twain of thoughts like these
As they wound along through the crowded trees,

Where never had rung the axeman's stroke
On the gnarled trunk of the rough-barked oak ; —
Climbing the dead tree's mossy log,
  Breaking the mesh of the bramble fine,
  Turning aside the wild grape vine,
And lightly crossing the quaking bog
Whose surface shakes at the leap of the frog,
And out of whose pools the ghostly fog
  Creeps into the chill moonshine !

Yet, even that Indian's ear had heard
The preaching of the Holy Word :
Sanchekantacket's isle of sand
Was once his father's hunting land,
Where zealous Hiacoomes * stood —
The wild apostle of the wood,
Shook from his soul the fear of harm,
And trampled on the Powwaw's charm ;
Until the wizard's curses hung
Suspended on his palsying tongue,
And the fierce warrior, grim and tall,
Trembled before the forest Paul !

A cottage hidden in the wood —
  Red through its seams a light is glowing,
On rock and bough and tree-trunk rude,
  A narrow lustre throwing.

* Hiacoomes, the first Christian preacher on Martha's Vineyard; for a biography of whom the reader is referred to Increase Mayhew's account of the Praying Indians, 1726. The following is related of him: "One Lord's day, after meeting, where Hiacoomes had been preaching, there came in a Powwaw very angry, and said, 'I know all the meeting Indians are liars. You say you do n't care for the Powwaws;' — then, calling two or three of them by name, he railed at them, and told them they were deceived, for the Powwaws could kill all the meeting Indians, if they set about it. But Hiacoomes told him that he would be in the midst of all the Powwaws in the island, and they should do the utmost they could against him; and when they should do their worst by their witchcraft to kill him, he would without fear set himself against them, by remembering Jehovah. He told them also he did put all the Powwaws under his heel. Such was the faith of this good man. Nor were these Powwaws ever able to do these Christian Indians any hurt, though others were frequently hurt and killed by them." — *Mayhew's Book*, pp. 6, 7, c. 1.

"Who 's there?" a clear, firm voice demands:
  "Hold, Ruth — 'tis I, the Sagamore!"
Quick, at the summons, hasty hands
  Unclose the bolted door;
And on the outlaw's daughter shine
The flashes of the kindled pine.

Tall and erect the maiden stands,
  Like some young priestess of the wood,
The free born child of Solitude,
  And bearing still the wild and rude,
Yet noble trace of Nature's hands.
Her dark brown cheek has caught its stain
More from the sunshine than the rain;
Yet, where her long fair hair is parting,
A pure white brow into light is starting;
And, where the folds of her blanket sever,
Are a neck and bosom as white as ever
The foam-wreaths rise on the leaping river.
But, in the convulsive quiver and grip
Of the muscles around her bloodless lip,
  There is something painful and sad to see;
And her eye has a glance more sternly wild
Than even that of a forest child
  In its fearless and untamed freedom should be.

Yet, seldom in hall or court are seen
So queenly a form and so noble a mien,
  As freely and smiling she welcomes them there!
Her outlawed sire and Mogg Megone:
  "Pray, father, how does thy hunting fare?
  And, Sachem, say — does Scamman wear,
In spite of thy promise, a scalp of his own?"
Hurried and light is the maiden's tone;
  But a fearful meaning lurks within
Her glance, as it questions the eye of Megone —
  An awful meaning of guilt and sin! —
The Indian hath opened his blanket, and there
Hangs a human scalp by its long damp hair!

With hand upraised, with quick-drawn breath,
She meets that ghastly sign of death.
In one long, glassy, spectral stare
The enlarging eye is fastened there,
As if that mesh of pale brown hair
 Had power to change at sight alone,
Even as the fearful locks which wound
Medusa's fatal forehead round,
 The gazer into stone.
With such a look Herodias read
The features of the bleeding head,
So looked the mad Moor on his dead,
Or the young Cenci as she stood,
O'er-dabbled with a father's blood!

Look! — feeling melts that frozen glance,
It moves that marble countenance,
As if at once within her strove
Pity with shame, and hate with love.
The Past recalls its joy and pain,
Old memories rise before her brain —
The lips which love's embraces met,
The hand her tears of parting wet,
The voice whose pleading tones beguiled
The pleased ear of the forest-child, —
And tears she may no more repress
Reveal her lingering tenderness.

Oh! woman wronged, can cherish hate
 More deep and dark than manhood may;
But, when the mockery of Fate
 Hath left Revenge its chosen way,
And the fell curse, which years have nursed,
Full on the spoiler's head hath burst —
When all her wrong, and shame, and pain,
Burns fiercely on his heart and brain —
Still lingers something of the spell
 Which bound her to the traitor's bosom —
Still, midst the vengeful fires of hell,
 Some flowers of old affection blossom.

John Bonython's eye-brows together are drawn
With a fierce expression of wrath and scorn —
He hoarsely whispers, "Ruth, beware!
  Is this the time to be playing the fool —
Crying over a paltry lock of hair,
  Like a love-sick girl at school? —
Curse on it! — an Indian can see and hear:
Away — and prepare our evening cheer!"

How keenly the Indian is watching now
Her tearful eye and her varying brow —
  With a serpent eye, which kindles and burns,
  Like a fiery star in the upper air:
On sire and daughter his fierce glance turns: —
  "Has my old white father a scalp to spare?
  For his young one loves the pale brown hair
Of the scalp of an English dog, far more
Than Mogg Megone, or his wigwam floor:
  Go — Mogg is wise: he will keep his land —
  And Sagamore John, when he feels with his hand,
Shall miss his scalp where it grew before."

The moment's gust of grief is gone —
  The lip is clenched — the tears are still —
God pity thee, Ruth Bonython!
  With what a strength of will
Are nature's feelings in thy breast,
As with an iron hand repressed!
And how, upon that nameless woe,
Quick as the pulse can come and go,
While shakes the unsteadfast knee, and yet
The bosom heaves — the eye is wet —
Has thy dark spirit power to stay
The heart's wild current on its way?
  And whence that baleful strength of guile,
Which over that still working brow
And tearful eye and cheek, can throw
  The mockery of a smile?
Warned by her father's blackening frown,
With one strong effort crushing down

Grief, hate, remorse, she meets again
  The savage murderer's sullen gaze,
  And scarcely look or tone betrays
How the heart strives beneath its chain.

"Is the Sachem angry — angry with Ruth,
Because she cries with an ache in her tooth,*
Which would make a Sagamore jump and cry,
And look about with a woman's eye?
No — Ruth will sit in the Sachem's door,
And braid the mats for his wigwam floor,
And broil his fish and tender fawn,
And weave his wampum, and grind his corn, —
For she loves the brave and the wise, and none
Are braver and wiser than Mogg Megone!"

The Indian's brow is clear once more:
  With grave, calm face, and half-shut eye,
He sits upon the wigwam floor,
  And watches Ruth go by,
Intent upon her household care;
  And ever and anon, the while,
Or on the maiden, or her fare,
Which smokes in grateful promise there,
  Bestows his quiet smile.

Ah, Mogg Megone! — what dreams are thine,
  But those which love's own fancies dress —
  The sum of Indian happiness! —
A wigwam, where the warm sunshine
Looks in among the groves of pine —
A stream, where, round thy light canoe,
The trout and salmon dart in view,
And the fair girl, before thee now,
Spreading thy mat with hand of snow,
Or plying, in the dews of morn,

*"The tooth-ache," says Roger Williams, in his observations upon the language and customs of the New England tribes, "is the only paine which will force their stoute hearts to cry." He afterwards remarks that even the Indian women never cry as he has heard "some of their men in this paine."

Her hoe amidst thy patch of corn,
Or offering up, at eve, to thee,
Thy birchen dish of hominy!

From the rude board of Bonython,
Venison and suckatash have gone —
For long these dwellers of the wood
Have felt the gnawing want of food.
But untasted of Ruth is the frugal cheer —
With head averted, yet ready ear,
She stands by the side of her austere sire,
Feeding, at times, the unequal fire,
With the yellow knots of the pitch-pine tree,
Whose flaring light, as they kindle, falls
On the cottage-roof, and its black log walls,
And over its inmates three.

From Sagamore Bonython's hunting flask
  The fire-water burns at the lip of Megone:
"Will the Sachem hear what his father shall ask?
  Will he make his mark, that it may be known,
On the speaking-leaf, that he gives the land,
From the Sachem's own, to his father's hand?"

The fire-water shines in the Indian's eyes,
  As he rises, the white man's bidding to do:
"Wuttamuttata — weekan!* Mogg is wise —
  For the water he drinks is strong and new, —
Mogg's heart is great! — will he shut his hand,
When his father asks for a little land?" —
With unsteady fingers, the Indian has drawn
  On the parchment the shape of a hunter's bow:
"Boon water — boon water — Sagamore John!
  Wuttamuttata — weekan! our hearts will grow!"
He drinks yet deeper — he mutters low —
He reels on his bear-skin to and fro —

* *Wuttamuttata*, "Let us drink." *Weekan*, "It is sweet." Vide Roger Williams's Key to the Indian Language, "in that parte of America called New England." London, 1643, p. 35.

His head falls down on his naked breast —
He struggles, and sinks to a drunken rest.

"Humph — drunk as a beast!" — and Bonython's brow
  Is darker than ever with evil thought —
"The fool has signed his warrant; but how
  And when shall the deed be wrought?
Speak, Ruth! why, what the devil is there,
To fix thy gaze in that empty air? —
Speak, Ruth! — by my soul, if I thought that tear,
Which shames thyself and our purpose here,
Were shed for that cursed and pale-faced dog,
Whose green scalp hangs from the belt of Mogg,
  And whose beastly soul is in Satan's keeping —
This — this!" — he dashes his hand upon
The rattling stock of his loaded gun —
  "Should send thee with him to do thy weeping!"

"Father!" — the eye of Bonython
Sinks, at that low, sepulchral tone,
Hollow and deep, as it were spoken
  By the unmoving tongue of death —
Or from some statue's lips had broken —
A sound without a breath!
"Father! — my life I value less
Than yonder fool his gaudy dress;
And how it ends it matters not,
By heart-break or by rifle-shot:
But spare awhile the scoff and threat —
Our business is not finished yet."

"True, true, my girl — I only meant
To draw up again the bow unbent.
Harm thee, my Ruth! I only sought
To frighten off thy gloomy thought; —
Come — let 's be friends!" He seeks to clasp
His daughter's cold, damp hand in his.
Ruth startles from her father's grasp,
As if each nerve and muscle felt,

Instinctively, the touch of guilt,
Through all their subtle sympathies.

He points her to the sleeping Mogg
"What shall be done with yonder dog?
Scamman is dead, and revenge is thine —
The deed is signed and the land is mine;
And this drunken fool is of use no more,
Save as thy hopeful bridegroom, and sooth,
'T were Christian mercy to finish him Ruth,
Now, while he lies like a beast on our floor, —
If not for thine, at least for his sake,
Rather than let the poor dog awake,
To drain my flask, and claim as his bride
Such a forest devil to run by his side —
Such a Wetuomanit * as thou wouldst make!"

He laughs at his jest. Hush — what is there? —
The sleeping Indian is striving to rise,
With his knife in his hand, and glaring eyes! —
"Wagh! — Mogg will have the pale-face's hair,
For his knife is sharp and his fingers can help
The hair to pull and the skin to peel —
Let him cry like a woman and twist like an eel,
The great Captain Scamman must lose his scalp!
And Ruth, when she sees it, shall dance with Mogg."
His eyes are fixed — but his lips draw in —
With a low, hoarse chuckle, and fiendish grin, —
And he sinks again, like a senseless log.

Ruth does not speak — she does not stir;
But she gazes down on the murderer,

* *Wetuomanit* — a house god, or demon. "They — the Indians — have given me the names of thirty-seven gods, which I have, all which in their solemne Worships they invocate!" R. Williams's Briefe Observations of the Customs, Manners, Worships, &c., of the Natives, in Peace and Warre, in Life and Death: on all which is added Spiritual Observations, General and Particular, of Chiefe and Special use — upon all occasions — to all the English inhabiting these parts; yet Pleasant and Profitable to the view of all Mene. p. 110, c. 21.

Whose broken and dreamful slumbers tell,
Too much for her ear, of that deed of hell.
She sees the knife, with its slaughter red,
And the dark fingers clenching the bear-skin bed!
What thoughts of horror and madness whirl
Through the burning brain of that fallen girl!

John Bonython lifts his gun to his eye,
  Its muzzle is close to the Indian's ear —
But he drops it again. "Some one may be nigh,
  And I would not that even the wolves should hear."
He draws his knife from its deer-skin belt —
Its edge with his fingers is slowly felt; —
Kneeling down on one knee, by the Indian's side,
From his throat he opens the blanket wide;
And twice or thrice he feebly essays
A trembling hand with the knife to raise.

"I cannot" — he mutters — "did he not save
My life from a cold and wintry grave,
When the storm came down from Agioochook,
And the north-wind howled, and the tree-tops shook —
And I strove, in the drifts of the rushing snow,
Till my knees grew weak and I could not go,
And I felt the cold to my vitals creep,
And my heart's blood stiffen, and pulses sleep!
I cannot strike him — Ruth Bonython!
In the devil's name, tell me — what's to be done?"

    Oh! when the soul, once pure and high,
    Is stricken down from Virtue's sky,
    As, with the downcast star of morn,
    Some gems of light are with it drawn —
    And, through its night of darkness, play
    Some tokens of its primal day —
    Some lofty feelings linger still —
      The strength to dare, the nerve to meet
      Whatever threatens with defeat
    Its all-indomitable will! —
    But lacks the mean of mind and heart,

Though eager for the gains of crime,
Oft, at this chosen place and time,
The strength to bear this evil part;
And, shielded by this very Vice,
Escapes from Crime by Cowardice.

Ruth starts erect — with bloodshot eye,
And lips drawn tight across her teeth,
Showing their locked embrace beneath,
In the red fire-light: — "Mogg must die!
Give me the knife!" — The outlaw turns,
Shuddering in heart and limb, away —
But, fitfully there, the hearth-fire burns,
And he sees on the wall strange shadows play.
A lifted arm, a tremulous blade,
Are dimly pictured, in light and shade,
Plunging down in the darkness. Hark, that cry!
Again — and again — he sees it fall —
That shadowy arm down the lighted wall!
He hears quick footsteps — a shape flits by! —
The door on its rusted hinges creaks: —
"Ruth — daughter Ruth!" the outlaw shrieks
But no sound comes back — he is standing alone
By the mangled corse of Mogg Megone!

MOGG MEGONE.

PART II.

'Tis morning over Norridgewock —
On tree and wigwam, wave and rock.
Bathed in the autumnal sunshine, stirred
At intervals by breeze and bird,
And wearing all the hues which glow
In heaven's own pure and perfect bow,
  That glorious picture of the air,
Which summer's light-robed angel forms
On the dark ground of fading storms,
  With pencil dipped in sunbeams there —
And, stretching out, on either hand,
O'er all that wide and unshorn land,
Till, weary of its gorgeousness,
The aching and the dazzled eye
Rests gladdened, on the calm blue sky —
  Slumbers the mighty wilderness!
The oak, upon the windy hill,
  Its dark green burthen upward heaves —
The hemlock broods above its rill,
Its cone-like foliage darker still,
  While the white birch's graceful stem
And the rough walnut bough receives
The sun upon their crowded leaves,
  Each colored like a topaz gem;
  And the tall maple wears with them
The coronal which autumn gives,
  The brief, bright sign of ruin near,
  The hectic of a dying year!

The hermit priest, who lingers now
On the Bald Mountain's shrubless brow,
The grey and thunder-smitten pile
Which marks afar the Desert Isle,*
While gazing on the scene below,
May half forget the dreams of home,
That nightly with his slumbers come,—
The tranquil skies of sunny France,
The peasant's harvest song and dance,
The vines around the hill-sides wreathing,
The soft airs midst their clusters breathing,
The wings which dipped, the stars which shone
Within thy bosom, blue Garronne!
And round the Abbey's shadowed wall,
At morning spring and even-fall,
Sweet voices in the still air singing—
The chant of many a holy hymn—
The solemn bell of vespers ringing—
And hallowed torch-light falling dim
On pictured saint and seraphim!
For here beneath him lies unrolled,
Bathed deep in morning's flood of gold,
A vision gorgeous as the dream
Of the beatified may seem,
When, as his Church's legends say,
Borne upward in exstatic bliss,
The rapt enthusiast soars away
Unto a brighter world than this:
A mortal's glimpse beyond the pale—
A moment's lifting of the veil!

Far eastward o'er the lovely bay,
Penobscot's clustered wigwams lay;
And gently from that Indian town
The verdant hill-side slopes adown,

* Mt. Desert Island, the Bald Mountain upon which overlooks Frenchman's and Penobscot Bay. It was upon this island that the Jesuits made their earliest settlement.

To where the sparkling waters play
  Upon the yellow sands below;
And shooting round the winding shores
  Of narrow capes, and isles which lie
  Slumbering to ocean's lullaby —
With birchen boat and glancing oars,
  The red men to their fishing go;
While from their planting ground is borne
The treasure of the golden corn,
By laughing girls, whose dark eyes glow
Wild through the locks which o'er them flow.
The wrinkled squaw, whose toil is done,
Sits on her bear-skin in the sun,
Watching the huskers, with a smile
For each full ear which swells the pile;
And the old chief, who never more
May bend the bow or pull the oar,
Smokes gravely in his wigwam door,
Or slowly shapes, with axe of stone
The arrow-head from flint and bone

Beneath the westward turning eye
A thousand wooded islands lie —
Gems of the waters! — with each hue
Of brightness set in ocean's blue.
Each bears aloft its tuft of trees
  Touched by the pencil of the frost,
And, with the motion of each breeze,
  A moment seen — a moment lost —
  Changing and blent, confused and tossed,
  The brighter with the darker crossed,
Their thousand tints of beauty glow
Down in the restless waves below,
  And tremble in the sunny skies,
As if, from waving bough to bough,
  Flitted the birds of paradise.
There sleep Placentia's group — and there
Pere Breteaux marks the hour of prayer;

And there, beneath the sea-worn cliff,
  On which the Father's hut is seen,
The Indian stays his rocking skiff,
  And peers the hemlock boughs between,
Half trembling, as he seeks to look
Upon the Jesuit's Cross and Book.*
There, gloomily against the sky
The Dark Isles rear their summits high;
And Desert Rock, abrupt and bare,
Lifts its grey turrets in the air —
Seen from afar, like some strong hold
Built by the ocean kings of old;
And, faint as smoke-wreath white and thin,
Swells in the north vast Katadin:
And, wandering from its marshy feet,
The broad Penobscot comes to meet
  And mingle with his own bright bay.
Slow sweep his dark and gathering floods,
Arched over by the ancient woods,
Which Time, in those dim solitudes,
  Wielding the dull axe of Decay,
  Alone hath ever shorn away.

Not thus, within the woods which hide
The beauty of thy azure tide,
  And with their falling timbers block
Thy broken currents, Kennebeck!
Gazes the white man on the wreck
  Of the down-trodden Norridgewock —
In one lone village hemmed at length,
In battle shorn of half their strength,
Turned, like the panther in his lair,
  With his fast-flowing life-blood wet,
For one last struggle of despair,
  Wounded and faint, but tameless yet!

*Father Hennepin, a missionary among the Iroquois, mentions that the Indians believed him to be a conjuror, and that they were particularly afraid of a bright silver chalice which he had in his possession. "The Indians," says Pere Jerome Lallamant, "fear us as the greatest sorcerers on earth."

Unreaped, upon the planting lands,
The scant, neglected harvest stands:
No shout is there — no dance — no song:
The aspect of the very child
Scowls with a meaning sad and wild
Of bitterness and wrong.
The almost infant Norridgewock
Essays to lift the tomahawk;
And plucks his fathers knife away,
To mimic, in his frightful play,
The scalping of an English foe:
Wreaths on his lip a horrid smile,
Burns, like a snake's, his small eye, while
Some bough or sapling meets his blow.
The fisher, as he drops his line,
Starts, when he sees the hazles quiver
Along the margin of the river,
Looks up and down the ripling tide,
And grasps the firelock at his side.
For Bomazeen * from Tacconock
Has sent his runners to Norridgewock,
With tidings that Moulton and Harmon of York
Far up the river have come:
They have left their boats — they have entered the [wood,
And filled the depths of the solitude
With the sound of the ranger's drum.

On the brow of a hill, which slopes to meet
The flowing river, and bathe its feet —
The bare-washed rock, and the drooping grass,
And the creeping vine, as the waters pass —
A rude and unshapely chapel stands,
Built up in that wild by unskilled hands;
Yet the traveller knows it a place of prayer,
For the holy sign of the cross is there:

* Bomazeen is spoken of by Penhallow, as "the famous warrior and chieftain of Norridgewock." He was killed in the attack of the English upon Norridgewock, in 1724.

And should he chance at that place to be,
Of a sabbath morn, or some hallowed day,
When prayers are made and masses are said,
Some for the living and some for the dead,
Well might that traveller start to see
The tall dark forms, that take their way
From the birch canoe, on the river-shore,
And the forest paths, to that chapel door;
And marvel to mark the naked knees
And the dusky foreheads bending there,
While, in coarse white vesture, over these
In blessing or in prayer,
Stretching abroad his thin pale hands,
Like a shrouded ghost, the Jesuit* stands.

* Pere Ralle, or Rasles, was one of the most zealous and indefatigable of that band of Jesuit missionaries who, at the beginning of the seventeenth century, penetrated the forests of America, with the avowed object of converting the heathen. The first religious mission of the Jesuits, to the savages in North America, was in 1611. The zeal of the fathers for the conversion of the Indians to the Catholic faith, knew no bounds. For this, they plunged into the depths of the wilderness; habituated themselves to all the hardships and privations of the natives; suffered cold, hunger, and some of them death itself, by the extremest tortures. Pere Brebeuf, after laboring in the cause of his mission for twenty years, together with his companion, Pere Lallamant, was burned alive. To these might be added the names of those Jesuits who were put to death by the Iroquois — Daniel, Garnier, Buteaux, La Riborerde, Goupil, Constantin, and Liegeouis. "For bed," says Father Lallamant, in his *Relation de ce qui s'est dans le pays des Hurons*, 1640, c. 3, "we have nothing but a miserable piece of bark of a tree; for nourishment, a handful or two of corn, either roasted or soaked in water, which seldom satisfies our hunger; and after all, not venturing to perform even the ceremonies of our religion, without being considered as sorcerers." Their success among the natives, however, by no means equalled their exertions. Pere Lallamant says — "With respect to adult persons, in good health, there is little apparent success; on the contrary, there have been nothing but storms and whirlwinds from that quarter."

Sebastien Ralle established himself, sometime about the year 1670, at Norridgewock, where he continued more than forty years. He was accused, and perhaps not without justice, of exciting his praying Indians against the English, whom he looked upon as the enemies not only of his king, but also of the Catholic religion. He was killed by the English, in 1724, at the foot of the cross, which his own hands had planted. This Indian church was broken up, and its members either killed outright or dispersed.

H. Billings del. E. L. Glover Sc.

Two forms are now in that chapel dim,
The Jesuit, silent and sad and pale,
Anxiously heeding some fearful tale,
Which a stranger is telling him.

Page 55

Two forms are now in that chapel dim,
  The Jesuit, silent and sad and pale,
  Anxiously heeding some fearful tale,
Which a stranger is telling him.
That stranger's garb is soiled and torn,
And wet with dew and loosely worn;
Her fair neglected hair falls down
O'er cheeks with wind and sunshine brown;
Yet still, in that disordered face,
The Jesuit's cautious eye can trace
Those elements of former grace,
Which, half effaced, seem scarcely less,
Even now, than perfect loveliness.

With drooping head, and voice so low
  That scarce it meets the Jesuit's ears —
While through her clasp'd fingers flow,
From the heart's fountain, hot and slow,
  Her penitential tears —
She tells the story of the wo
  And evil of her years.

"Oh Father, bear with me; my heart
  Is sick and death-like, and my brain
  Seems girdled with a fiery chain,
Whose scorching links will never part,
  And never cool again.
Bear with me while I speak — but turn
  Away that gentle eye, the while —

In a letter written by Ralle to his nephew, he gives the following account of his church, and his own labors. "All my converts repair to the church regularly twice every day; first, very early in the morning, to attend mass, and again in the evening, to assist in the prayers at sunset. As it is necessary to fix the imagination of savages, whose attention is easily distracted, I have composed prayers, calculated to inspire them with just sentiments of the august sacrifice of our altars: they chant, or at least recite them aloud, during mass. Besides preaching to them on Sundays and saint's days, I seldom let a working day pass, without making a concise exhortation, for the purpose of inspiring them with horror at those vices to which they are most addicted, or to confirm them in the practice of some particular virtue." Vide *Lettres Edifiantes et Cur.*, vol. 6, page 127.

The fires of guilt more fiercely burn
  Beneath its holy smile;
For half I fancy I can see
My mother's sainted look in thee.

"My dear lost mother! sad and pale,
  Mournfully sinking day by day,
And with a hold on life as frail
  As frosted leaves, that, thin and gray,
  Hang feebly on their parent spray,
And tremble in the gale;
Yet watching o'er my childishness
With patient fondness — not the less
For all the agony which kept
Her blue eye wakeful, while I slept;
And checking every tear and groan
That haply might have waked my own;
And bearing still, without offence,
My idle words, and petulance;
  Reproving with a tear — and, while
The tooth of pain was keenly preying
Upon her very heart, repaying
  My brief repentance with a smile.

"Oh, in her meek, forgiving eye
  There was a brightness not of mirth —
A light, whose clear intensity
  Was borrowed not of earth.
Along her cheek a deepening red
Told where the feverish hectic fed;
  And yet, each fatal token gave
To the mild beauty of her face
A newer and a dearer grace,
  Unwarning of the grave.
'T was like the hue which autumn gives
To yonder changed and dying leaves,
  Breathed over by his frosty breath;
Scarce can the gazer feel that this
Is but the spoiler's treacherous kiss,
  The mocking-smile of Death!

"Sweet were the tales she used to tell
  When summer's eve was dear to us,
And, fading from the darkening dell,
The glory of the sunset fell
  On wooded Agamenticus, —
When, sitting by our cottage wall,
The murmur of the Saco's fall,
  And the south wind's expiring sighs
Came, softly blending, on my ear,
With the low tones I loved to hear:
  Tales of the pure — the good — the wise —
The holy men and maids of old,
In the all-sacred pages told; —
Of Rachel, stooped at Haran's fountains,
  Amid her father's thirsty flock,
Beautiful to her kinsman seeming
As the bright angels of his dreaming,
  On Padan-aran's holy rock;
Of gentle Ruth — and her who kept
  Her awful vigil on the mountains,
By Israel's virgin daughters wept;
Of Miriam, with her maidens, singing
  The song for grateful Israel meet,
While every crimson wave was bringing
  The spoils of Egypt at her feet;
Of her — Samaria's humble daughter,
  Who paused to hear, beside her well,
  Lessons of love and truth, which fell
Softly as Shiloh's flowing water;
  And saw, beneath his pilgrim guise,
The Promised One, so long foretold
By holy seer and bard of old,
  Revealed before her wondering eyes!

"Slowly she faded. Day by day
Her step grew weaker in our hall,
And fainter, at each even-fall,
  Her sad voice died away.
Yet on her thin, pale lip, the while,

8

Sat Resignation's holy smile:
And even my father checked his tread,
And hushed his voice, beside her bed:
Beneath the calm and sad rebuke
Of her meek eye's imploring look,
The scowl of hate his brow forsook,
  And, in his stern and gloomy eye,
At times, a few unwonted tears
Wet the dark lashes, which for years
  Hatred and pride had kept so dry.

"Calm as a child to slumber soothed,
As if an angel's hand had smoothed
  The still, white features into rest,
Silent and cold, without a breath
  To stir the drapery on her breast,
Pain, with its keen and poisoned fang,
The horror of the mortal pang,
The suffering look her brow had worn,
The fear, the strife, the anguish gone —
  She slept at last in death!

"Oh, tell me, father, *can* the dead
  Walk on the earth, and look on us,
And lay upon the living's head
  Their blessing or their curse?
For, oh, last night she stood by me,
As I lay beneath the woodland tree!"

The Jesuit crosses himself in awe —
"Jesu! what was it my daughter saw?"

"*She* came to me last night.
  The dried leaves did not feel her tread;
She stood by me in the wan moonlight,
  In the white robes of the dead!
Pale, and very mournfully
She bent her light form over me.
I heard no sound, I felt no breath
Breathe o'er me from that face of death:

Its blue eyes rested on my own,
Rayless and cold as eyes of stone;
Yet, in their fixed, unchanging gaze,
Something, which spoke of early days —
A sadness in their quiet glare,
As if love's smile were frozen there —
Came o'er me with an icy thrill;
Oh God! I feel its presence still!"

The Jesuit makes the holy sign —
"How passed the vision, daughter mine?"

"All dimly in the wan moonshine,
As a wreath of mist will twist and twine,
And scatter, and melt into the light —
So scattering — melting on my sight,
  The pale, cold vision passed;
But those sad eyes were fixed on mine
  Mournfully to the last."

"God help thee, daughter, tell me why
That spirit passed before thine eye!"

"Father, I know not, save it be
  That deeds of mine have summoned her
  From the unbreathing sepulchre,
To leave her last rebuke with me.
Ah, wo for me! my mother died
Just at the moment when I stood
Close on the verge of womanhood,
A child in every thing beside;
And when my wild heart needed most
Her gentle counsels, they were lost.

"My father lived a stormy life,
Of frequent change and daily strife;
And — God forgive him! left his child
To feel, like him, a freedom wild;
To love the red man's dwelling place,
  The birch boat on his shaded floods,

The wild excitement of the chase
  Sweeping the ancient woods,
The camp-fire, blazing on the shore
  Of the still lakes, the clear stream, where
  The idle fisher sets his wear,
Or angles in the shade, far more
  Than that restraining awe I felt
Beneath my gentle mother's care,
  When nightly at her knee I knelt,
With childhood's simple prayer.

"There came a change. The wild, glad mood
  Of unchecked freedom passed.
Amid the ancient solitude
Of unshorn grass and waving wood,
  And waters glancing bright and fast,
A softened voice was in my ear,
  Sweet as those lulling sounds and fine
The hunter lifts his head to hear,
Now far and faint, now full and near —
  The murmur of the wind-swept pine.
A manly form was ever nigh,
A bold, free hunter, with an eye
  Whose dark, keen glance had power to wake
Both fear and love — to awe and charm;
  'T was as the wizard rattlesnake,
Whose evil glances lure to harm —
Whose cold and small and glittering eye,
And brilliant coil, and changing dye,
Draw, step by step, the gazer near,
With drooping wing and cry of fear,
Yet powerless all to turn away,
A conscious, but a willing prey!

Fear, doubt, thought, life itself, ere long
Merged in one feeling deep and strong.
Faded the world which I had known,
  A poor vain shadow, cold and waste,
In the warm present bliss alone
  Seemed I of actual life to taste.

Fond longings dimly understood,
The glow of passion's quickening blood,
And cherished fantasies which press
The young lip with a dream's caress, —
The heart's forecast and prophecy
Took form and life before my eye,
Seen in the glance which met my own,
Heard in the soft and pleading tone,
Felt in the arms around me cast,
And warm heart-pulses beating fast.
Ah ! scarcely yet to God above
With deeper trust, with stronger love
Has prayerful saint his meek heart lent,
Or cloistered nun at twilight bent,
Than I, before a human shrine,
As mortal and as frail as mine,
With heart, and soul, and mind, and form,
Knelt madly to a fellow worm.

" Full soon, upon that dream of sin,
An awful light came bursting in.
The shrine was cold, at which I knelt ;
  The idol of that shrine was gone ;
A humbled thing of shame and guilt,
  Outcast, and spurned and lone,
Wrapt in the shadows of my crime,
  With withering heart and burning brain,
  And tears that fell like fiery rain,
I passed a fearful time.

" There came a voice — it checked the tear —
  In heart and soul it wrought a change ; —
My father's voice was in my ear ;
  It whispered of revenge !
A new and fiercer feeling swept
  All lingering tenderness away ;
And tiger passions, which had slept
  In childhood's better day,
Unknown, unfelt, arose at length
In all their own demoniac strength.

"A youthful warrior of the wild,
By words deceived, by smiles beguiled,
Of crime the cheated instrument,
Upon our fatal errands went.
  Through camp and town and wilderness
He tracked his victim; and, at last,
Just when the tide of hate had passed,
And milder thoughts came warm and fast,
Exulting, at my feet he cast
  The bloody token of success.

"Oh God! with what an awful power
  I saw the buried past uprise,
And gather, in a single hour,
  Its ghost-like memories!
And then I felt — alas! too late —
That underneath the mask of hate,
That shame and guilt and wrong had thrown
O'er feelings which they might not own,
  The heart's wild love had known no change;
And still, that deep and hidden love,
With its first fondness, wept above
  The victim of its own revenge!
There lay the fearful scalp, and there
The blood was on its pale brown hair!
I thought not of the victim's scorn,
  I thought not of his baleful guile,
My deadly wrong, my outcast name,
The characters of sin and shame
On heart and forehead drawn;
  I only saw that victim's smile —
The still, green places where we met —
The moon-lit branches, dewy wet;
I only felt, I only heard
The greeting and the parting word —
The smile — the embrace — the tone, which made
An Eden of the forest shade.

"And oh, with what a loathing eye,
  With what a deadly hate, and deep,

H. Billings del. J. Andrews & S. A. Schoff sc.

MOGG MEGONE.

I only saw that victim's smile
The still green places where we met.

I saw that Indian murderer lie
  Before me, in his drunken sleep!
What though for me the deed was done,
And words of mine had sped him on!
Yet when he murmured, as he slept,
  The horrors of that deed of blood,
The tide of utter madness swept
  O'er brain and bosom, like a flood.
And, father, with this hand of mine" ——
  "Ha! what didst thou?" the Jesuit cries,
Shuddering, as smitten with sudden pain,
  And shading, with one thin hand, his eyes,
With the other he makes the holy sign ——
"I smote him as I would a worm; —
With heart as steeled — with nerves as firm:
  He never woke again!"

"Woman of sin and blood and shame,
Speak — I would know that victim's name."

"Father," she gasped, "a chieftain, known
As Saco's Sachem — MOGG MEGONE!"

Pale priest! What proud and lofty dreams,
What keen desires, what cherished schemes,
What hopes, that time may not recall,
Are darkened by that chieftain's fall!
Was he not pledged, by cross and vow,
  To lift the hatchet of his sire,
And, round his own, the Church's foe,
  To light the avenging fire?
Who now the Tarrantine shall wake,
For thine and for the Church's sake?
  Who summon to the scene
Of conquest and unsparing strife,
And vengeance dearer than his life,
  The fiery-souled Castine?*

* The character of Ralle has probably never been correctly delineated. By his brethren of the Romish Church, he has been nearly apotheosized. On the other hand, our Puritan historians have represented him as a demon in human

Three backward steps the Jesuit takes —
His long, thin frame as ague shakes :
  And loathing hate is in his eye,
As from his lips these words of fear
Fall hoarsely on the maiden's ear —
  "The soul that sinneth shall surely die !"

She stands, as stands the stricken deer,
  Checked midway in the fearful chase,
When bursts, upon his eye and ear,
The gaunt, gray robber, baying near,
  Between him and his hiding place ;
While still behind, with yell and blow,
Sweeps, like a storm, the coming foe.
"Save me, O holy man !" — her cry
  Fills all the void, as if a tongue,
  Unseen, from rib and rafter hung,
Thrilling with mortal agony ;
Her hands are clasping the Jesuit's knee,
  And her eye looks fearfully into his own ; —
"Off, woman of sin ! — nay, touch not me
  With those fingers of blood ; — begone !"
With a gesture of horror, he spurns the form
That writhes at his feet like a trodden worm.

Ever thus the spirit must,
  Guilty in the sight of Heaven,
  With a keener woe be riven,
For its weak and sinful trust
In the strength of human dust ;
  And its anguish thrill afresh,
For each vain reliance given
  To the failing arm of flesh.

form. He was undoubtedly sincere in his devotion to the interests of his church, and not over-scrupulous as to the means of advancing those interests. "The French," says the author of the History of Saco and Biddeford, "after the peace of 1713, secretly promised to supply the Indians with arms and ammunition, if they would renew hostilities. Their principal agent was the celebrated Ralle, the French Jesuit." p. 215.

MOGG MEGONE.

PART III.

Ah, weary Priest! — with pale hands pressed
On thy throbbing brow of pain,
Baffled in thy life-long quest,
Overworn with toiling vain,
How ill thy troubled musings fit
The holy quiet of a breast
With the Dove of Peace at rest,
Sweetly brooding over it.
Thoughts are thine which have no part
With the meek and pure of heart,
Undisturbed by outward things,
Resting in the heavenly shade,
By the overspreading wings
Of the Blessed Spirit made.
Thoughts of strife and hate and wrong
Sweep thy heated brain along —
Fading hopes, for whose success
It were sin to breathe a prayer; —
Schemes which heaven may never bless —
Fears which darken to despair.
Hoary priest! thy dream is done
Of a hundred red tribes won
To the pale of Holy Church;
And the heretic o'erthrown,
And his name no longer known,
And thy weary brethren turning,
Joyful from their years of mourning,
'Twixt the altar and the porch.

Hark! what sudden sound is heard
  In the wood and in the sky,
Shriller than the scream of bird —
  Than the trumpet's clang more high!
Every wolf-cave of the hills —
  Forest arch and mountain gorge,
  Rock and dell and river verge —
With an answering echo thrills.
Well does the Jesuit know that cry,
Which summons the Norridgewock to die,
And tells that the foe of his flock is nigh.
He listens, and hears the rangers come,
With loud hurra, and jar of drum,
And hurrying feet (for the chase is hot),
And the short, sharp sound of rifle shot,
And taunt and menace — answered well
By the Indians' mocking cry and yell —
The bark of dogs — the squaw's mad scream —
The dash of paddles along the stream —
The whistle of shot as it cuts the leaves
Of the maples around the church's eaves —
And the gride of hatchets, fiercely thrown,
On wigwam-log and tree and stone.

Black with the grime of paint and dust,
  Spotted and streaked with human gore,
A grim and naked head is thrust
  Within the chapel-door.
"Ha — Bomazeen! — In God's name say,
What mean these sounds of bloody fray?"
Silent, the Indian points his hand
  To where across the echoing glen
Sweep Harmon's dreaded ranger-band,
  And Moulton with his men.
"Where are thy warriors, Bomazeen?
Where are De Rouville * and Castine,
And where the braves of Sawga's queen?"

* Hertel de Rouville was an active and unsparing enemy of the English. He was the leader of the combined French and Indian forces which destroyed

"Let my father find the winter snow
Which the sun drank up long moons ago!
Under the falls of Tacconock,
The wolves are eating the Norridgewock;
Castine with his wives lies closely hid
Like a fox in the woods of Pemaquid!
On Sawga's banks the man of war
Sits in his wigwam like a squaw —
Squando has fled, and Mogg Megone,
Struck by the knife of Sagamore John,
Lies stiff and stark and cold as a stone."

Fearfully over the Jesuit's face,
Of a thousand thoughts, trace after trace,
Like swift cloud-shadows, each other chase.
One instant, his fingers grasp his knife,
For a last vain struggle for cherished life —
The next, he hurls the blade away,
And kneels at his altar's foot to pray;
Over his beads his fingers stray,
And he kisses the cross, and calls aloud
On the Virgin and her Son;
For terrible thoughts his memory crowd
  Of evil seen and done —
Of scalps brought home by his savage flock
From Casco and Sawga and Sagadahock,
  In the Church's service won.

No shrift the gloomy savage brooks,
As scowling on the priest he looks:
"Cowesass — cowesass — tawhich wessaseen?*
Let my father look upon Bomazeen —
My father's heart is the heart of a squaw,
But mine is so hard that it does not thaw:

Deerfield, and massacred its inhabitants, in 1703. He was afterwards killed in the attack upon Haverhill. Tradition says that on examining his dead body, his head and face were found to be perfectly smooth, without the slightest appearance of hair or beard.

* *Cowesass? — tawhich wessaseen?* Are you afraid? — why fear you?

Let my father ask his God to make
  A dance and a feast for a great sagamore,
When he paddles across the western lake
  With his dogs and his squaws to the spirit's shore.
Cowesass — cowesass — tawhich wessaseen ?
Let my father die like Bomazeen ! "

Through the chapel's narrow doors,
  And through each window in the walls,
Round the priest and warrior pours
  The deadly shower of English balls.
Low on his cross the Jesuit falls ;
While at his side the Norridgewock,
With failing breath, essays to mock
And menace yet the hated foe —
Shakes his scalp-trophies to and fro
  Exultingly before their eyes —
Till, cleft and torn by shot and blow,
  Defiant still, he dies.

" So fare all eaters of the frog !
Death to the Babylonish dog !
  Down with the beast of Rome ! "
With shouts like these, around the dead,
Unconscious on his bloody bed,
  The rangers crowding come.
Brave men ! the dead priest cannot hear
The unfeeling taunt — the brutal jeer ; —
Spurn — for he sees ye not — in wrath,
The symbol of your Saviour's death ; —
  Tear from his death-grasp, in your zeal,
And trample, as a thing accursed,
The cross he cherished in the dust :
  The dead man cannot feel !

Brutal alike in deed and word,
  With callous heart and hand of strife,
How like a fiend may man be made,
Plying the foul and monstrous trade
  Whose harvest-field is human life,

Whose sickle is the reeking sword!
Quenching, with reckless hand, in blood,
Sparks kindled by the breath of God;
Urging the deathless soul, unshriven,
  Of open guilt or secret sin,
Before the bar of that pure Heaven
  The holy only enter in!
Oh! by the widow's sore distress,
The orphan's wailing wretchedness,
By Virtue struggling in the accursed
Embraces of polluting Lust,
By the fell discord of the Pit,
And the pained souls that people it,
And by the blessed peace which fills
  The Paradise of God forever,
Resting on all its holy hills,
  And flowing with its crystal river—
Let Christian hands no longer bear
  In triumph on his crimson car
  The foul and idol god of war;
No more the purple wreaths prepare
To bind amid his snaky hair;
Nor Christian bards his glories tell,
Nor Christian tongues his praises swell.

Through the gun-smoke wreathing white,
Glimpses on the soldiers' sight
A thing of human shape I ween,
For a moment only seen,
With its loose hair backward streaming,
And its eyeballs madly gleaming,
Shrieking, like a soul in pain,
  From the world of light and breath,
Hurrying to its place again,
  Spectre-like it vanisheth!

Wretched girl! one eye alone
Notes the way which thou hast gone.
That great Eye, which slumbers never,
Watching o'er a lost world ever,

Tracks thee over vale and mountain,
By the gushing forest-fountain,
Plucking from the vine its fruit,
Searching for the ground-nut's root,
Peering in the she wolf's den,
Wading through the marshy fen,
Where the sluggish water-snake
Basks beside the sunny brake,
Coiling in his slimy bed,
Smooth and cold against thy tread —
Purposeless, thy mazy way
Threading through the lingering day.
And at night securely sleeping
Where the dogwood's dews are weeping!
Still, though earth and man discard thee,
Doth thy heavenly Father guard thee —
He who spared the guilty Cain,
  Even when a brother's blood,
  Crying in the ear of God,
Gave the earth its primal stain —
He whose mercy ever liveth,
Who repenting guilt forgiveth,
And the broken heart receiveth ; —
Wanderer of the wilderness,
  Haunted, guilty, crazed and wild,
He regardeth thy distress,
  And careth for his sinful child !

'T is spring time on the eastern hills !
Like torrents gush the summer rills ;
Through winter's moss and dry dead leaves
The bladed grass revives and lives,
Pushes the mouldering waste away,
And glimpses to the April day.
In kindly shower and sunshine bud
The branches of the dull gray wood ;
Out from its sunned and sheltered nooks
The blue eye of the violet looks ;

The south-west wind is warmly blowing,
And odors from the springing grass,
The pine-tree and the sassafras,
Are with it on its errands going.

A band is marching through the wood
Where rolls the Kennebec his flood —
The warriors of the wilderness,
Painted, and in their battle dress;
And with them one whose bearded cheek,
And white and wrinkled brow, bespeak
A wanderer from the shores of France.
A few long locks of scattering snow
Beneath a battered morion flow,
And from the rivets of the vest
Which girds in steel his ample breast,
The slanted sunbeams glance.
In the harsh outlines of his face
Passion and sin have left their trace;
Yet, save worn brow and thin gray hair,
No signs of weary age are there.
His step is firm, his eye is keen,
Nor years in broil and battle spent,
Nor toil, nor wounds, nor pain have bent
The lordly frame of old Castine.

No purpose now of strife and blood
Urges the hoary veteran on:
The fire of conquest, and the mood
Of chivalry have gone.
A mournful task is his — to lay
Within the earth the bones of those
Who perished in that fearful day,
When Norridgewock became the prey
Of all unsparing foes.
Sadly and still, dark thoughts between,
Of coming vengeance mused Castine,
Of the fallen chieftain Bomazeen,
Who bade for him the Norridgewocks,
Dig up their buried tomahawks

For firm defence or swift attack ;
And him whose friendship formed the tie
Which held the stern self-exile back
From lapsing into savagery ;
Whose garb and tone and kindly glance
Recalled a younger, happier day,
And prompted memory's fond essay,
To bridge the mighty waste which lay,
Between his wild home and that gray,
Tall chateau of his native France,
Whose chapel bell, with far-heard din
Ushered his birth hour gaily in,
And counted with its solemn toll,
The masses for his father's soul.

Hark ! from the foremost of the band
Suddenly bursts the Indian yell ;
For now on the very spot they stand
Where the Norridgewocks fighting fell.
No wigwam smoke is curling there ;
The very earth is scorched and bare :
And they pause and listen to catch a sound
Of breathing life — but there comes not one,
Save the fox's bark and the rabbit's bound ;
But here and there, on the blackened ground,
White bones are glistening in the sun.
And where the house of prayer arose,
And the holy hymn, at daylight's close,
And the aged priest stood up to bless
The children of the wilderness,
There is nought save ashes sodden and dank ;
And the birchen boats of the Norridgewock,
Tethered to tree and stump and rock,
Rotting along the river bank !

Blessed Mary ! — who is she
Leaning against that maple tree ?
The sun upon her face burns hot,
But the fixed eyelid moveth not ;

The squirrel's chirp is shrill and clear
From the dry bough above her ear;
Dashing from rock and root its spray,
  Close at her feet the river rushes;
  The black-bird's wing against her brushes,
  And sweetly through the hazel bushes
  The robbin's mellow music gushes;—
God save her! will she sleep alway?

Castine hath bent him over the sleeper:
 "Wake daughter — wake!" — but she stirs no limb:
 The eye that looks on him is fixed and dim;
And the sleep she is sleeping shall be no deeper,
 Until the angel's oath is said,
And the final blast of the trump goes forth
To the graves of the sea and the graves of earth.
 RUTH BONYTHON IS DEAD!

LEGENDARY.

THE MERRIMACK.

[" The Indians speak of a beautiful river, far to the South, which they call Merrimack." — Sieur de Monts: 1604.]

Stream of my fathers! sweetly still
The sunset rays thy valley fill;
Poured slantwise down the long defile,
Wave, wood, and spire beneath them smile.
I see the winding Powow fold
The green hill in its belt of gold,
And following down its wavy line,
Its sparkling waters blend with thine.
There 's not a tree upon thy side,
Nor rock, which thy returning tide
As yet hath left abrupt and stark
Above thy evening water-mark;
No calm cove with its rocky hem,
No isle whose emerald swells begem
Thy broad, smooth current; not a sail
Bowed to the freshening ocean gale;
No small boat with its busy oars,
Nor gray wall sloping to thy shores;
Nor farm-house with its maple shade,
Or rigid poplar colonnade,
But lies distinct and full in sight,
Beneath this gush of sunset light.

Centuries ago, that harbor-bar,
Stretching its length of foam afar,
And Salisbury's beach of shining sand,
And yonder island's wave-smoothed strand,
Saw the adventurer's tiny sail
Flit, stooping from the eastern gale ;*
And o'er these woods and waters broke
The cheer from Britain's hearts of oak,
As brightly on the voyager's eye,
Weary of forest, sea, and sky,
Breaking the dull continuous wood,
The Merrimack rolled down his flood ;
Mingling that clear pellucid brook,
Which channels vast Agioochook
When spring-time's sun and shower unlock
The frozen fountains of the rock,
And more abundant waters given
From that pure lake, "The Smile of Heaven," †
Tributes from vale and mountain side —
With ocean's dark, eternal tide !

On yonder rocky cape, which braves
The stormy challenge of the waves,
Midst tangled vine and dwarfish wood,
The hardy Anglo-Saxon stood,
Planting upon the topmost crag
The staff of England's battle-flag ;
And, while from out its heavy fold
Saint George's crimson cross unrolled,
Midst roll of drum and trumpet blare,
And weapons brandishing in air,
He gave to that lone promontory
The sweetest name in all his story ; ‡

* The celebrated Captain Smith, after resigning the government of the colony in Virginia, in his capacity of "Admiral of New England," made a careful survey of the coast from Penobscot to Cape Cod, in the summer of 1614.

† Lake Winnipiseogee — *The Smile of the Great Spirit* — the source of one of the branches of the Merrimack.

‡ Capt. Smith gave to the promontory, now called Cape Ann, the name of

Of her, the flower of Islam's daughters,
Whose harems look on Stamboul's waters —
Who, when the chance of war had bound
The Moslem chain his limbs around,
Wreathed o'er with silk that iron chain,
Soothed with her smiles his hours of pain,
And fondly to her youthful slave
A dearer gift than freedom gave.

But look ! — the yellow light no more
Streams down on wave and verdant shore ;
And clearly on the calm air swells
The twilight voice of distant bells.
From Ocean's bosom, white and thin
The mists come slowly rolling in ;
Hills, woods, the river's rocky rim,
Amidst the sea-like vapor swim,
While yonder lonely coast-light set
Within its wave-washed minaret,
Half quenched, a beamless star and pale,
Shines dimly through its cloudy veil !

Home of my fathers ! — I have stood
Where Hudson rolled his lordly flood :
Seen sunrise rest and sunset fade
Along his frowning Palisade ;
Looked down the Appalachian peak
On Juniata's silver streak ;
Have seen along his valley gleam
The Mohawk's softly winding stream ;
The level light of sunset shine
Through broad Potomac's hem of pine ;
And autumn's rainbow-tinted banner
Hang lightly o'er the Susquehanna ;
Yet, wheresoe'er his step might be,
Thy wandering child looked back to thee !

Tragabizanda, in memory of his young and beautiful mistress of that name, who, while he was a captive at Constantinople, like Desdemona, "loved him for the dangers he had passed."

Heard in his dreams thy river's sound
Of murmuring on its pebbly bound,
The unforgotten swell and roar
Of waves on thy familiar shore;
And saw amidst the curtained gloom
And quiet of his lonely room,
Thy sunset scenes before him pass;
As, in Agrippa's magic glass,
The loved and lost arose to view,
Remembered groves in greenness grew,
Bathed still in childhood's morning dew,
Along whose bowers of beauty swept
Whatever Memory's mourners wept,
Sweet faces, which the charnel kept,
Young, gentle eyes, which long had slept;
And while the gazer leaned to trace,
More near, some dear familiar face,
He wept to find the vision flown —
A phantom and a dream alone!

THE NORSEMEN.

[Some three or four years since, a fragment of a statue, rudely chiseled from dark gray stone, was found in the town of Bradford, on the Merrimack. Its origin must be left entirely to conjecture. The fact that the ancient Northmen visited New England, some centuries before the discoveries of Columbus, is now very generally admitted.]

Gift from the cold and silent Past!
A relic to the present cast;
Left on the ever-changing strand
Of shifting and unstable sand,
Which wastes beneath the steady chime
And beating of the waves of Time!
Who from its bed of primal rock
First wrenched thy dark, unshapely block?
Whose hand, of curious skill untaught,
Thy rude and savage outline wrought?

The waters of my native stream
Are glancing in the sun's warm beam:
From sail-urged keel and flashing oar
The circles widen to its shore;
And cultured field and peopled town
Slope to its willowed margin down.
Yet, while this morning breeze is bringing
The mellow sound of church-bells ringing,
And rolling wheel, and rapid jar
Of the fire-winged and steedless car,
And voices from the wayside near
Come quick and blended on my ear,
A spell is in this old gray stone —
My thoughts are with the Past alone!

A change ! — The steepled town no more
Stretches along the sail-thronged shore ;
Like palace-domes in sunset's cloud,
Fade sun-gilt spire and mansion proud !
Spectrally rising where they stood,
I see the old, primeval wood :
Dark, shadow-like, on either hand
I see its solemn waste expand :
It climbs the green and cultured hill,
It arches o'er the valley's rill ;
And leans from cliff and crag, to throw
Its wild arms o'er the stream below.
Unchanged, alone, the same bright river
Flows on, as it will flow forever !
I listen, and I hear the low
Soft ripple where its waters go ;
I hear behind the panther's cry,
The wild bird's scream goes thrilling by,
And shyly on the river's brink
The deer is stooping down to drink.

But hark ! — from wood and rock flung back,
What sound comes up the Merrimack ?
What sea-worn barks are those which throw
The light spray from each rushing prow ?
Have they not in the North Sea's blast
Bowed to the waves the straining mast ?
Their frozen sails the low, pale sun
Of Thulè's night has shone upon ;
Flapped by the sea-wind's gusty sweep
Round icy drift, and headland steep.
Wild Jutland's wives and Lochlin's daughters
Have watched them fading o'er the waters,
Lessening through driving mist and spray,
Like white-winged sea-birds on their way !

Onward they glide — and now I view
Their iron-armed and stalwart crew ;
Joy glistens in each wild blue eye,
Turned to green earth and summer sky :

Each broad, seamed breast has cast aside
Its cumbering vest of shaggy hide;
Bared to the sun and soft warm air,
Streams back the Norsemen's yellow hair.
I see the gleam of axe and spear,
The sound of smitten shields I hear,
Keeping a harsh and fitting time
To Saga's chant, and Runic rhyme;
Such lays as Zetland's Skald has sung,
His gray and naked isles among;
Or muttered low at midnight hour
Round Odin's mossy stone of power.
The wolf beneath the Arctic moon
Has answered to that startling rune;
The Gaal has heard its stormy swell,
The light Frank knows its summons well;
Iona's sable-stoled Culdee
Has heard it sounding o'er the sea,
And swept with hoary beard and hair
His altar's foot in trembling prayer!

'T is past — the 'wildering vision dies
In darkness on my dreaming eyes!
The forest vanishes in air —
Hill-slope and vale lie starkly bare;
I hear the common tread of men,
And hum of work-day life again:
The mystic relic seems alone
A broken mass of common stone;
And if it be the chiseled limb
Of Berserkar or idol grim —
A fragment of Valhalla's Thor,
The stormy Viking's god of War,
Or Praga of the Runic lay,
Or love awakening Siona,
I know not — for no graven line,
Nor Druid mark, nor Runic sign,
Is left me here, by which to trace
Its name, or origin, or place.

Yet, for this vision of the Past,
This glance upon its darkness cast,
My spirit bows in gratitude
Before the Giver of all good,
Who fashioned so the human mind,
That, from the waste of Time behind
A simple stone, or mound of earth,
Can summon the departed forth;
Quicken the Past to life again —
The Present lose in what hath been,
And in their primal freshness show
The buried forms of long ago.
As if a portion of that Thought
By which the Eternal will is wrought,
Whose impulse fills anew with breath
The frozen solitude of Death,
To mortal mind were sometimes lent,
To mortal musings sometimes sent,
To whisper — even when it seems
But Memory's phantasy of dreams —
Through the mind's waste of wo and sin,
Of an immortal origin!

CASSANDRA SOUTHWICK.

[In the following ballad, the author has endeavored to display the strong enthusiasm of the early Quaker, the short-sighted intolerance of the clergy and magistrates, and that sympathy with the oppressed, which the "common people," when not directly under the control of spiritual despotism, have ever evinced. He is not blind to the extravagance of language and action which characterized some of the pioneers of Quakerism in New England, and which furnished persecution with its solitary but most inadequate excuse.

The ballad has its foundation upon a somewhat remarkable event in the history of Puritan intolerance. Two young persons, son and daughter of Lawrence Southwick, of Salem, who had himself been imprisoned and deprived of all his property for having entertained two Quakers at his house, were fined ten pounds each for non-attendance at church, which they were unable to pay. The case being represented to the General Court, at Boston, that body issued an order, which may still be seen on the court records, bearing the signature of Edward Rawson, Secretary, by which the treasurer of the County was "fully empowered to *sell the said persons* to any of the English nation *at Virginia or Barbadoes*, to answer said fines." An attempt was made to carry this barbarous order into execution, but no shipmaster was found willing to convey them to the West Indies. — Vide Sewall's History, pp. 225–6, G. Bishop.]

To the God of all sure mercies let my blessing rise to-day,
From the scoffer and the cruel He hath plucked the spoil away,—
Yea, He who cooled the furnace around the faithful three,
And tamed the Chaldean lions, hath set His handmaid free!

Last night I saw the sunset melt through my prison bars,
Last night across my damp earth-floor fell the pale gleam of stars;
In the coldness and the darkness all through the long night time,
My grated casement whitened with Autumn's early rime.

Alone, in that dark sorrow, hour after hour crept by;
Star after star looked palely in and sank adown the sky;

No sound amid night's stillness, save that which seemed to be
The dull and heavy beating of the pulses of the sea;

All night I sat unsleeping, for I knew that on the morrow
The ruler and the cruel priest would mock me in my sorrow,
Dragged to their place of market, and bargained for and sold,
Like a lamb before the shambles, like a heifer from the fold!

Oh, the weakness of the flesh was there — the shrinking and the shame;
And the low voice of the Tempter like whispers to me came:
"Why sit'st thou thus forlornly!" the wicked murmur said,
"Damp walls thy bower of beauty, cold earth thy maiden bed?

"Where be the smiling faces, and voices soft and sweet,
Seen in thy father's dwelling, heard in the pleasant street?
Where be the youths, whose glances the summer Sabbath through
Turned tenderly and timidly unto thy father's pew?

"Why sit'st thou here, Cassandra? — Bethink thee with what mirth
Thy happy schoolmates gather around the warm bright hearth;
How the crimson shadows tremble on foreheads white and fair,
On eyes of merry girlhood, half hid in golden hair.

Not for thee the hearth-fire brightens, not for thee kind words are spoken,
Not for thee the nuts of Wenham woods by laughing boys are broken,
No first-fruits of the orchard within thy lap are laid,
For thee no flowers of Autumn the youthful hunters braid.

"Oh! weak, deluded maiden! — by crazy fancies led,
With wild and raving railers an evil path to tread;
To leave a wholesome worship, and teaching pure and sound;
And mate with maniac women, loose-haired and sack-cloth-bound.

"Mad scoffers of the priesthood, who mock at things divine,
Who rail against the pulpit, and holy bread and wine;
Sore from their cart-tail scourgings, and from the pillory lame,
Rejoicing in their wretchedness, and glorying in their shame.

"And what a fate awaits thee? — a sadly toiling slave,
Dragging the slowly lengthening chain of bondage to the grave!
Think of thy woman's nature, subdued in hopeless thrall,
The easy prey of any, the scoff and scorn of all!"

Oh! — ever as the Tempter spoke, and feeble Nature's fears
Wrung drop by drop the scalding flow of unavailing tears,
I wrestled down the evil thoughts, and strove in silent prayer,
To feel, oh, Helper of the weak! — that Thou indeed wert there!

I thought of Paul and Silas, within Phillippi's cell,
And how from Peter's sleeping limbs the prison-shackles fell,
Till I seemed to hear the trailing of an angel's robe of white,
And to feel a blessed presence invisible to sight.

Bless the Lord for all His mercies! — for the peace and love I felt,
Like dew of Hermon's holy hill, upon my spirit melt;
When, "Get behind me, Satan!" was the language of my heart,
And I felt the Evil Tempter with all his doubts depart.

Slow broke the gray cold morning; again the sunshine fell,
Flecked with the shade of bar and grate within my lonely cell;
The hoar frost melted on the wall, and upward from the street
Came careless laugh and idle word, and tread of passing feet.

At length the heavy bolts fell back, my door was open cast,
And slowly at the sheriff's side, up the long street I passed;
I heard the murmur round me, and felt, but dared not see,
How, from every door and window, the people gazed on me.

And doubt and fear fell on me, shame burned upon my cheek,
Swam earth and sky around me, my trembling limbs grew weak:
"Oh, Lord! support thy handmaid; and from her soul cast out
The fear of man, which brings a snare — the weakness and the doubt."

Then the dreary shadows scattered like a cloud in morning's breeze,
And a low deep voice within me seemed whispering words like these:

"Though thy earth be as the iron, and thy heaven a brazen
wall,
Trust still His loving kindness whose power is over all."

We paused at length, where at my feet the sunlit waters broke
On glaring reach of shining beach, and shingly wall of rock;
The merchant-ships lay idly there, in hard clear lines on high,
Tracing with rope and slender spar their net-work on the sky.

And there were ancient citizens, cloak-wrapped and grave and
cold,
And grim and stout sea-captains with faces bronzed and old,
And on his horse, with Rawson, his cruel clerk at hand,
Sat dark and haughty Endicott, the ruler of the land.

And poisoning with his evil words the ruler's ready ear,
The priest leaned o'er his saddle, with laugh and scoff and jeer;
It stirred my soul, and from my lips the seal of silence broke,
As if through woman's weakness a warning spirit spoke.

I cried, "The Lord rebuke thee, thou smiter of the meek,
Thou robber of the righteous, thou trampler of the weak!
Go light the dark, cold hearth-stones — go turn the prison lock
Of the poor hearts thou hast hunted, thou wolf amid the flock!"

Dark lowered the brows of Endicott, and with a deeper red
O'er Rawson's wine-empurpled cheek the flush of anger spread;
"Good people," quoth the white-lipped priest, "heed not her
words so wild,
Her Master speaks within her — the Devil owns his child!"

But gray heads shook, and young brows knit, the while the
sheriff read
That law the wicked rulers against the poor have made,
Who to their house of Rimmon and idol priesthood bring
No bended knee of worship, nor gainful offering.

Then to the stout sea-captains the sheriff turning said:
"Which of ye, worthy seamen, will take this Quaker maid?
In the Isle of fair Barbadoes, or on Virginia's shore,
You may hold her at a higher price than Indian girl or Moor."

Grim and silent stood the captains ; and when again he cried,
"Speak out, my worthy seamen!" — no voice, no sign replied ;
But I felt a hard hand press my own, and kind words met my ear :
"God bless thee, and preserve thee, my gentle girl and dear!"

A weight seemed lifted from my heart, — a pitying friend was nigh,
I felt it in his hard, rough hand, and saw it in his eye ;
And when again the sheriff spoke, that voice, so kind to me,
Growled back its stormy answer like the roaring of the sea :

"Pile my ship with bars of silver — pack with coins of Spanish gold,
From keel-piece up to deck-plank, the roomage of her hold,
By the living God who made me! — I would sooner in your bay
Sink ship and crew and cargo, than bear this child away!"

"Well answered, worthy captain, shame on their cruel laws!"
Ran through the crowd in murmurs loud the people's just applause.
"Like the herdsman of Tekoa, in Israel of old,
Shall we see the poor and righteous again for silver sold?"

I looked on haughty Endicott ; with weapon half way drawn,
Swept round the throng his lion glare of bitter hate and scorn ;
Fiercely he drew his bridle rein, and turned in silence back,
And sneering priest and baffled clerk rode murmuring in his track.

Hard after them the sheriff looked, in bitterness of soul ;
Thrice smote his staff upon the ground, and crushed his parchment roll.
"Good friends," he said, "since both have fled, the ruler and the priest,
Judge ye, if from their further work I be not well released."

Loud was the cheer which, full and clear, swept round the silent bay,
As, with kind words and kinder looks, he bade me go my way ;

For He who turns the courses of the streamlet of the glen,
And the river of great waters, had turned the hearts of men.

Oh, at that hour the very earth seemed changed beneath my eye,
A holier wonder round me rose the blue walls of the sky,
A lovelier light on rock and hill, and stream and woodland lay,
And softer lapsed on sunnier sands the waters of the bay.

Thanksgiving to the Lord of life! — to Him all praises be,
Who from the hands of evil men hath set His handmaid free;
All praise to Him before whose power the mighty are afraid,
Who takes the crafty in the snare, which for the poor is laid!

Sing, oh, my soul, rejoicingly, on evening's twilight calm
Uplift the loud thanksgiving — pour forth the grateful psalm;
Let all dear hearts with me rejoice, as did the saints of old,
When of the Lord's good angel the rescued Peter told.

And weep and howl, ye evil priests and mighty men of wrong,
The Lord shall smite the proud and lay His hand upon the strong.
Wo to the wicked rulers in His avenging hour!
Wo to the wolves who seek the flocks to raven and devour:

But let the humble ones arise, — the poor in heart be glad,
And let the mourning ones again with robes of praise be clad,
For He who cooled the furnace, and smoothed the stormy wave,
And tamed the Chaldean lions, is mighty still to save!

FUNERAL TREE OF THE SOKOKIS.*

AROUND Sebago's lonely lake
There lingers not a breeze to break
The mirror which its waters make.

The solemn pines along its shore,
The firs which hang its gray rocks o'er,
Are painted on its glassy floor.

The sun looks o'er, with hazy eye,
The snowy mountain-tops which lie
Piled coldly up against the sky.

Dazzling and white ! save where the bleak,
Wild winds have bared some splintering peak,
Or snow-slide left its dusky streak.

Yet green are Saco's banks below,
And belts of spruce and cedar show,
Dark fringing round those cones of snow.

The earth hath felt the breath of spring,
Though yet on her deliverer's wing
The lingering frosts of winter cling.

* Polan, a chief of the Sokokis Indians, the original inhabitants of the country lying between Agamenticus and Casco bay, was killed in a skirmish at Windham, on the Sebago lake, in the spring of 1756. He claimed all the lands on both sides of the Presumpscot river to its mouth at Casco, as his own. He was shrewd, subtle, and brave. After the white men had retired, the surviving Indians "swayed" or bent down a young tree until its roots were turned up, placed the body of their chief beneath them, and then released the tree to spring back to its former position

Fresh grasses fringe the meadow-brooks,
And mildly from its sunny nooks
The blue eye of the violet looks.

And odors from the springing grass,
The sweet birch and the sassafras,
Upon the scarce-felt breezes pass.

Her tokens of renewing care
Hath Nature scattered everywhere,
In bud and flower, and warmer air.

But in their hour of bitterness,
What reck the broken Sokokis,
Beside their slaughtered chief, of this?

The turf's red stain is yet undried —
Scarce have the death-shot echoes died
Along Sebago's wooded side:

And silent now the hunters stand,
Grouped darkly, where a swell of land
Slopes upward from the lake's white sand.

Fire and the axe have swept it bare,
Save one lone beech, unclosing there
Its light leaves in the vernal air.

With grave, cold looks, all sternly mute,
They break the damp turf at its foot,
And bare its coiled and twisted root.

They heave the stubborn trunk aside,
The firm roots from the earth divide —
The rent beneath yawns dark and wide.

And there the fallen chief is laid,
In tasseled garb of skins arrayed,
And girded with his wampum-braid.

The silver cross he loved is pressed
Beneath the heavy arms, which rest
Upon his scarred and naked breast.*

'T is done: the roots are backward sent,
The beechen tree stands up unbent —
The Indian's fitting monument!

When of that sleeper's broken race
Their green and pleasant dwelling-place
Which knew them once, retains no trace;

O! long may sunset's light be shed
As now upon that beech's head —
A green memorial of the dead!

There shall his fitting requiem be,
In northern winds, that, cold and free,
Howl nightly in that funeral tree.

To their wild wail the waves which break
Forever round that lonely lake
A solemn under-tone shall make!

And who shall deem the spot unblest,
Where Nature's younger children rest,
Lulled on their sorrowing mother's breast?

Deem ye that mother loveth less
These bronzed forms of the wilderness
She foldeth in her long caress?

As sweet o'er them her wild flowers blow,
As if with fairer hair and brow
The blue-eyed Saxon slept below.

* The Sokokis were early converts to the Catholic faith. Most of them, prior to the year 1756, had removed to the French settlements on the St. François.

What though the places of their rest
No priestly knee hath ever pressed —
No funeral rite nor prayer hath blessed ?

What though the bigot's ban be there,
And thoughts of wailing and despair,
And cursing in the place of prayer ! *

Yet Heaven hath angels watching round
The Indian's lowliest forest-mound —
And *they* have made it holy ground.

There ceases man's frail judgment ; all
His powerless bolts of cursing fall
Unheeded on that grassy pall.

O, peeled, and hunted, and reviled,
Sleep on, dark tenant of the wild !
Great Nature owns her simple child !

And Nature's God, to whom alone
The secret of the heart is known —
The hidden language traced thereon ;

Who from its many cumberings
Of form and creed, and outward things,
To light the naked spirit brings ;

Not with our partial eye shall scan —
Not with our pride and scorn shall ban
The spirit of our brother man !

* The brutal and unchristian spirit of the early settlers of New England toward the red man, is strikingly illustrated in the conduct of the man who shot down the Sokokis chief. He used to say he always noticed the anniversary of that exploit, as "the day on which he sent the devil a present." — *Williamson's History of Maine.*

ST. JOHN.

[THE fierce rivalship of the two French officers, left by the death of RAZILLA in the possession of Acadia, or Nova Scotia, forms one of the most romantic passages in the history of the New World. CHARLES ST. ESTIENNE, inheriting from his father the title of Lord DE LA TOUR, whose seat was at the mouth of the St. John's river, was a Protestant; DE AULNEY CHARNISY, whose fortress was at the mouth of the Penobscot, or ancient *Pentagoet*, was a Catholic. The incentives of a false religious feeling, sectarian intolerance, and personal interest and ambition, conspired to render their feud bloody and unspairing. The Catholic was urged on by the Jesuits, who had found protection from Puritan gallows-ropes under his jurisdiction; the Huguenot still smarted under the recollection of his wrongs and persecutions in France. Both claimed to be champions of that cross from which went upward the holy petition of the Prince of Peace: "*Father, forgive them.*" LA TOUR received aid in several instances from the Puritan colonies of Massachusetts. During one of his voyages for the purpose of obtaining arms and provisions for his establishment at St. John, his castle was attacked by DE AULNEY, and successfully defended by its high-spirited mistress. A second attack, however, followed in the 4th mo. 1647. Lady LA TOUR defended her castle with a desperate perseverance. After a furious cannonade, DE AULNEY stormed the walls, and put the entire garrison to the sword. Lady LA TOUR languished a few days only in the hands of her inveterate enemy, and died of grief, greatly regretted by the colonists of Boston, to whom, as a devoted Protestant, she was well known.]

"To the winds give our banner!
  Bear homeward again!"
Cried the lord of Acadia,
  Cried Charles of Estienne;
From the prow of his shallop
  He gazed, as the sun,
From its bed in the ocean,
  Streamed up the St. John.

O'er the blue western waters
  That shallop had passed,

Where the mists of Penobscot
  Clung damp on her mast.
St. Saviour* had look'd
  On the heretic sail,
As the songs of the Huguenot
  Rose on the gale.

The pale, ghostly fathers
  Remembered her well,
And had cursed her while passing,
  With taper and bell,
But the men of Monhegan,†
  Of Papists abhorr'd,
Had welcomed and feasted
  The heretic Lord.

They had loaded his shallop
  With dun-fish and ball,
With stores for his larder,
  And steel for his wall.
Pemequid, from her bastions
  And turrets of stone,
Had welcomed his coming
  With banner and gun.

And the prayers of the elders
  Had followed his way,
As homeward he glided,
  Down Pentecost Bay.
O! well sped La Tour!
  For, in peril and pain,
His lady kept watch
  For his coming again.

O'er the Isle of the Pheasant
  The morning sun shone,
On the plane trees which shaded
  The shores of St. John.

* The settlement of the Jesuits on the island of Mount Desert was called St. Saviour.

† The isle of Monhegan was one of the first settled on the coast of Maine.

"Now, why from yon battlements
  Speaks not my love!
Why waves there no banner
  My fortress above?"

Dark and wild, from his deck
  St. Estienne gazed about,
On fire-wasted dwellings,
  And silent redoubt;
From the low, shattered walls
  Which the flame had o'errun,
There floated no banner,
  There thunder'd no gun!

But, beneath the low arch
  Of its doorway there stood
A pale priest of Rome,
  In his cloak and his hood.
With the bound of a lion,
  La Tour sprang to land,
On the throat of the Papist
  He fastened his hand.

"Speak, son of the Woman,
  Of scarlet and sin!
What wolf has been prowling
  My castle within?"
From the grasp of the soldier
  The Jesuit broke,
Half in scorn, half in sorrow,
  He smiled as he spoke:

"No wolf, Lord of Estienne,
  Has ravaged thy hall,
But thy red-handed rival,
  With fire, steel, and ball!
On an errand of mercy
  I hitherward came,
While the walls of thy castle
  Yet spouted with flame.

"Pentagoet's dark vessels
Were moored in the bay,
Grim sea-lions, roaring
Aloud for their prey."
"But what of my lady?"
Cried Charles of Estienne:
"On the shot-crumbled turret
Thy lady was seen:

"Half-veiled in the smoke-cloud,
Her hand grasped thy pennon,
While her dark tresses swayed
In the hot breath of cannon!
But wo to the heretic,
Evermore wo!
When the son of the church
And the cross is his foe!

"In the track of the shell,
In the path of the ball,
Pentagoet swept over
The breach of the wall!
Steel to steel, gun to gun,
One moment — and then
Alone stood the victor,
Alone with his men!

"Of its sturdy defenders,
Thy lady alone
Saw the cross-blazon'd banner
Float over St. John."
"Let the dastard look to it!"
Cried fiery Estienne,
"Were D'Aulney King Louis,
I 'd free her again!"

"Alas, for thy lady!
No service from thee
Is needed by her
Whom the Lord hath set free:

Nine days, in stern silence,
  Her thraldom she bore,
But the tenth morning came,
  And Death opened her door!"

As if suddenly smitten
  La Tour stagger'd back;
His hand grasped his sword-hilt,
  His forehead grew black.
He sprang on the deck
  Of his shallop again:
"We cruise now for vengeance!
  Give way!" cried Estienne.

"Massachusetts shall hear
  Of the Huguenot's wrong,
And from island and creek-side
  Her fishers shall throng!
Pentagoet shall rue
  What his Papists have done,
When his palisades echo
  The Puritan's gun!"

O! the loveliest of heavens
  Hung tenderly o'er him,
There were waves in the sunshine,
  And green isles before him:
But a pale hand was beckoning
  The Huguenot on;
And in blackness and ashes
  Behind was St. John!

PENTUCKET.

[The village of Haverhill, on the Merrimack, called by the Indians, Pentucket, was for nearly seventeen years a frontier town, and during thirty years endured all the horrors of savage warfare. In the year 1708, a combined body of French and Indians, under the command of De Challions, and Hertel de Rouville, the infamous and bloody sacker of Deerfield, made an attack upon the village, which at that time contained only thirty houses. Sixteen of the villagers were massacred, and a still larger number made prisoners. About thirty of the enemy also fell, and among them Hertel de Rouville. The minister of the place, Benjamin Rolfe, was killed by a shot through his own door.]

How sweetly on the wood-girt town
The mellow light of sunset shone!
Each small, bright lake, whose waters still
Mirror the forest and the hill,
Reflected from its waveless breast
The beauty of a cloudless West,
Glorious as if a glimpse were given
Within the western gates of Heaven,
Left, by the spirit of the star
Of sunset's holy hour, ajar!

Beside the river's tranquil flood
The dark and low-wall'd dwellings stood,
Where many a rood of open land
Stretch'd up and down on either hand,
With corn-leaves waving freshly green
The thick and blacken'd stumps between.
Behind, unbroken, deep and dread,
The wild, untravel'd forest spread,
Back to those mountains, white and cold,
Of which the Indian trapper told,
Upon whose summits never yet
Was mortal foot in safety set.

Quiet and calm, without a fear
Of danger darkly lurking near,
The weary laborer left his plough —
The milk-maid carol'd by her cow —
From cottage door and household hearth
Rose songs of praise, or tones of mirth.
At length the murmur died away,
And silence on that village lay —
So slept Pompeii, tower and hall,
Ere the quick earthquake swallow'd all,
Undreaming of the fiery fate
Which made its dwellings desolate!

Hours pass'd away. By moonlight sped
The Merrimack along his bed.
Bathed in the pallid lustre, stood
Dark cottage-wall and rock and wood,
Silent, beneath that tranquil beam,
As the hush'd grouping of a dream.
Yet on the still air crept a sound —
No bark of fox — nor rabbit's bound —
Nor stir of wings — nor waters flowing —
Nor leaves in midnight breezes blowing.

Was that the tread of many feet,
Which downward from the hill-side beat?
What forms were those which darkly stood
Just on the margin of the wood? —
Charr'd tree-stumps in the moonlight dim,
Or paling rude, or leafless limb?
No — through the trees fierce eye-balls glow'd,
Dark human forms in moonshine show'd,
Wild from their native wilderness,
With painted limbs and battle-dress!

A yell, the dead might wake to hear,
Swell'd on the night air, far and clear —
Then smote the Indian tomahawk
On crashing door and shattering lock —
Then rang the rifle-shot — and then
The shrill death-scream of stricken men —

Sank the red axe in woman's brain,
And childhood's cry arose in vain —
Bursting through roof and window came,
Red, fast and fierce, the kindled flame ;
And blended fire and moonlight glared
On still dead men and weapons bared.

The morning sun looked brightly through
The river willows, wet with dew.
No sound of combat fill'd the air, —
No shout was heard, — nor gun-shot there :
Yet still the thick and sullen smoke
From smouldering ruins slowly broke ;
And on the green sward many a stain,
And, here and there, the mangled slain,
Told how that midnight bolt had sped,
Pentucket, on thy fated head !

Even now, the villager can tell
Where Rolfe beside his hearth-stone fell,
Still show the door of wasting oak
Through which the fatal death-shot broke,
And point the curious stranger where
De Rouville's corse lay grim and bare —
Whose hideous head, in death still fear'd,
Bore not a trace of hair or beard —
And still, within the churchyard ground,
Heaves darkly up the ancient mound,
Whose grass-grown surface overlies
The victims of that sacrifice.

THE FAMILIST'S HYMN.

[The "Pilgrims" of New England, even in their wilderness home, were not exempted from the sectarian contentions which agitated the mother country after the downfall of Charles the First, and of the established Episcopacy. The Quakers, Baptists, and Catholics were banished, on pain of death, from the Massachusetts Colony. One Samuel Gorton, a bold and eloquent declaimer, after preaching for a time in Boston, against the doctrines of the Puritans, and declaring that their churches were mere human devices, and their sacrament and baptism an abomination, was driven out of the State's jurisdiction, and compelled to seek a residence among the savages. He gathered round him a considerable number of converts, who, like the primitive Christians, shared all things in common. His opinions, however, were so troublesome to the leading clergy of the Colony, that they instigated an attack upon his "Family" by an armed force, which seized upon the principal men in it, and brought them into Massachusetts, where they were sentenced to be kept at hard labor in several towns (one only in each town), during the pleasure of the General Court, they being forbidden, under severe penalties, to utter any of their religious sentiments, except to such ministers as might labor for their conversion. They were unquestionably sincere in their opinions, and, whatever may have been their errors, deserve to be ranked among those who have in all ages suffered for the freedom of conscience.]

FATHER! to thy suffering poor
  Strength and grace and faith impart,
And with Thy own love restore
  Comfort to the broken heart!
Oh, the failing ones confirm
  With a holier strength of zeal!—
Give Thou not the feeble worm
  Helpless to the spoiler's heel!

Father! for Thy holy sake
  We are spoiled and hunted thus;
Joyful, for Thy truth we take
  Bonds and burthens unto us:

Poor, and weak, and robbed of all,
  Weary with our daily task,
That Thy truth may never fall
  Through our weakness, Lord, we ask.

Round our fired and wasted homes
  Flits the forest-bird unscared,
And at noon the wild beast comes
  Where our frugal meal was shared;
For the song of praises there
  Shrieks the crow the livelong day,
For the sound of evening prayer
  Howls the evil beast of prey!

Sweet the songs we loved to sing
  Underneath Thy holy sky —
Words and tones that used to bring
  Tears of joy in every eye, —
Dear the wrestling hours of prayer,
  When we gathered knee to knee,
Blameless youth and hoary hair,
  Bow'd, O God, alone to Thee.

As Thine early children, Lord,
  Shared their wealth and daily bread,
Even so, with one accord,
  We, in love, each other fed.
Not with us the miser's hoard,
  Not with us his grasping hand;
Equal round a common board,
  Drew our meek and brother band!

Safe our quiet Eden lay
  When the war-whoop stired the land,
And the Indian turn'd away
  From our homes his bloody hand.
Well that forest-ranger saw,
  That the burthen and the curse
Of the white man's cruel law
  Rested also upon us.

Torn apart, and driven forth
  To our toiling hard and long,
Father! from the dust of earth
  Lift we still our grateful song!
Grateful — that in bonds we share
  In Thy love which maketh free;
Joyful — that the wrongs we bear,
  Draw us nearer, Lord, to Thee!

Grateful! — that where'er we toil —
  By Wachuset's wooded side,
On Nantucket's sea-worn isle,
  Or by wild Neponset's tide —
Still, in spirit, we are near,
  And our evening hymns which rise
Separate and discordant here,
  Meet and mingle in the skies!

Let the scoffer scorn and mock,
  Let the proud and evil priest
Rob the needy of his flock,
  For his wine-cup and his feast, —
Redden not Thy bolts in store
  Through the blackness of Thy skies?
For the sighing of the poor
  Wilt Thou not, at length, arise?

Worn and wasted, oh, how long
  Shall Thy trodden poor complain?
In Thy name they bear the wrong,
  In Thy cause the bonds of pain!
Melt oppression's heart of steel,
  Let the haughty priesthood see,
And their blinded followers feel,
  That in us they mock at Thee!

In Thy time, O Lord of hosts,
  Stretch abroad that hand to save
Which of old, on Egypt's coasts,
  Smote apart the Red Sea's wave!

Lead us from this evil land,
  From the spoiler set us free,
And once more our gather'd band,
  Heart to heart, shall worship Thee!

THE FOUNTAIN.

[On the declivity of a hill, in Salisbury, Essex county, is a beautiful fountain of clear water, gushing out from the very roots of a majestic and venerable oak. It is about two miles from the junction of the Powow river with the Merrimack.]

TRAVELLER ! on thy journey toiling
  By the swift Powow,
With the summer sunshine falling
  On thy heated brow,
Listen, while all else is still
To the brooklet from the hill.

Wild and sweet the flowers are blowing
  By that streamlet's side,
And a greener verdure showing
  Where its waters glide —
Down the hill-slope murmuring on,
Over root and mossy stone.

Where yon oak his broad arms flingeth
  O'er the sloping hill,
Beautiful and freshly springeth
  That soft-flowing rill,
Through its dark roots wreath'd and bare,
Gushing up to sun and air.

Brighter waters sparkled never
  In that magic well,
Of whose gift of life for ever
  Ancient legends tell, —
In the lonely desert wasted,
And by mortal lip untasted.

Waters which the proud Castilian *
  Sought with longing eyes,
Underneath the bright pavilion
  Of the Indian skies;
Where his forest pathway lay
Through the blooms of Florida.

Years ago a lonely stranger,
  With the dusky brow
Of the outcast forest-ranger,
  Crossed the swift Powow;
And betook him to the rill,
And the oak upon the hill.

O'er his face of moody sadness
  For an instant shone
Something like a gleam of gladness,
  As he stooped him down
To the fountain's grassy side
And his eager thirst supplied.

With the oak its shadow throwing
  O'er his mossy seat,
And the cool, sweet waters flowing
  Softly at his feet,
Closely by the fountain's rim
That lone Indian seated him.

Autumn's earliest frost had given
  To the woods below
Hues of beauty, such as Heaven
  Lendeth to its bow;
And the soft breeze from the west
Scarcely broke their dreamy rest.

Far behind was Ocean striving
  With his chains of sand;
Southward, sunny glimpses giving,
  'Twixt the swells of land,

* De Soto, in the sixteenth century, penetrated into the wilds of the new world in search of gold and the fountain of perpetual youth.

Of its calm and silvery track,
Rolled the tranquil Merrimack.

Over village, wood and meadow,
  Gazed that stranger man
Sadly, till the twilight shadow
  Over all things ran,
Save where spire and westward pane
Flashed the sunset back again.

Gazing thus upon the dwelling
  Of his warrior sires,
Where no lingering trace was telling
  Of their wigwam fires,
Who the gloomy thoughts might know
Of that wandering child of woe?

Naked lay, in sunshine glowing,
  Hills that once had stood
Down their sides the shadows throwing
  Of a mighty wood,
Where the deer his covert kept,
And the eagle's pinion swept!

Where the birch canoe had glided
  Down the swift Powow,
Dark and gloomy bridges strided
  Those clear waters now;
And where once the beaver swam,
Jarred the wheel and frowned the dam.

For the wood-bird's merry singing,
  And the hunter's cheer,
Iron clang and hammer's ringing
  Smote upon his ear;
And the thick and sullen smoke
From the blackened forges broke.

Could it be, his fathers ever,
  Loved to linger here?
These bare hills — this conquer'd river —
  Could they hold them dear,

With their native loveliness
Tamed and tortured into this?

Sadly, as the shades of even
  Gathered o'er the hill,
While the western half of Heaven
  Blushed with sunset still,
From the fountain's mossy seat
Turned the Indian's weary feet.

Year on year hath flown for ever,
  But he came no more
To the hill-side or the river
  Where he came before.
But the villager can tell
Of that strange man's visit well.

And the merry children, laden
  With their fruits or flowers —
Roving boy and laughing maiden,
  In their school-day hours,
Love the simple tale to tell
Of the Indian and his well.

THE EXILES.

[THE incidents upon which the following ballad has its foundation, occurred about the year 1660. Thomas Macey was one of the first, if not *the* first white settler of Nantucket. A quaint description of his singular and perilous voyage, in his own hand-writing, is still preserved.]

THE goodman sat beside his door
  One sultry afternoon,
With his young wife singing at his side
  An old and goodly tune.

A glimmer of heat was in the air, —
  The dark green woods were still ;
And the skirts of a heavy thunder-cloud
  Hung over the western hill.

Black, thick, and vast, arose that cloud
  Above the wilderness,
As some dark world from upper air
  Were stooping over this.

At times, the solemn thunder pealed,
  And all was still again,
Save a low murmur in the air
  Of coming wind and rain.

Just as the first big rain-drop fell,
  A weary stranger came,
And stood before the farmer's door,
  With travel soiled and lame.

Sad seemed he, yet sustaining hope
  Was in his quiet glance,
And peace, like autumn's moonlight, clothed
  His tranquil countenance.

A look, like that his Master wore
  In Pilate's council-hall:
It told of wrongs — but of a love
  Meekly forgiving all.

"Friend! wilt thou give me shelter here?"
  The stranger meekly said;
And, leaning on his oaken staff,
  The goodman's features read.

"My life is hunted — evil men
  Are following in my track;
The traces of the torturer's whip
  Are on my aged back.

"And much, I fear, 't will peril thee
  Within thy doors to take
A hunted seeker of the Truth,
  Oppressed for conscience sake."

Oh, kindly spoke the goodman's wife —
  "Come in, old man!" quoth she, —
"We will not leave thee to the storm
  Whoever thou may'st be."

Then came the aged wanderer in,
  And silent sat him down;
While all within grew dark as night
  Beneath the storm-cloud's frown.

But while the sudden lightning's blaze
  Filled every cottage nook,
And with the jarring thunder-roll
  The loosened casements shook,

A heavy tramp of horses' feet
  Came sounding up the lane,
And half a score of horse, or more,
  Came plunging through the rain.

"Now, Goodman Macey, ope thy door,—
  We would not be house-breakers;
A rueful deed thou 'st done this day,
  In harboring banished Quakers."

Out looked the cautious goodman then,
  With much of fear and awe,
For there, with broad wig drenched with rain,
  The parish priest he saw.

"Open thy door, thou wicked man,
  And let thy pastor in,
And give God thanks, if forty stripes
  Repay thy deadly sin."

"What seek ye?" quoth the goodman,—
  "The stranger is my guest;
He is worn with toil and grievous wrong,—
  Pray let the old man rest.

"Now, out upon thee, canting knave!"
  And strong hands shook the door,
"Believe me, Macey," quoth the priest,—
  "Thou 'lt rue thy conduct sore."

Then kindled Macey's eye of fire:
  "No priest who walks the earth,
Shall pluck away the stranger-guest
  Made welcome to my hearth."

Down from his cottage wall he caught
  The matchlock, hotly tried
At Preston-pans and Marston-moor,
  By fiery Ireton's side;

Where Puritan, and Cavalier,
  With shout and psalm contended;
And Rupert's oath, and Cromwell's prayer,
  With battle-thunder blended.

Up rose the ancient stranger then:
  "My spirit is not free
To bring the wrath and violence
  Of evil men on thee:

"And for thyself, I pray forbear,—
  Bethink thee of thy Lord,
Who healed again the smitten ear,
  And sheathed his follower's sword.

"I go, as to the slaughter led:
  Friends of the poor, farewell!"
Beneath his hand the oaken door,
  Back on its hinges fell.

  "Come forth, old grey-beard, yea and nay;"
The reckless scoffers cried,
  As to a horseman's saddle-bow
The old man's arms were tied.

And of his bondage hard and long
  In Boston's crowded jail,
Where suffering woman's prayer was heard,
  With sickening childhood's wail,

It suits not with our tale to tell:
  Those scenes have passed away—
Let the dim shadows of the past
  Brood o'er that evil day.

"Ho, sheriff!" quoth the ardent priest—
  "Take goodman Macey too;
The sin of this day's heresy,
  His back or purse shall rue."

And priest and sheriff, both together
Upon his threshold stood,
When Macey, through another door,
Sprang out into the wood.

"Now goodwife, haste thee!" Macey cried,
She caught his manly arm: —
Behind, the parson urged pursuit,
With outcry and alarm.

Ho! speed the Maceys, neck or nought, —
The river course was near: —
The plashing on its pebbled shore
Was music to their ear.

A grey rock, tasseled o'er with birch
Above the waters hung,
And at its base, with every wave,
A small light wherry swung.

A leap — they gain the boat — and there
The goodman wields his oar:
"Ill luck betide them all" — he cried, —
"The laggards upon the shore."

Down through the crashing under-wood,
The burly sheriff came: —
"Stand, goodman Macey — yield thyself;
Yield in the King's own name."

"Now out upon thy hangman's face!"
Bold Macey answered then, —
"Whip *women*, on the village green,
But meddle not with *men*."

The priest came panting to the shore, —
His grave cocked hat was gone:
Behind him, like some owl's nest, hung
His wig upon a thorn.

"Come back — come back!" the parson cried,
  "The church's curse beware."
"Curse an' thou wilt," said Macey, "but
  Thy blessing prithee spare."

"Vile scoffer!" cried the baffled priest, —
  "Thou 'lt yet the gallows see."
"Who's born to be hanged, will not be drowned,"
  Quoth Macey merrily;

"And so, sir sheriff and priest, good bye!"
  He bent him to his oar,
And the small boat glided quietly
  From the twain upon the shore.

Now in the west, the heavy clouds
  Scattered and fell asunder,
While feebler came the rush of rain,
  And fainter growled the thunder.

And through the broken clouds, the sun
  Looked out serene and warm,
Painting its holy symbol-light
  Upon the passing storm.

Oh, beautiful! that rainbow span,
  O'er dim Crane-neck was bended; —
One bright foot touched the eastern hills,
  And one with ocean blended.

By green Pentucket's southern slope
  The small boat glided fast, —
The watchers of "the Block-house" saw
  The strangers as they passed.

That night a stalwart garrison
  Sat shaking in their shoes,
To hear the dip of Indian oars, —
  The glide of birch canoes.

The fisher-wives of Salisbury,
  (The men were all away),
Looked out to see the stranger oar
  Upon their waters play.

Deer-Island's rocks and fir-trees threw
  Their sunset-shadows o'er them,
And Newbury's spire and weathercock
  Peered o'er the pines before them.

Around the Black Rocks, on their left,
  The marsh lay broad and green;
And on their right, with dwarf shrubs crowned,
  Plum Island's hills were seen.

With skilful hand and wary eye
  The harbor-bar was crossed;—
A plaything of the restless wave,
  The boat on ocean tossed.

The glory of the sunset heaven
  On land and water lay,—
On the steep hills of Agawam,
  On cape, and bluff, and bay.

They passed the grey rocks of Cape Ann,
  And Gloucester's harbor-bar;
The watch-fire of the garrison
  Shone like a setting star.

How brightly broke the morning
  On Massachusetts' Bay!
Blue wave, and bright green island,
  Rejoicing in the day.

On passed the bark in safety
  Round isle and headland steep—
No tempest broke above them,
  No fog-cloud veiled the deep.

Far round the bleak and stormy Cape
  The vent'rous Macey passed,
And on Nantucket's naked isle,
  Drew up his boat at last.

And how, in log-built cabin,
  They braved the rough sea-weather;
And there, in peace and quietness,
  Went down life's vale together:

How others drew around them,
  And how their fishing sped,
Until to every wind of heaven
  Nantucket's sails were spread:

How pale want alternated
  With plenty's golden smile;
Behold, is it not written
  In the annals of the isle?

And yet that isle remaineth
  A refuge of the free,
As when true-hearted Macey
  Beheld it from the sea.

Free as the winds that winnow
  Her shrubless hills of sand —
Free as the waves that batter
  Along her yielding land.

Than hers, at duty's summons,
  No loftier spirit stirs, —
Nor falls o'er human suffering
  A readier tear than hers.

God bless the sea-beat island! —
  And grant for evermore,
That charity and freedom dwell,
  As now upon her shore!

THE NEW WIFE AND THE OLD.

[The following Ballad is founded upon one of the marvellous legends connected with the famous Gen. M., of Hampton, N. H., who was regarded by his neighbors as a Yankee Faust, in league with the adversary. I give the story, as I heard it when a child, from a venerable family visitant.]

Dark the halls, and cold the feast —
Gone the bridemaids, gone the priest!
All is over — all is done,
Twain of yesterday are one!
Blooming girl and manhood grey,
Autumn in the arms of May!

Hushed within and hushed without,
Dancing feet and wrestlers' shout;
Dies the bonfire on the hill;
All is dark and all is still,
Save the starlight, save the breeze
Moaning through the grave-yard trees;
And the great sea-waves below,
Like the night's pulse, beating slow.

From the brief dream of a bride
She hath wakened, at his side.
With half uttered shriek and start —
Feels she not his beating heart?
And the pressure of his arm,
And his breathing near and warm?

Lightly from the bridal bed
Springs that fair dishevelled head,
And a feeling, new, intense,
Half of shame, half innocence,

Maiden fear and wonder speaks
Through her lips and changing cheeks.

From the oaken mantel glowing
Faintest light the lamp is throwing
On the mirror's antique mould,
High-backed chair, and wainscot old,
And, through faded curtains stealing,
His dark sleeping face revealing.

Listless lies the strong man there,
Silver-streaked his careless hair;
Lips of love have left no trace
On that hard and haughty face;
And that forehead's knitted thought
Love's soft hand hath not unwrought.

"Yet," she sighs, "he loves me well,
More than these calm lips will tell.
Stooping to my lowly state,
He hath made me rich and great,
And I bless him, though he be
Hard and stern to all save me!"

While she speaketh, falls the light
O'er her fingers small and white;
Gold and gem, and costly ring
Back the timid lustre fling —
Love's selectest gifts, and rare,
His proud hand had fastened there.

Gratefully she marks the glow
From those tapering lines of snow;
Fondly o'er the sleeper bending
His black hair with golden blending,
In her soft and light caress,
Cheek and lip together press.

Ha! — that start of horror! — Why
That wild stare and wilder cry,
Full of terror, full of pain?
Is there madness in her brain?

Hark ! that gasping, hoarse and low :
" Spare me — spare me — let me go ! "

God have mercy ! — Icy cold
Spectral hands her own enfold,
Drawing silently from them
Love's fair gifts of gold and gem,
" Waken ! save me ! " still as death
At her side he slumbereth.

Ring and bracelet all are gone,
And that ice-cold hand withdrawn ;
But she hears a murmur low,
Full of sweetness, full of woe,
Half a sigh and half a moan :
" Fear not ! give the dead her own ! "

Ah ! — the dead wife's voice she knows !
That cold hand whose pressure froze,
Once in warmest life had borne
Gem and band her own hath worn.
" Wake thee ! wake thee ! " Lo, his eyes
Open with a dull surprise.

In his arms the strong man folds her,
Closer to his breast he holds her ;
Trembling limbs his own are meeting,
And he feels her heart's quick beating :
" Nay, my dearest, why this fear ? "
" Hush ! " she saith, " the dead is here ! "

" Nay, a dream — an idle dream."
But before the lamp's pale gleam
Tremblingly her hand she raises, —
There no more the diamond blazes,
Clasp of pearl, or ring of gold, —
" Ah ! " she sighs, " her hand was cold ! "

Broken words of cheer he saith,
But his dark lip quivereth,
And as o'er the past he thinketh,
From his young wife's arms he shrinketh ;

Can those soft arms round him lie,
Underneath his dead wife's eye?

She her fair young head can rest
Soothed and child-like on his breast,
And in trustful innocence
Draw new strength and courage thence;
He, the proud man, feels within
But the cowardice of sin!

She can murmur in her thought
Simple prayers her mother taught,
And His blessed angels call,
Whose great love is over all;
He, alone, in prayerless pride,
Meets the dark Past at her side!

One, who living shrank with dread,
From his look, or word, or tread,
Unto whom her early grave
Was as freedom to the slave,
Moves him at this midnight hour,
With the dead's unconscious power!

Ah, the dead, the unforgot!
From their solemn homes of thought,
Where the cypress shadows blend
Darkly over foe and friend,
Or in love or sad rebuke,
Back upon the living look.

And the tenderest ones and weakest,
Who their wrongs have borne the meekest,
Lifting from those dark, still places,
Sweet and sad-remembered faces,
O'er the guilty hearts behind
An unwitting triumph find.

H. Billings del. A. C. Warren Sc.

The blast which Freedom's Angel blew
O'er her green Islands, echoes through
Each valley of our forest land.

VOICES OF FREEDOM.

TOUSSAINT L'OUVERTURE.

[TOUSSAINT L'OUVERTURE, the black chieftain of Hayti, was a slave on the plantation "de Libertas," belonging to M. BAYOU. When the rising of the negroes took place, in 1791, TOUSSAINT refused to join them until he had aided M. BAYOU and his family to escape to Baltimore. The white man had discovered in TOUSSAINT many noble qualities, and had instructed him in some of the first branches of education; and the preservation of his life was owing to the negro's gratitude for this kindness.

In 1797, TOUSSAINT L'OUVERTURE was appointed, by the French government, General-in-Chief of the armies of St. Domingo, and, as such, signed the Convention with General MAITLAND, for the evacuation of the island by the British. From this period, until 1801, the island, under the government of TOUSSAINT was happy, tranquil, and prosperous. The miserable attempt of NAPOLEON to reëstablish slavery in St. Domingo, although it failed of its intended object, proved fatal to the negro chieftain. Treacherously seized by LE CLERC, he was hurried on board a vessel by night, and conveyed to France, where he was confined in a cold subterranean dungeon, at Besançon, where, in April, 1803, he died. The treatment of TOUSSAINT finds a parallel only in the murder of the DUKE D'ENGHEIN. It was the remark of GODWIN, in his Lectures, that the West India Islands, since their first discovery by COLUMBUS, could not boast of a single name which deserves comparison with that of TOUSSAINT L'OUVERTURE.]

'TWAS night. The tranquil moonlight smile
With which Heaven dreams of Earth, shed down
Its beauty on the Indian isle —
On broad green field and white-walled town;
And inland waste of rock and wood,
In searching sunshine, wild and rude,

Rose, mellowed through the silver gleam,
Soft as the landscape of a dream,
All motionless and dewy wet,
Tree, vine, and flower in shadow met:
The myrtle with its snowy bloom,
Crossing the nightshade's solemn gloom —
The white cecropia's silver rind
Relieved by deeper green behind, —
The orange with its fruit of gold, —
The lithe paullinia's verdant fold, —
The passion-flower, with symbol holy,
Twining its tendrils long and lowly, —
The rhexias dark, and cassia tall,
And proudly rising over all,
The kingly palm's imperial stem,
Crowned with its leafy diadem, —
Star-like, beneath whose sombre shade,
The fiery-winged cucullo played!

Yes — lovely was thine aspect, then,
  Fair island of the Western Sea!
Lavish of beauty, even when
Thy brutes were happier than thy men,
  For they, at least, were free!
Regardless of thy glorious clime,
  Unmindful of thy soil of flowers,
The toiling negro sighed, that Time
  No faster sped his hours.
For, by the dewy moonlight still,
He fed the weary-turning mill,
Or bent him in the chill morass,
To pluck the long and tangled grass,
And hear above his scar-worn back
The heavy slave-whip's frequent crack;
While in his heart one evil thought
In solitary madness wrought, —
One baleful fire surviving still
  The quenching of the immortal mind —
  One sterner passion of his kind,

Which even fetters could not kill, —
The savage hope, to deal, ere long,
A vengeance bitterer than his wrong!

Hark to that cry! — long, loud, and shrill,
From field and forest, rock and hill,
Thrilling and horrible it rang,
  Around, beneath, above; —
The wild beast from his cavern sprang —
  The wild bird from her grove!
Nor fear, nor joy, nor agony
Were mingled in that midnight cry;
But, like the lion's growl of wrath,
When falls that hunter in his path,
Whose barbed arrow, deeply set,
Is rankling in his bosom yet,
It told of hate, full, deep, and strong, —
Of vengeance kindling out of wrong;
It was as if the crimes of years —
The unrequited toil — the tears —
The shame and hate, which liken well
Earth's garden to the nether hell,
Had found in Nature's self a tongue,
On which the gathered horror hung;
As if from cliff, and stream, and glen,
Burst, on the startled ears of men,
That voice which rises unto God,
Solemn and stern — the cry of blood!
It ceased — and all was still once more,
Save ocean chafing on his shore,
The sighing of the wind between
The broad banana's leaves of green,
Or bough by restless plumage shook,
Or murmuring voice of mountain brook.

Brief was the silence. Once again
  Pealed to the skies that frantic yell —
Glowed on the heavens a fiery stain,
  And flashes rose and fell;

And, painted on the blood-red sky,
Dark, naked arms were tossed on high;
And, round the white man's lordly hall,
  Trode, fierce and free, *the brute he made;*
And those who crept along the wall,
And answered to his lightest call
  With more than spaniel dread —
The creatures of his lawless beck —
Were trampling on his very neck!
And, on the night-air, wild and clear,
Rose woman's shriek of more than fear;
For bloodied arms were round her thrown,
And dark cheeks pressed against her own!

Then, injured Afric! — for the shame
Of thy own daughters, vengeance came
Full on the scornful hearts of those,
Who mocked thee in thy nameless woes,
And to thy hapless children gave
One choice — pollution, or the grave!

Where then was he, whose fiery zeal
Had taught the trampled heart to feel,
Until despair itself grew strong,
And vengeance fed its torch from wrong?
Now — when the thunder-bolt is speeding;
Now — when oppression's heart is bleeding;
Now — when the latent curse of Time
  Is raining down in fire and blood —
That curse which, through long years of crime,
  Has gathered, drop by drop, its flood —
Why strikes he not, the foremost one,
Where murder's sternest deeds are done?

He stood the aged palms beneath,
  That shadowed o'er his humble door,
Listening, with half-suspended breath,
To the wild sounds of fear and death —
  Toussaint l'Ouverture!

What marvel that his heart beat high!
  The blow for freedom had been given;
And blood had answered to the cry
  Which earth sent up to Heaven!
What marvel, that a fierce delight
Smiled grimly o'er his brow of night,
As groan, and shout, and bursting flame,
Told where the midnight tempest came,
With blood and fire along its van,
And death behind! — he was a MAN!

Yes, dark-souled chieftain! — if the light
  Of mild Religion's heavenly ray
Unveiled not to thy mental sight
    The lowlier and the purer way,
In which the Holy Sufferer trod,
  Meekly amidst the sons of crime, —
That calm reliance upon God
  For justice, in his own good time, —
That gentleness, to which belongs
  Forgiveness for its many wrongs,
Even as the primal martyr, kneeling
For mercy on the evil-dealing, —
Let not the favored white man name
Thy stern appeal, with words of blame.
Has *he* not, with the light of heaven
  Broadly around him, made the same?
Yea, on his thousand war-fields striven,
  And gloried in his ghastly shame? —
Kneeling amidst his brother's blood,
To offer mockery unto God,
As if the High and Holy One
Could smile on deeds of murder done! —
As if a human sacrifice
Were purer in his Holy eyes,
Though offered up by Christian hands,
Than the foul rites of Pagan lands!

*   *   *   *

Sternly, amidst his household band,
His carbine grasped within his hand,
  The white man stood, prepared and still,
Waiting the shock of maddened men,
Unchained, and fierce as tigers, when
  The horn winds through their caverned hill.
And one was weeping in his sight —
  The sweetest flower of all the isle, —
The bride who seemed but yesternight
  Love's fair embodied smile.
And, clinging to her trembling knee,
Looked up the form of infancy,
With tearful glance in either face,
The secret of its fear to trace.

"Ha — stand, or die!" The white man's eye
  His steady musket gleamed along,
As a tall Negro hastened nigh,
  With fearless step and strong.
"What, ho, Toussaint!" A moment more,
His shadow crossed the lighted floor.
"Away," he shouted; "fly with me, —
The white man's bark is on the sea; —
Her sails must catch the seaward wind,
For sudden vengeance sweeps behind.
Our brethren from their graves have spoken,
The yoke is spurned — the chain is broken;
On all the hills our fires are glowing —
Through all the vales red blood is flowing!
No more the mocking White shall rest
His foot upon the Negro's breast;
No more, at morn or eve, shall drip
The warm blood from the driver's whip; —
Yet, though Toussaint has vengeance sworn
For all the wrongs his race have borne, —
Though for each drop of Negro blood
The white man's veins shall pour a flood;
Not all alone the sense of ill
Around his heart is lingering still,
Nor deeper can the white man feel

The generous warmth of grateful zeal.
Friends of the Negro! fly with me—
The path is open to the sea:
Away, for life!"—He spoke, and pressed
The young child to his manly breast,
As, headlong, through the cracking cane,
Down swept the dark insurgent train—
Drunken and grim, with shout and yell
Howled through the dark, like sounds from hell!

Far out, in peace, the white man's sail
Swayed free before the sunrise gale.
Cloud-like that island hung afar,
  Along the bright horizon's verge,
O'er which the curse of servile war
  Rolled its red torrent, surge on surge.
And he—the Negro champion—where
  In the fierce tumult, struggled he?
Go trace him by the fiery glare
Of dwellings in the midnight air—
The yells of triumph and despair—
  The streams that crimson to the sea!

Sleep calmly in thy dungeon-tomb,
  Beneath Besançon's alien sky,
Dark Haytien!—for the time shall come,
Yea, even now is nigh—
When, every where, thy name shall be
Redeemed from *color's infamy;*
And men shall learn to speak of thee,
As one of earth's great spirits, born
In servitude, and nursed in scorn,
Casting aside the weary weight
And fetters of its low estate,
In that strong majesty of soul,
  Which knows no color, tongue or clime—
Which still hath spurned the base control
  Of tyrants through all time!
Far other hands than mine may wreath
The laurel round thy brow of death,

And speak thy praise, as one whose word
A thousand fiery spirits stirred, —
Who crushed his foeman as a worm —
Whose step on human hearts fell firm : —*
Be mine the better task to find
A tribute for thy lofty mind,
Amidst whose gloomy vengeance shone
Some milder virtues all thine own, —
Some gleams of feeling pure and warm,
Like sunshine on a sky of storm, —
Proofs that the Negro's heart retains
Some nobleness amidst its chains, —
That kindness to the wronged is never
  Without its excellent reward, —
Holy to human-kind, and ever
  Acceptable to God.

* The reader may, perhaps, call to mind the beautiful sonnet of William Wordsworth, addressed to Toussaint L'Ouverture, during his confinement in France.

"Toussaint! — thou most unhappy man of men!
  Whether the whistling rustic tends his plough
  Within thy hearing, or thou liest now
Buried in some deep dungeon's earless den;
Oh, miserable chieftain! — where and when
  Wilt thou find patience? — Yet, die not; do thou
  Wear rather in thy bonds a cheerful brow:
Though fallen thyself, never to rise again,
Live and take comfort. Thou hast left behind
  Powers that will work for thee; air, earth, and skies, —
There 's not a breathing of the common wind
  That will forget thee: thou hast great allies.
Thy friends are exultations, agonies,
  And love, and man's unconquerable mind."

THE SLAVE SHIPS.

"———— That fatal, that perfidious bark,
Built i' the eclipse, and rigged with curses dark."

Milton's Lycidas.

[The French ship Le Rodeur, with a crew of twenty-two men, and with one hundred and sixty negro slaves, sailed from Bonny, in Africa, April, 1819. On approaching the line, a terrible malady broke out — an obstinate disease of the eyes — contagious, and altogether beyond the resources of medicine. It was aggravated by the scarcity of water among the slaves (only half a wine glass per day being allowed to an individual), and by the extreme impurity of the air in which they breathed. By the advice of the physician, they were brought upon deck occasionally; but some of the poor wretches, locking themselves in each other's arms, leaped overboard, in the hope, which so universally prevails among them, of being swiftly transported to their own homes in Africa. To check this, the captain ordered several, who were stopped in the attempt, to be shot, or hanged, before their companions. The disease extended to the crew; and one after another were smitten with it, until only *one* remained unaffected. Yet even this dreadful condition did not preclude calculation: to save the expense of supporting slaves rendered unsaleable, and to obtain grounds for a claim against the underwriters, *thirty-six of the negroes, having become blind, were thrown into the sea and drowned!*

In the midst of their dreadful fears lest the solitary individual, whose sight remained unaffected, should also be seized with the malady, a sail was discovered. It was the Spanish slaver, Leon. The same disease had been there; and, horrible to tell, all the crew had become blind! Unable to assist each other, the vessels parted. The Spanish ship has never since been heard of. The Rodeur reached Gaudaloupe on the 21st of June; the only man who had escaped the disease, and had thus been enabled to steer the slaver into port, caught it in three days after its arrival. — *Speech of M. Benjamin Constant, in the French Chamber of Deputies*, June 17, 1820.]

"All ready?" cried the captain;
"Ay, ay!" the seamen said;
"Heave up the worthless lubbers —
The dying and the dead."

Up from the slave-ship's prison
  Fierce, bearded heads were thrust —
"Now let the sharks look to it —
  Toss up the dead ones first!"

Corpse after corpse came up, —
  Death had been busy there;
Where every blow is mercy,
  Why should the spoiler spare?
Corpse after corpse they cast
  Sullenly from the ship,
Yet bloody with the traces
  Of fetter-link and whip.

Gloomily stood the captain,
  With his arms upon his breast,
With his cold brow sternly knotted,
  And his iron lip compressed.
"Are all the dead dogs over?"
  Growled through that matted lip —
"The blind ones are no better,
  Let 's lighten the good ship."

Hark! from the ship's dark bosom,
  The very sounds of hell!
The ringing clank of iron —
  The maniac's short, sharp yell! —
The hoarse, low curse, throat-stifled —
  The starving infant's moan —
The horror of a breaking heart
  Poured through a mother's groan!

Up from that loathsome prison
  The stricken blind ones came:
Below, had all been darkness —
  Above, was still the same.
Yet the holy breath of heaven
  Was sweetly breathing there,
And the heated brow of fever
  Cooled in the soft sea air.

"Overboard with them, shipmates!"
  Cutlass and dirk were plied;
Fettered and blind, one after one,
  Plunged down the vessel's side.
The sabre smote above —
  Beneath, the lean shark lay,
Waiting with wide and bloody jaw
  His quick and human prey.

God of the earth! what cries
  Rang upward unto Thee?
Voices of agony and blood,
  From ship-deck and from sea.
The last dull plunge was heard —
  The last wave caught its stain —
And the unsated shark looked up
  For human hearts in vain.

* * * *

Red glowed the western waters —
  The setting sun was there,
Scattering alike on wave and cloud
  His fiery mesh of hair.
Amidst a group in blindness,
  A solitary eye
Gazed, from the burdened slaver's deck,
  Into that burning sky.

"A storm," spoke out the gazer,
  "Is gathering and at hand —
Curse on 't — I 'd give my other eye
  For one firm rood of land."
And then he laughed — but only
  His echoed laugh replied —
For the blinded and the suffering
  Alone were at his side.

Night settled on the waters,
  And on a stormy heaven,
While fiercely on that lone ship's track
  The thunder-gust was driven.

"A sail! — thank God, a sail!"
  And, as the helmsman spoke,
Up through the stormy murmur,
  A shout of gladness broke.

Down came the stranger vessel
  Unheeding on her way,
So near, that on the slaver's deck
  Fell off her driven spray.
"Ho! for the love of mercy —
  We're perishing and blind!"
A wail of utter agony
  Came back upon the wind:

"Help *us!* for we are stricken
  With blindness every one;
Ten days we've floated fearfully,
  Unnoting star or sun.
Our ship's the slaver Leon —
  We've but a score on board —
Our slaves are all gone over —
  Help — for the love of God!"

On livid brows of agony
  The broad red lightning shone —
But the roar of wind and thunder
  Stifled the answering groan.
Wailed from the broken waters
  A last despairing cry,
As, kindling in the stormy light,
  The stranger ship went by.

* * * *

In the sunny Guadaloupe
  A dark hulled vessel lay —
With a crew who noted never
  The night-fall or the day.
The blossom of the orange
  Was white by every stream,
And tropic leaf, and flower, and bird
  Were in the warm sun-beam.

And the sky was bright as ever,
  And the moonlight slept as well,
On the palm trees by the hill-side,
  And the streamlet of the dell;
And the glances of the Creole
  Were still as archly deep,
And her smiles as full as ever
  Of passion and of sleep.

But vain were bird and blossom,
  The green earth and the sky,
And the smile of human faces,
  To the slaver's darkened eye;
At the breaking of the morning,
  At the star-lit evening time,
O'er a world of light and beauty,
  Fell the blackness of his crime.

STANZAS.

["The despotism which our fathers could not bear in their native country is expiring, and the sword of justice in her reformed hands has applied its exterminating edge to slavery. Shall the United States — the free United States, which could not bear the bonds of a king, cradle the bondage which a king is abolishing? Shall a Republic be less free than a Monarchy? Shall we, in the vigor and buoyancy of our manhood, be less energetic in righteousness than a kingdom in its age?" — *Dr. Follen's Address.*

"Genius of America! — Spirit of our free institutions — where art thou? — How art thou fallen, O Lucifer! son of the morning — how art thou fallen from Heaven! Hell from beneath is moved for thee, to meet thee at thy coming! — The kings of the earth cry out to thee, Aha! Aha! — ART THOU BECOME LIKE UNTO US?" — *Speech of Samuel J. May.*]

Our fellow-countrymen in chains!
  Slaves — in a land of light and law!
Slaves — crouching on the very plains
  Where rolled the storm of Freedom's war!

A groan from Eutaw's haunted wood —
  A wail where Camden's martyrs fell —
By every shrine of patriot blood,
  From Moultrie's wall and Jasper's well!

By storied hill and hallowed grot,
  By mossy wood and marshy glen,
Whence rang of old the rifle-shot,
  And hurrying shout of Marion's men!
The groan of breaking hearts is there —
  The falling lash — the fetter's clank!
Slaves — SLAVES are breathing in that air,
  Which old De Kalb and Sumter drank!

What, ho! — *our* countrymen in chains!
  The whip on WOMAN'S shrinking flesh!
Our soil yet reddening with the stains,
  Caught from her scourging, warm and fresh!
What! mothers from their children riven!
  What! God's own image bought and sold!
AMERICANS to market driven,
  And bartered as the brute for gold!

Speak! shall their agony of prayer
  Come thrilling to our hearts in vain?
To us whose fathers scorned to bear
  The paltry *menace* of a chain;
To us, whose boast is loud and long
  Of holy Liberty and Light —
Say, shall these writhing slaves of Wrong,
  Plead vainly for their plundered Right?

What! shall we send, with lavish breath,
  Our sympathies across the wave,
Where Manhood, on the field of death,
  Strikes for his freedom, or a grave?
Shall prayers go up, and hymns be sung
  For Greece, the Moslem fetter spurning,
And millions hail with pen and tongue
  Our light on all her altars burning?

Shall Belgium feel, and gallant France,
By Vendome's pile and Schoenbrun's wall,
And Poland, gasping on her lance,
The impulse of our cheering call?
And shall the SLAVE, beneath our eye,
Clank o'er *our* fields his hateful chain?
And toss his fettered arms on high,
And groan for Freedom's gift, in vain?

Oh, say, shall Prussia's banner be
A refuge for the stricken slave?
And shall the Russian serf go free
By Baikal's lake and Neva's wave?
And shall the wintry-bosomed Dane
Relax the iron hand of pride,
And bid his bondmen cast the chain
From fettered soul and limb, aside?

Shall every flap of England's flag
Proclaim that all around are free,
From "farthest Ind" to each blue crag
That beetles o'er the Western Sea?
And shall we scoff at Europe's kings,
When Freedom's fire is dim with us,
And round our country's altar clings
The damning shade of Slavery's curse?

Go — let us ask of Constantine
To loose his grasp on Poland's throat;
And beg the lord of Mahmoud's line
To spare the struggling Suliote —
Will not the scorching answer come
From turbaned Turk, and scornful Russ:
"Go, loose your fettered slaves at home,
Then turn, and ask the like of us!"

Just God! and shall we calmly rest,
The Christian's scorn — the heathen's mirth —
Content to live the lingering jest
And by-word of a mocking Earth?

Shall our own glorious land retain
That curse which Europe scorns to bear?
Shall our own brethren drag the chain
Which not even Russia's menials wear?

Up, then, in Freedom's manly part,
From gray-beard eld to fiery youth,
And on the nation's naked heart
Scatter the living coals of Truth!
Up — while ye slumber, deeper yet
The shadow of our fame is growing!
Up — while ye pause, our sun may set
In blood, around our altars flowing!

Oh! rouse ye, ere the storm comes forth —
The gathered wrath of God and man —
Like that which wasted Egypt's earth,
When hail and fire above it ran.
Hear ye no warnings in the air?
Feel ye no earthquake underneath?
Up — up — why will ye slumber where
The sleeper only wakes in death?

Up *now* for Freedom! — not in strife
Like that your sterner fathers saw —
The awful waste of human life —
The glory and the guilt of war:
But break the chain — the yoke remove,
And smite to earth oppression's rod,
With those mild arms of Truth and Love,
Made mighty through the living God!

Down let the shrine of Moloch sink,
And leave no traces where it stood;
Nor longer let its idol drink
His daily cup of human blood:
But rear another altar there,
To Truth and Love and Mercy given,
And Freedom's gift, and Freedom's prayer,
Shall call an answer down from Heaven!

THE YANKEE GIRL.

She sings by her wheel, at that low cottage-door,
Which the long evening shadow is stretching before,
With a music as sweet as the music which seems
Breathed softly and faint in the ear of our dreams!

How brilliant and mirthful the light of her eye,
Like a star glancing out from the blue of the sky!
And lightly and freely her dark tresses play
O'er a brow and a bosom as lovely as they!

Who comes in his pride to that low cottage-door —
The haughty and rich to the humble and poor?
'T is the great Southern planter — the master who waves
His whip of dominion o'er hundreds of slaves.

"Nay, Ellen — for shame! Let those Yankee fools spin,
Who would pass for our slaves with a change of their skin;
Let them toil as they will at the loom or the wheel,
Too stupid for shame, and too vulgar to feel!

But thou art too lovely and precious a gem
To be bound to their burdens and sullied by them —
For shame, Ellen, shame! — cast thy bondage aside,
And away to the South, as my blessing and pride.

Oh, come where no winter thy footsteps can wrong,
But where flowers are blossoming all the year long,
Where the shade of the palm-tree is over my home,
And the lemon and orange are white in their bloom!

Oh, come to my home, where my servants shall all
Depart at thy bidding and come at thy call;
They shall heed thee as mistress with trembling and awe,
And each wish of thy heart shall be felt as a law."

Oh, could ye have seen her — that pride of our girls —
Arise and cast back the dark wealth of her curls,
With a scorn in her eye which the gazer could feel,
And a glance like the sunshine that flashes on steel!

"Go back, haughty Southron! thy treasures of gold
Are dim with the blood of the hearts thou hast sold;
Thy home may be lovely, but round it I hear
The crack of the whip and the footsteps of fear!

And the sky of thy South may be brighter than ours,
And greener thy landscapes, and fairer thy flowers;
But, dearer the blast round our mountains which raves,
Than the sweet summer zephyr which breathes over slaves!

Full low at thy bidding thy negroes may kneel,
With the iron of bondage on spirit and heel;
Yet know that the Yankee girl sooner would be
In fetters with them, than in freedom with thee!"

TO W. L. G.

Champion of those who groan beneath
Oppression's iron hand:
In view of penury, hate, and death,
I see thee fearless stand.
Still bearing up thy lofty brow,
In the steadfast strength of truth,
In manhood sealing well the vow
And promise of thy youth.

Go on! — for thou hast chosen well;
On in the strength of God!
Long as one human heart shall swell
Beneath the tyrant's rod.
Speak in a slumbering nation's ear,
As thou hast ever spoken,
Until the dead in sin shall hear —
The fetter's link be broken!

I love thee with a brother's love,
I feel my pulses thrill,
To mark thy spirit soar above
The cloud of human ill.
My heart hath leaped to answer thine,
And echo back thy words,
As leaps the warrior's at the shine
And flash of kindred swords!

They tell me thou art rash and vain —
A searcher after fame —
That thou art striving but to gain
A long enduring name —

That thou hast nerved the Afric's hand,
 And steeled the Afric's heart,
To shake aloft his vengeful brand,
 And rend his chain apart.

Have I not known thee well, and read
 Thy mighty purpose long!
And watched the trials which have made
 Thy human spirit strong?
And shall the slanderer's demon breath
 Avail with one like me,
To dim the sunshine of my faith
 And earnest trust in thee?

Go on — the dagger's point may glare
 Amid thy pathway's gloom —
The fate which sternly threatens there
 Is glorious martyrdom!
Then onward with a martyr's zeal —
 Press on to thy reward —
The hour when man shall only kneel
 Before his Father — God.

1833.

SONG OF THE FREE.

["Living, I shall assert the right of FREE DISCUSSION; dying, I shall assert it; and, should I leave no other inheritance to my children, by the blessing of God I will leave them the inheritance of FREE PRINCIPLES, and the example of a manly and independent defence of them." — *Daniel Webster.*]

PRIDE of New England!
Soul of our fathers!
Shrink we all craven-like,
When the storm gathers?
What though the tempest be
Over us lowering,
Where's the New Englander
Shamefully cowering?
Graves green and holy
Around us are lying, —
Free were the sleepers all,
Living and dying!

Back with the Southerner's
Padlocks and scourges!
Go — let him fetter down
Ocean's free surges!
Go — let him silence
Winds, clouds, and waters —
Never New England's own
Free sons and daughters!
Free as our rivers are
Ocean-ward going —
Free as the breezes are
Over us blowing.

Up to our altars, then,
  Haste we, and summon
Courage and loveliness,
  Manhood and woman!
Deep let our pledges be:
  Freedom for ever!
Truce with oppression,
  Never, oh! never!
By our own birthright-gift,
  Granted of Heaven—
Freedom for heart and lip,
  Be the pledge given!

If we have whispered truth,
  Whisper no longer;
Speak as the tempest does,
  Sterner and stronger;
Still be the tones of truth
  Louder and firmer,
Startling the haughty South
  With the deep murmur:
God and our charter's right,
  Freedom for ever!
Truce with oppression,
  Never, oh! never!

1836.

THE HUNTERS OF MEN.

Written on reading the report of the proceedings of the American Colonization Society, at its annual meeting in 1834.

Have ye heard of our hunting, o'er mountain and glen,
Through cane-brake and forest — the hunting of men ?
The lords of our land to this hunting have gone,
As the fox-hunter follows the sound of the horn :
Hark ! — the cheer and the hallo ! — the crack of the whip,
And the yell of the hound as he fastens his grip !
All blithe are our hunters, and noble their match —
Though hundreds are caught, there are millions to catch.
So speed to their hunting, o'er mountain and glen,
Through cane-brake and forest — the hunting of men !

Gay luck to our hunters ! — how nobly they ride
In the glow of their zeal, and the strength of their pride ! —
The priest with his cassock flung back on the wind,
Just screening the politic statesman behind —
The saint and the sinner, with cursing and prayer —
The drunk and the sober, ride merrily there.
And woman — kind woman — wife, widow, and maid —
For the good of the hunted, is lending her aid :
Her foot 's in the stirrup — her hand on the rein —
How blithely she rides to the hunting of men !

Oh ! goodly and grand is our hunting to see,
In this "land of the brave and this home of the free."
Priest, warrior, and statesman, from Georgia to Maine,
All mounting the saddle — all grasping the rein —
Right merrily hunting the black man, whose sin
Is the curl of his hair and the hue of his skin !

Woe, now, to the hunted who turns him at bay!
Will our hunters be turned from their purpose and prey?
Will their hearts fail within them? — their nerves tremble, when
All roughly they ride to the hunting of men?

Ho! — ALMS for our hunters! all weary and faint
Wax the curse of the sinner and prayer of the saint.
The horn is wound faintly — the echoes are still,
Over cane-brake and river, and forest and hill.
Haste — alms for our hunters! the hunted once more
Have turned from their flight with their backs to the shore:
What right have *they* here in the home of the white,
Shadowed o'er by *our* banner of Freedom and Right?
Ho! — alms for the hunters! or never again
Will they ride in their pomp to the hunting of men!

ALMS — ALMS for our hunters! why *will* ye delay,
When their pride and their glory are melting away?
The parson has turned; for, on charge of his own,
Who goeth a warfare, or hunting, alone?
The politic statesman looks back with a sigh —
There is doubt in his heart — there is fear in his eye.
Oh! haste, lest that doubting and fear shall prevail,
And the head of his steed take the place of the tail.
Oh! haste, ere he leave us! for who will ride then,
For pleasure or gain, to the hunting of men?

CLERICAL OPPRESSORS.

[In the Report of the celebrated pro-slavery meeting in Charleston, S. C., on the 4th of the 9th month, 1835, published in the Courier of that city, it is stated, "*The* CLERGY *of all denominations attended in a body*, LENDING THEIR SANCTION TO THE PROCEEDINGS, and adding by their presence to the impressive character of the scene!"]

Just God! — and these are they
Who minister at Thine altar, God of Right!
Men who their hands with prayer and blessing lay
On Israel's Ark of light!

What! preach, and kidnap men?
Give thanks — and rob Thy own afflicted poor?
Talk of Thy glorious liberty, and then
Bolt hard the captive's door?

What! servants of Thy own
Merciful Son, who came to seek and save
The homeless and the outcast, — fettering down
The tasked and plundered slave!

Pilate and Herod, friends!
Chief priests and rulers, as of old, combine!
Just God and holy! is that church, which lends
Strength to the spoiler, Thine?

Paid hypocrites, who turn
Judgment aside, and rob the Holy Book
Of those high words of truth which search and burn
In warning and rebuke;

Feed fat, ye locusts, feed!
And, in your tasseled pulpits, thank the Lord
That, from the toiling bondman's utter need,
Ye pile your own full board.

How long, O Lord! how long
Shall such a priesthood barter truth away,
And, in Thy name, for robbery and wrong
At Thy own altars pray?

Is not Thy hand stretched forth
Visibly in the heavens, to awe and smite?
Shall not the living God of all the earth,
And heaven above, do right?

Woe, then, to all who grind
Their brethren of a common Father down!
To all who plunder from the immortal mind
Its bright and glorious crown!

Woe to the priesthood! woe
To those whose hire is with the price of blood —
Perverting, darkening, changing as they go,
The searching truths of God!

Their glory and their might
Shall perish; and their very names shall be
Vile before all the people, in the light
Of a world's liberty.

Oh! speed the moment on
When Wrong shall cease — and Liberty, and Love,
And Truth, and Right, throughout the earth be known
As in their home above.

THE CHRISTIAN SLAVE.

[In a late publication of L. F. Tasistro, "Random Shots and Southern Breezes," is a description of a slave auction at New Orleans, at which the auctioneer recommended the woman on the stand as "a good Christian!"]

A Christian! going, gone!
Who bids for God's own image? — for His grace
Which that poor victim of the market-place
Hath in her suffering won?

My God! can such things be?
Hast thou not said that whatsoe'er is done
Unto Thy weakest and Thy humblest one,
Is even done to Thee?

In that sad victim, then,
Child of Thy pitying love, I see Thee stand —
Once more the jest-word of a mocking band,
Bound, sold, and scourged again!

A Christian up for sale!
Wet with her blood your whips — o'ertask her frame,
Make her life loathsome with your wrong and shame,
Her patience shall not fail!

A heathen hand might deal
Back on your heads the gathered wrong of years,
But her low, broken prayer and nightly tears,
Ye neither heed nor feel.

Con well thy lesson o'er,
Thou *prudent* teacher — tell the toiling slave
No dangerous tale of Him who came to save
The outcast and the poor.

But wisely shut the ray
Of God's free Gospel from her simple heart,
And to her darkened mind alone impart
One stern command — "OBEY!" *

So shalt thou deftly raise
The market price of human flesh; and while
On thee, their pampered guest, the planters smile,
Thy church shall praise.

Grave, reverend men shall tell
From Northern pulpits how thy work was blest,
While in that vile South Sodom, first and best,
Thy poor disciples sell.

Oh, shame! the Moslem thrall,
Who, with his master, to the Prophet kneels,
While turning to the sacred Kebla feels
His fetters break and fall.

Cheers for the turbaned Bey
Of robber-peopled Tunis! he hath torn
The dark slave-dungeons open, and hath borne
Their inmates into day:

But our poor slave in vain
Turns to the Christian shrine his aching eyes —
Its rites will only swell his market price,
And rivet on his chain.†

* There is in Liberty county, Georgia, an Association for the religious instruction of Negroes. Their seventh annual report contains an address by the *Rev.* Josiah Spry Law, from which we extract the following: — "There is a growing interest, in this community, in the religious instruction of Negroes. There is a conviction that religious instruction promotes the *quiet* and *order* of the people, and the pecuniary *interest* of the owners."

† We often see advertisements in the Southern papers, in which individual

God of all right! how long
Shall priestly robbers at Thine altar stand,
Lifting in prayer to Thee, the bloody hand
And haughty brow of wrong?

Oh, from the fields of cane,
From the low rice-swamp, from the trader's cell —
From the black slave-ship's foul and loathsome hell,
And coffle's weary chain, —

Hoarse, horrible, and strong,
Rises to Heaven that agonizing cry,
Filling the arches of the hollow sky,
HOW LONG, OH GOD, HOW LONG?

---

slaves, or several of a lot, are recommended as "*pious*," or as "*members of churches*." Lately we saw a slave advertised, who, among other qualifications, was described as "*a Baptist preacher*."

STANZAS FOR THE TIMES.*

Is this the land our fathers loved,
  The freedom which they toiled to win?
Is this the soil whereon they moved?
  Are these the graves they slumber in?
Are *we* the sons by whom are borne
The mantles which the dead have worn?

And shall we crouch above these graves,
  With craven soul and fettered lip?
Yoke in with marked and branded slaves,
  And tremble at the driver's whip?
Bend to the earth our pliant knees,
And speak — but as our masters please?

Shall outraged Nature cease to feel?
  Shall Mercy's tears no longer flow?
Shall ruffian threats of cord and steel —
  The dungeon's gloom — the assassin's blow,
Turn back the spirit roused to save
The Truth, our Country, and the Slave?

Of human skulls that shrine was made,
  Round which the priests of Mexico
Before their loathsome idol prayed —
  Is Freedom's altar fashioned so?

* The "Times" alluded to, were those evil times of the pro-slavery meeting in Faneuil Hall, for the suppression of freedom of speech, lest it should endanger the foundations of commercial society. In view of the outrages which a careful observation of the times had enabled him to foresee must spring from the false witness borne against the abolitionists by the speakers at that meeting, well might Garrison say of them, "I consider the man who fires a city, guiltless in comparison."

And must we yield to Freedom's God,
As offering meet, the negro's blood?

Shall tongues be mute, when deeds are wrought
Which well might shame extremest hell?
Shall freemen lock the indignant thought?
Shall Pity's bosom cease to swell?
Shall Honor bleed? — Shall Truth succumb?
Shall pen, and press, and soul be dumb?

No — by each spot of haunted ground,
Where Freedom weeps her children's fall —
By Plymouth's rock, and Bunker's mound —
By Griswold's stained and shattered wall —
By Warren's ghost — by Langdon's shade —
By all the memories of our dead!

By their enlarging souls, which burst
The bands and fetters round them set —
By the free Pilgrim spirit nursed
Within our inmost bosoms, yet, —
By all above — around — below —
Be ours the indignant answer — NO!

No — guided by our country's laws,
For truth, and right, and suffering man,
Be ours to strive in Freedom's cause,
As Christians *may* — as freemen *can!*
Still pouring on unwilling ears
That truth oppression only fears.

What! shall we guard our neighbor still,
While woman shrieks beneath his rod,
And while he tramples down at will
The image of a common God!
Shall watch and ward be round him set,
Of Northern nerve and bayonet?

And shall we know and share with him
The danger and the growing shame?
And see our Freedom's light grow dim,
Which should have filled the world with flame?

And, writhing, feel, where'er we turn,
A world's reproach around us burn?

Is 't not enough that this is borne?
  And asks our hearty neighbor more?
Must fetters which his slaves have worn,
  Clank round the Yankee farmer's door?
Must he be told, beside his plough,
What he must speak, and when, and how?

Must he be told his freedom stands
  On Slavery's dark foundations strong —
On breaking hearts and fettered hands,
  On robbery, and crime, and wrong?
That all his fathers taught is vain —
That Freedom's emblem is the chain?

Its life — its soul, from slavery drawn?
  False — foul — profane! Go — teach as well
Of holy Truth from Falsehood born!
  Of Heaven refreshed by airs from Hell!
Of Virtue in the arms of Vice!
Of Demons planting Paradise!

Rail on, then, "brethren of the South" —
  Ye shall not hear the truth the less —
No seal is on the Yankee's mouth,
  No fetter on the Yankee's press!
From our Green Mountains to the Sea,
One voice shall thunder — WE ARE FREE!

LINES,

WRITTEN on reading the spirited and manly remarks of Governor RITNER, of Pennsylvania, in his Message of 1836, on the subject of Slavery.

THANK God for the token! — one lip is still free —
One spirit untrammeled — unbending one knee!
Like the oak of the mountain, deep-rooted and firm,
Erect, when the multitude bends to the storm;
When traitors to Freedom, and Honor, and God,
Are bowed at an Idol polluted with blood;
When the recreant North has forgotten her trust,
And the lip of her honor is low in the dust, —
Thank God, that one arm from the shackle has broken!
Thank God, that one man, as a *freeman*, has spoken!

O'er thy crags, Alleghany, a blast has been blown!
Down thy tide, Susquehanna, the murmur has gone!
To the land of the South — of the charter and chain —
Of Liberty sweetened with Slavery's pain;
Where the cant of Democracy dwells on the lips
Of the forgers of fetters, and wielders of whips!
Where "chivalric" honor means really no more
Than scourging of women, and robbing the poor!
Where the Moloch of Slavery sitteth on high,
And the words which he utters are — WORSHIP, OR DIE!

Right onward, oh, speed it! Wherever the blood
Of the wronged and the guiltless is crying to God;
Wherever a slave in his fetters is pining;
Wherever the lash of the driver is twining;
Wherever from kindred, torn rudely apart,
Comes the sorrowful wail of the broken of heart;

Wherever the shackles of tyranny bind,
In silence and darkness, the God-given mind;
There, God speed it onward! — its truth will be felt —
The bonds shall be loosened — the iron shall melt!

And oh, will the land where the free soul of PENN
Still lingers and breathes over mountain and glen —
Will the land where a BENEZET'S spirit went forth
To the peeled, and the meted, and outcast of Earth —
Where the words of the Charter of Liberty first
From the soul of the sage and the patriot burst —
Where first for the wronged and the weak of their kind,
The Christian and statesman their efforts combined —
Will that land of the free and the good wear a chain?
Will the call to the rescue of Freedom be vain?

No, RITNER! — her "Friends," at thy warning shall stand
Erect for the truth, like their ancestral band;
Forgetting the feuds and the strife of past time,
Counting coldness injustice, and silence a crime;
Turning back from the cavil of creeds, to unite
Once again for the poor in defence of the Right;
Breasting calmly, but firmly, the full tide of Wrong,
Overwhelmed, but not borne on its surges along;
Unappalled by the danger, the shame, and the pain,
And counting each trial for Truth as their gain!

And that bold-hearted yeomanry, honest and true,
Who, haters of fraud, give to labor its due;
Whose fathers, of old, sang in concert with thine,
On the banks of Swetara, the songs of the Rhine —
The German-born pilgrims, who first dared to brave
The scorn of the proud in the cause of the slave: * —
Will the sons of such men yield the lords of the South
One brow for the brand — for the padlock one mouth?
They cater to tyrants? — They rivet the chain,
Which their fathers smote off, on the negro again?

* It is a remarkable fact, that the first testimony of a religious body against negro slavery, was that of a Society of German "Friends" in Pennsylvania.

No, never! — one voice, like the sound in the cloud,
When the roar of the storm waxes loud and more loud,
Wherever the foot of the freeman hath pressed
From the Delaware's marge to the Lake of the West,
On the South-going breezes shall deepen and grow
Till the land it sweeps over shall tremble below!
The voice of a PEOPLE — uprisen — awake —
Pennsylvania's watchword, with Freedom at stake,
Thrilling up from each valley, flung down from each height,
"OUR COUNTRY AND LIBERTY! — GOD FOR THE RIGHT!"

LINES,

WRITTEN on reading the famous "PASTORAL LETTER" of the Massachusetts General Association, 1837.

So, this is all — the utmost reach
  Of priestly power the mind to fetter!
When laymen think — when women preach —
  A war of words — a "Pastoral Letter!"
Now, shame upon ye, parish Popes!
  Was it thus with those, your predecessors,
Who sealed with racks, and fire, and ropes
  Their loving kindness to transgressors?

A "Pastoral Letter," grave and dull —
  Alas! in hoof and horns and features,
How different is your Brookfield bull,
  From him who bellows from St. Peter's!
Your pastoral rights and powers from harm,
  Think ye, can words alone preserve them?
Your wiser fathers taught the arm
  And sword of temporal power to serve them.

Oh, glorious days — when church and state
  Were wedded by your spiritual fathers!
And on submissive shoulders sat
  Your Wilsons and your Cotton Mathers.

No vile "itinerant" then could mar
  The beauty of your tranquil Zion,
But at his peril of the scar
  Of hangman's whip and branding-iron.

Then, wholesome laws relieved the church
  Of heretic and mischief-maker,
And priest and bailiff joined in search,
  By turns, of Papist, witch, and Quaker!
The stocks were at each church's door,
  The gallows stood on Boston Common,
A Papist's ears the pillory bore, —
  The gallows-rope, a Quaker woman!

Your fathers dealt not as ye deal
  With "non-professing" frantic teachers;
They bored the tongue with red-hot steel,
  And flayed the backs of "female preachers."
Old Newbury, had her fields a tongue,
  And Salem's streets could tell their story,
Of fainting woman dragged along,
  Gashed by the whip, accursed and gory!

And will ye ask me, why this taunt
  Of memories sacred from the scorner?
And why with reckless hand I plant
  A nettle on the graves ye honor?
Not to reproach New England's dead
  This record from the past I summon,
Of manhood to the scaffold led,
  And suffering and heroic woman.

No — for yourselves alone, I turn
  The pages of intolerance over,
That, in their spirit, dark and stern,
  Ye haply may your own discover!
For, if ye claim the "pastoral right"
  To silence Freedom's voice of warning,
And from your precincts shut the light
  Of Freedom's day around ye dawning;

If when an earthquake voice of power,
 And signs in earth and heaven are showing
That, forth, in its appointed hour,
 The Spirit of the Lord is going!
And, with that Spirit, Freedom's light
 On kindred, tongue, and people breaking,
Whose slumbering millions, at the sight,
 In glory and in strength are waking!

When for the sighing of the poor,
 And for the needy, God hath risen,
And chains are breaking, and a door
 Is opening for the souls in prison!
If then ye would, with puny hands,
 Arrest the very work of Heaven,
And bind anew the evil bands
 Which God's right arm of power hath riven —

What marvel that, in many a mind,
 Those darker deeds of bigot madness
Are closely with your own combined,
 Yet "less in anger than in sadness?"
What marvel, if the people learn
 To claim the right of free opinion?
What marvel, if at times they spurn
 The ancient yoke of your dominion?

Oh, how contrast, with such as ye,
 A LEAVITT'S free and generous bearing!
A PERRY'S calm integrity,
 A PHELPS' zeal and Christian daring!
A FOLLEN'S soul of sacrifice,
 And MAY'S with kindness overflowing!
How green and lovely in the eyes
 Of freemen are their graces growing!

Ay, there 's a glorious remnant yet,
 Whose lips are wet at Freedom's fountains,
The coming of whose welcome feet
 Is beautiful upon our mountains!

Men, who the gospel tidings bring
  Of Liberty and Love for ever,
Whose joy is one abiding spring,
  Whose peace is as a gentle river!

But ye, who scorn the thrilling tale
  Of Carolina's high-souled daughters,
Which echoes here the mournful wail
  Of sorrow from Edisto's waters,
Close while ye may the public ear —
  With malice vex, with slander wound them —
The pure and good shall throng to hear,
  And tried and manly hearts surround them.

Oh, ever may the power which led
  Their way to such a fiery trial,
And strengthened womanhood to tread
  The wine-press of such self-denial,
Be round them in an evil land,
  With wisdom and with strength from Heaven,
With Miriam's voice, and Judith's hand,
  And Deborah's song for triumph given!

And what are ye who strive with God,
  Against the ark of his salvation,
Moved by the breath of prayer abroad,
  With blessings for a dying nation?
What, but the stubble and the hay
  To perish, even as flax consuming,
With all that bars His glorious way,
  Before the brightness of His coming?

And thou sad Angel, who so long
  Hast waited for the glorious token,
That Earth from all her bonds of wrong
  To liberty and light has broken —
Angel of Freedom! soon to thee
  The sounding trumpet shall be given,
And over Earth's full jubilee
  Shall deeper joy be felt in Heaven!

LINES,

WRITTEN for the meeting of the Anti-Slavery Society, at Chatham Street Chapel, N. Y., held on the 4th of the 7th month, 1834.

O THOU, whose presence went before
Our fathers in their weary way,
As with thy chosen moved of yore
The fire by night — the cloud by day!

When from each temple of the free,
A nation's song ascends to Heaven,
Most Holy Father! unto Thee
May not our humble prayer be given?

Thy children all — though hue and form
Are varied in Thine own good will —
With Thy own holy breathings warm,
And fashioned in Thine image still.

We thank Thee, Father! — hill and plain
Around us wave their fruits once more,
And clustered vine, and blossomed grain,
Are bending round each cottage door.

And peace is here; and hope and love
Are round us as a mantle thrown,
And unto Thee, supreme above,
The knee of prayer is bowed alone.

But oh, for those this day can bring,
As unto us, no joyful thrill —
For those who, under Freedom's wing,
Are bound in Slavery's fetters still:

For those to whom Thy living word
  Of light and love is never given —
For those whose ears have never heard
  The promise and the hope of Heaven!

For broken heart, and clouded mind,
  Whereon no human mercies fall —
Oh, be Thy gracious love inclined,
  Who, as a father, pitiest all!

And grant, O Father! that the time
  Of Earth's deliverance may be near,
When every land, and tongue, and clime,
  The message of Thy love shall hear —

When, smitten as with fire from heaven,
  The captive's chain shall sink in dust,
And to his fettered soul be given
  The glorious freedom of the just!

LINES,

WRITTEN for the celebration of the Third Anniversary of British Emancipation, at the Broadway Tabernacle, N. Y., "First of August," 1837.

O HOLY FATHER! — just and true
  Are all thy works and words and ways,
And unto Thee alone are due
  Thanksgiving and eternal praise!
As children of Thy gracious care,
  We veil the eye — we bend the knee,
With broken words of praise and prayer,
  Father and God, we come to Thee.

For Thou hast heard, O God of Right,
  The sighing of the island slave;
And stretched for him the arm of might,
  Not shortened that it could not save.

The laborer sits beneath his vine,
  The shackled soul and hand are free —
Thanksgiving ! — for the work is Thine !
  Praise ! — for the blessing is of Thee !

And oh, we feel Thy presence here —
  Thy awful arm in judgment bare !
Thine eye hath seen the bondman's tear —
  Thine ear hath heard the bondman's prayer !
Praise ! — for the pride of man is low,
  The counsels of the wise are nought,
The fountains of repentance flow ;
  What hath our God in mercy wrought ?

Speed on Thy work, Lord God of Hosts !
  And when the bondman's chain is riven,
And swells from all our guilty coasts
  The anthem of the free to Heaven,
Oh, not to those whom Thou hast led,
  As with Thy cloud and fire before,
But unto Thee, in fear and dread,
  Be praise and glory ever more.

LINES,

WRITTEN for the Anniversary celebration of the First of August, at Milton, 1846.

A FEW brief years have passed away
  Since Britain drove her million slaves
Beneath the tropic's fiery ray :
God willed their freedom ; and to-day
  Life blooms above those island graves !

He spoke ! across the Carib sea,
  We heard the clash of breaking chains,
And felt the heart-throb of the free,
The first, strong pulse of liberty
  Which thrilled along the bondman's veins.

Though long delayed, and far, and slow,
  The Briton's triumph shall be ours :
Wears slavery here a prouder brow
Than that which twelve short years ago
  Scowled darkly from her island bowers ?

Mighty alike for good or ill
  With mother-land, we fully share
The Saxon strength — the nerve of steel —
The tireless energy of will, —
  The power to do, the pride to dare.

What she has done can we not do ?
  Our hour and men are both at hand;
The blast which Freedom's angel blew
O'er her green islands, echoes through
  Each valley of our forest land.

Hear it, old Europe ! we have sworn
  The death of slavery. — When it falls
Look to your vassals in their turn,
Your poor dumb millions, crushed and worn,
  Your prisons and your palace walls !

Oh kingly mockers ! — scoffing show
  What deeds in Freedom's name we do ;
Yet know that every taunt ye throw
Across the waters, goads our slow
  Progression towards the right and true.

Not always shall your outraged poor,
  Appalled by democratic crime,
Grind as their fathers ground before, —
The hour which sees our prison door
  Swing wide shall be *their* triumph time.

On then, my brothers ! every blow
  Ye deal is felt the wide earth through ;
Whatever here uplifts the low
Or humbles Freedom's hateful foe,
  Blesses the Old World through the New.

Take heart! The promised hour draws near —
I hear the downward beat of wings,
And Freedom's trumpet sounding clear —
Joy to the people! — woe and fear
To new world tyrants, old world kings!"

THE FAREWELL

OF A VIRGINIA SLAVE MOTHER TO HER DAUGHTERS, SOLD INTO SOUTHERN BONDAGE.

Gone, gone — sold and gone,
To the rice-swamp dank and lone.
Where the slave-whip ceaseless swings,
Where the noisome insect stings,
Where the fever demon strews
Poison with the falling dews;
Where the sickly sunbeams glare
Through the hot and misty air, —
Gone, gone — sold and gone,
To the rice-swamp dank and lone,
From Virginia's hills and waters, —
Woe is me, my stolen daughters!

Gone, gone — sold and gone,
To the rice-swamp dank and lone.
There no mother's eye is near them,
There no mother's ear can hear them;
Never, when the torturing lash
Seams their back with many a gash,
Shall a mother's kindness bless them,
Or a mother's arms caress them.
Gone, gone — sold and gone,
To the rice-swamp dank and lone,
From Virginia's hills and waters —
Woe is me, my stolen daughters!

Gone, gone — sold and gone,
To the rice-swamp dank and lone.
Oh, when weary, sad, and slow,
From the fields at night they go,
Faint with toil, and racked with pain,
To their cheerless homes again —
There no brother's voice shall greet them —
There no father's welcome meet them.
Gone, gone — sold and gone,
To the rice-swamp dank and lone,
From Virginia's hills and waters —
Woe is me, my stolen daughters !

Gone, gone — sold and gone,
To the rice-swamp dank and lone,
From the tree whose shadow lay
On their childhood's place of play —
From the cool spring where they drank —
Rock, and hill, and rivulet bank —
From the solemn house of prayer,
And the holy counsels there —
Gone, gone — sold and gone,
To the rice-swamp dank and lone,
From Virginia's hills and waters, —
Woe is me, my stolen daughters !

Gone, gone — sold and gone,
To the rice-swamp dank and lone —
Toiling through the weary day,
And at night the spoiler's prey.
Oh, that they had earlier died,
Sleeping calmly, side by side,
Where the tyrant's power is o'er,
And the fetter galls no more !
Gone, gone — sold and gone,
To the rice-swamp dank and lone,
From Virginia's hills and waters, —
Woe is me, my stolen daughters !

Gone, gone — sold and gone,
To the rice-swamp dank and lone.
By the holy love He beareth —
By the bruised reed He spareth —
Oh, may He, to whom alone
All their cruel wrongs are known,
Still their hope and refuge prove,
With a more than a mother's love.
Gone, gone — sold and gone,
To the rice-swamp dank and lone,
From Virginia's hills and waters, —
Woe is me, my stolen daughters!

ADDRESS,

WRITTEN for the opening of "PENNSYLVANIA HALL," dedicated to Free Discussion, Virtue, Liberty, and Independence, on the 15th of the 5th month, 1838.

NOT with the splendors of the days of old,
The spoil of nations, and "barbaric gold" —
No weapons wrested from the fields of blood,
Where dark and stern the unyielding Roman stood,
And the proud eagles of his cohorts saw
A world, war-wasted, crouching to his law —
Nor blazoned car — nor banners floating gay,
Like those which swept along the Appian way,
When, to the welcome of imperial Rome,
The victor warrior came in triumph home,
And trumpet-peal, and shoutings wild and high,
Stirred the blue quiet of the Italian sky;
But calm and grateful, prayerful and sincere,
As Christian freemen, only, gathering here,
We dedicate our fair and lofty Hall,
Pillar and arch, entablature and wall,
As Virtue's shrine — as Liberty's abode —
Sacred to Freedom, and to Freedom's God!

Oh ! loftier halls, 'neath brighter skies than these,
Stood darkly mirrored in the Ægean seas,
Pillar and shrine — and life-like statues seen,
Graceful and pure, the marble shafts between,
Where glorious Athens from her rocky hill
Saw Art and Beauty subject to her will —
And the chaste temple, and the classic grove —
The hall of sages — and the bowers of love,
Arch, fane, and column, graced the shores, and gave
Their shadows to the blue Saronic wave ;
And statelier rose, on Tiber's winding side,
The Pantheon's dome — the Coliseum's pride —
The Capitol, whose arches backward flung
The deep, clear cadence of the Roman tongue,
Whence stern decrees, like words of fate, went forth
To the awed nations of a conquered earth,
Where the proud Cæsars in their glory came,
And Brutus lightened from his lips of flame !

Yet in the porches of Athena's halls,
And in the shadows of her stately walls,
Lurked the sad bondman, and his tears of woe
Wet the cold marble with unheeded flow ;
And fetters clanked beneath the silver dome
Of the proud Pantheon of imperious Rome.
Oh ! not for him — the chained and stricken slave —
By Tiber's shore, or blue Ægina's wave,
In the thronged forum, or the sages' seat,
The bold lip pleaded, and the warm heart beat ;
No soul of sorrow melted at his pain,
No tear of pity rusted on his chain !

But this fair Hall, to Truth and Freedom given,
Pledged to the Right before all Earth and Heaven,
A free arena for the strife of mind,
To caste, or sect, or color unconfined,
Shall thrill with echoes, such as ne'er of old
From Roman hall, or Grecian temple rolled ;
Thoughts shall find utterance, such as never yet
The Propylea or the Forum met.

Beneath its roof no gladiator's strife
Shall win applauses with the waste of life;
No lordly lictor urge the barbarous game —
No wanton Lais glory in her shame.
But here the tear of sympathy shall flow,
As the ear listens to the tale of woe;
Here, in stern judgment of the oppressor's wrong —
Shall strong rebukings thrill on Freedom's tongue —
No partial justice hold the unequal scale —
No pride of caste a brother's rights assail —
No tyrant's mandates echo from this wall,
Holy to Freedom and the Rights of All!
But a fair field, where mind may close with mind,
Free as the sunshine and the chainless wind;
Where the high trust is fixed on Truth alone,
And bonds and fetters from the soul are thrown;
Where wealth, and rank, and worldly pomp, and might,
Yield to the presence of the True and Right.

And fitting is it that this Hall should stand
Where Pennsylvania's Founder led his band,
From thy blue waters, Delaware! — to press
The virgin verdure of the wilderness.
Here, where all Europe with amazement saw
The soul's high freedom trammeled by no law;
Here, where the fierce and warlike forest-men
Gathered in peace, around the home of PENN,
Awed by the weapons Love alone had given,
Drawn from the holy armory of Heaven;
Where Nature's voice against the bondman's wrong
First found an earnest and indignant tongue;
Where LAY's bold message to the proud was borne,
And KEITH's rebuke, and FRANKLIN's manly scorn—
Fitting it is that here, where Freedom first
From her fair feet shook off the Old World's dust,
Spread her white pinions to our Western blast,
And her free tresses to our sunshine cast,
One Hall should rise redeemed from Slavery's ban —
One Temple sacred to the Rights of Man!

Oh! if the spirits of the parted come,
Visiting angels, to their olden home;
If the dead fathers of the land look forth
From their far dwellings, to the things of earth —
Is it a dream, that with their eyes of love,
They gaze now on us from the bowers above?
LAY's ardent soul — and BENEZET the mild,
Steadfast in faith, yet gentle as a child —
Meek-hearted WOOLMAN, — and that brother-band,
The sorrowing exiles from their "FATHER LAND,"
Leaving their homes in Krieshiem's bowers of vine,
And the blue beauty of their glorious Rhine,
To seek amidst our solemn depths of wood
Freedom from man and holy peace with God;
Who first of all their testimonial gave
Against the oppressor, — for the outcast slave, —
Is it a dream that such as these look down,
And with their blessing our rejoicings crown?

Let us rejoice, that, while the pulpit's door
Is barred against the pleaders for the poor;
While the church, wrangling upon points of faith,
Forgets her bondmen suffering unto death;
While crafty traffic and the lust of gain
Unite to forge oppression's triple chain,
One door is open, and one Temple free —
As a resting place for hunted Liberty!
Where men may speak, unshackled and unawed,
High words of truth, for Freedom and for God.

And when that truth its perfect work hath done,
And rich with blessings o'er our land hath gone;
When not a slave beneath his yoke shall pine,
From broad Potomac to the far Sabine;
When unto angel-lips at last is given
The silver trump of Jubilee to Heaven;
And from Virginia's plains — Kentucky's shades,
And through the dim Floridian everglades,
Rises, to meet that angel-trumpet's sound,
The voice of millions from their chains unbound —

Then, though this Hall be crumbling in decay,
Its strong walls blending with the common clay,
Yet, round the ruins of its strength shall stand
The best and noblest of a ransomed land —
Pilgrims, like those who throng around the shrine
Of Mecca, or of holy Palestine! —
A prouder glory shall that ruin own
Than that which lingers round the Parthenon.

Here shall the child of after years be taught
The work of Freedom which his fathers wrought —
Told of the trials of the present hour,
Our weary strife with prejudice and power, —
How the high errand quickened woman's soul,
And touched her lip as with a living coal —
How Freedom's martyrs kept their lofty faith,
True and unwavering, unto bonds and death. —
The pencil's art shall sketch the ruined Hall,
The Muses' garland crown its aged wall,
And History's pen for after times record
Its consecration unto FREEDOM'S GOD!

THE MORAL WARFARE.

When Freedom, on her natal day,
Within her war-rocked cradle lay,
An iron race around her stood,
Baptized her infant brow in blood
And, through the storm which round her swept,
Their constant ward and watching kept.

Then, where our quiet herds repose,
The roar of baleful battle rose,
And brethren of a common tongue
To mortal strife as tigers sprung,
And every gift on Freedom's shrine
Was man for beast, and blood for wine!

Our fathers to their graves have gone;
Their strife is past — their triumph won;
But sterner trials wait the race
Which rises in their honored place —
A moral warfare with the crime
And folly of an evil time.

So let it be. In God's own might
We gird us for the coming fight,
And, strong in Him whose cause is ours
In conflict with unholy powers,
We grasp the weapons He has given, —
The Light, and Truth, and Love of Heaven!

THE RESPONSE.

["To agitate the question (Slavery) anew, is not only impolitic, but it is a virtual breach of good faith to our brethren of the South; an unwarrantable interference with their domestic relations and institutions." "I can never, in the official station which I occupy, consent to *countenance* a course which may jeopard the peace and harmony of the Union." — *Gov. Porter's Inaugural Message*, 1838.]

No "countenance" of his, forsooth!
  Who asked it at his vassal hands?
Who looked for homage done to Truth,
  By party's vile and hateful bands?
Who dreamed that one by them possessed,
Would lay for her his spear in rest?

His "countenance!" well, let it light
  The human robber to his spoil! —
Let those who track the bondman's flight,
  Like bloodhounds o'er our once free soil,
Bask in its sunshine while they may,
And howl its praises on their way;

We ask no boon: our rights we claim —
  Free press and thought — free tongue and pen —
The right to speak in Freedom's name,
  As Pennsylvanians and as men;
To do, by Lynch law unforbid,
What our own Rush and Franklin did.

Ay, there we stand, with planted feet,
  Steadfast, where those old worthies stood: —
Upon us let the tempest beat,
  Around us swell and surge the flood:

We fail or triumph on that spot
God helping us, we falter not.

"A breach of plighted faith?" for shame!—
  Who voted for that "breach?" Who gave
In the state councils, vote and name
  For freedom for the District slave?
Consistent patriot! go, forswear,
Blot out, "expunge" the record there! *

Go, eat thy words. Shall H—— C——
  Turn round—a moral harlequin?
And arch V—— B—— wipe away
  The stains of his Missouri sin?
And shall that one unlucky vote
Stick, burr-like, in *thy* honest throat?

No—do thy part in "*putting down*" †
  The friends of Freedom:—summon out
The parson in his saintly gown,
  To curse the outlawed roundabout,
In concert with the Belial brood—
The Balaam of "the brotherhood!"

Quench every free discussion light—
  Clap on the legislative snuffers,
And caulk with "resolutions" tight
  The ghastly rents the Union suffers!
Let church and state brand Abolition
As heresy and rank sedition.

Choke down, at once, each breathing thing,
  That whispers of the Rights of Man:—
Gag the free girl who dares to sing
  Of freedom o'er her dairy pan:—

* It ought to be borne in mind, that DAVID R. PORTER voted in the Legislature to instruct the congressional delegation of Pennsylvania to use their influence for the abolition of slavery in the District of Columbia.

† "He (Martin Van Buren) thinks the abolitionists may be put down."—*Richmond (Va.) Enquirer.*

Dog the old farmer's steps about,
And hunt his cherished treason out.

Go, hunt sedition. — Search for that
  In every pedlar's cart of rags;
Pry into every Quaker's hat,
  And DOCTOR FUSSELL'S saddle bags!
Lest treason wrap, with all its ills,
Around his powders and his pills.

Where Chester's oak and walnut shades
  With slavery-laden breezes stir,
And on the hills, and in the glades
  Of Bucks and honest Lancaster,
Are heads which think and hearts which feel —
Flints to the Abolition steel!

Ho! send ye down a corporal's guard
  With flow of flag and beat of drum —
Storm LINDLEY COATES'S poultry yard,
  Beleaguer THOMAS WHITSON'S home!
Beat up the Quaker quarters — show
Your valor to an unarmed foe!

Do more. Fill up your loathsome jails
  With faithful men and women — set
The scaffold up in these green vales,
  And let their verdant turf be wet
With blood of unresisting men —
Ay, do all this, and more, — WHAT THEN?

Think ye, one heart of man or child
  Will falter from its lofty faith,
At the mob's tumult, fierce and wild —
  The prison cell — the shameful death?
No! — nursed in storm and trial long,
The weakest of our band is strong!

Oh! while before us visions come
  Of slave ships on Virginia's coast —
Of mothers in their childless home,
  Like Rachel, sorrowing o'er the lost —

The slave-gang scourged upon its way —
The blood-hound and his human prey —

We cannot falter! Did we so,
  The stones beneath would murmur out,
And all the winds that round us blow
  Would whisper of our shame about.
No! let the tempest rock the land,
Our faith shall live — our truth shall stand.

True as the Vaudois hemmed around
  With Papal fire and Roman steel —
Firm as the Christian heroine bound
  Upon Domitian's torturing wheel,
We 'bate no breath — we curb no thought —
Come what may come, WE FALTER NOT!

THE WORLD'S CONVENTION

OF THE FRIENDS OF EMANCIPATION, HELD IN LONDON IN 1840.

Yes, let them gather! — Summon forth
The pledged philanthrophy of Earth,
From every land, whose hills have heard
  The bugle blast of Freedom waking;
Or shrieking of her symbol-bird
  From out his cloudy eyrie breaking;
Where Justice hath one worshipper,
Or truth one altar built to her;
Where'er a human eye is weeping
  O'er wrongs which Earth's sad children know —
Where'er a single heart is keeping
  Its prayerful watch with human woe:
Thence let them come, and greet each other,
And know in each, a friend and brother!

Yes, let them come! from each green vale
  Where England's old baronial halls
  Still bear upon their storied walls
The grim crusader's rusted mail,
Battered by Paynim spear and brand
On Malta's rock or Syria's sand!
And mouldering pennon-staves once set
  Within the soil of Palestine,
By Jordan and Genessaret;
  Or, borne with England's battle line,
O'er Acre's shattered turrets stooping,
Or, 'midst the camp their banners drooping,
  With dews from hallowed Hermon wet,

A holier summons now is given
  Than that grey hermit's voice of old,
Which unto all the winds of heaven
  The banners of the Cross unrolled!
Not for the long deserted shrine, —
  Not for the dull unconscious sod,
Which tells not by one lingering sign
  That there the hope of Israel trod; —
But for that TRUTH, for which alone
  In pilgrim eyes are sanctified
The garden moss, the mountain stone,
Whereon His holy sandals pressed —
The fountain which His lip hath blessed —
Whate'er hath touched His garment's hem
At Bethany or Bethlehem,
  Or Jordan's river side.
For FREEDOM, in the name of Him
  Who came to raise Earth's drooping poor,
To break the chain from every limb —
  The bolt from every prison door!
For these, o'er all the earth hath passed
An ever-deepening trumpet blast,
As if an angel's breath had lent
Its vigor to the instrument.

And Wales, from Snowden's mountain wall,
Shall startle at that thrilling call,
  As if she heard her bards again;
And Erin's "harp on Tara's wall"
  Give out its ancient strain,
Mirthful and sweet, yet sad withal —
  The melody which Erin loves,
When o'er that harp, mid bursts of gladness
And slogan cries and lyke-wake sadness,
  The hand of her O'Connell moves:
Scotland, from lake and tarn and rill,
And mountain hold, and heathery hill,
  Shall catch and echo back the note,
As if she heard upon her air

Once more her Cameronian's prayer
  And song of Freedom float.
And cheering echoes shall reply
From each remote dependency,
Where Britain's mighty sway is known,
In tropic sea or frozen zone;
Where'er her sunset flag is furling,
Or morning gun-fire's smoke is curling;
From Indian Bengal's groves of palm
And rosy fields and gales of balm,
Where Eastern pomp and power are rolled
Through regal Ava's gates of gold;
And from the lakes and ancient woods
And dim Canadian solitudes,
Whence, sternly from her rocky throne,
Queen of the North, Quebec looks down;
And from those bright and ransomed Isles
Where all unwonted Freedom smiles,
And the dark laborer still retains
The scar of slavery's broken chains!

From the hoar Alps, which sentinel
The gateways of the land of Tell,
Where morning's keen and earliest glance
  On Jura's rocky wall is thrown,
And from the olive bowers of France
  And vine groves garlanding the Rhone, —
"Friends of the Blacks," as true and tried
As those who stood by Oge's side —
Brissot and eloquent Gregoire —
When with free lip and heart of fire
The Haytien told his country's wrong,
Shall gather at that summons strong —
Broglie, Passy, and him, whose song
Breathed over Syria's holy sod,
And in the paths which Jesus trod,
And murmured midst the hills which hem
Crownless and sad Jerusalem,

Hath echoes whereso'er the tone
Of Israel's prophet-lyre is known.

Still let them come — from Quito's walls,
And from the Oronoco's tide,
From Lima's Inca-haunted halls,
From Santa Fe and Yucatan,—
Men who by swart Guerrero's side
Proclaimed the deathless RIGHTS OF MAN,
Broke every bond and fetter off,
And hailed in every sable serf
A free and brother Mexican!
Chiefs who across the Andes' chain
Have followed Freedom's flowing pennon,
And seen on Junin's fearful plain,
Glare o'er the broken ranks of Spain,
The fire-burst of Bolivar's cannon!
And Hayti, from her mountain land,
Shall send the sons of those who hurled
Defiance from her blazing strand —
The war-gage from her Petion's hand,
Alone against a hostile world.

Nor all unmindful, thou, the while,
Land of the dark and mystic Nile! —
Thy Moslem mercy yet may shame
All tyrants of a Christian name —
When in the shade of Gezeh's pile,
Or, where from Abyssinian hills
El Gerek's upper fountain fills,
Or where from mountains of the Moon
El Abiad bears his watery boon,
Where'er thy lotus blossoms swim
Within their ancient hallowed waters —
Where'er is heard thy prophet's hymn,
Or song of Nubia's sable daughters, —
The curse of SLAVERY and the crime,
Thy bequest from remotest time,

At thy dark Mehemet's decree
For evermore shall pass from thee;
  And chains forsake each captive's limb
Of all those tribes, whose hills around
Have echoed back the cymbal sound
  And victor horn of Ibrahim.

And thou whose glory and whose crime
To earth's remotest bound and clime,
In mingled tones of awe and scorn,
The echoes of a world have borne,
My country! glorious at thy birth,
A day-star flashing brightly forth—
  The herald-sign of Freedom's dawn!
Oh! who could dream that saw thee then,
  And watched thy rising from afar,
That vapors from oppression's fen
  Would cloud the upward tending star?
Or, that earth's tyrant powers, which heard,
  Awe-struck, the shout which hailed thy dawning,
Would rise so soon, prince, peer, and king,
To mock thee with their welcoming,
Like Hades when her thrones were stirred
  To greet the down-cast Star of Morning!
"Aha! and art thou fallen thus?
Art THOU become as one of *us?*"

Land of my fathers!—there will stand,
Amidst that world-assembled band,
Those owning thy maternal claim
Unweakened by thy crime and shame,—
The sad reprovers of thy wrong—
The children thou hast spurned so long.
Still with affection's fondest yearning
To their unnatural mother turning.
No traitors they!—but tried and leal,
Whose own is but thy general weal,
Still blending with the patriot's zeal

The Christian's love for human kind,
To caste and climate unconfined.

A holy gathering! — peaceful all —
No threat of war — no savage call
  For vengeance on an erring brother;
But in their stead the God-like plan
To teach the brotherhood of man
  To love and reverence one another,
As sharers of a common blood —
The children of a common God! —
Yet, even at its lightest word,
Shall Slavery's darkest depths be stirred:
Spain watching from her Moro's keep
Her slave-ships traversing the deep,
And Rio, in her strength and pride,
Lifting, along her mountain side,
Her snowy battlements and towers —
Her lemon groves and tropic bowers,
With bitter hate and sullen fear
Its freedom-giving voice shall hear;
And where my country's flag is flowing,
On breezes from Mount Vernon blowing
  Above the Nation's council halls,
Where Freedom's praise is loud and long,
  While, close beneath the outward walls,
The driver plies his reeking thong —
  The hammer of the man-thief falls,
O'er hypocritic cheek and brow
The crimson flush of shame shall glow:
And all who for their native land
Are pledging life and heart and hand —
Worn watchers o'er her changing weal,
Who for her tarnished honor feel —
Through cottage-door and council-hall
Shall thunder an awakening call.
The pen along its page shall burn
With all intolerable scorn —

And eloquent rebuke shall go
On all the winds that Southward blow ;
From priestly lips, now sealed and dumb,
Warning and dread appeal shall come,
Like those which Israel heard from him,
The Prophet of the Cherubim —
Or those which sad Esaias hurled
Against a sin-accursed world !
Its wizard-leaves the Press shall fling
Unceasing from its iron wing,
With characters inscribed thereon,
 As fearful in the despot's hall
As to the pomp of Babylon
 The fire-sign on the palace wall !
And, from her dark iniquities,
Methinks I see my country rise :
Not challenging the nations round
 To note her tardy justice done —
Her captives from their chains unbound,
 Her prisons opening to the sun ; —
But tearfully her arms extending
Over the poor and unoffending ;
 Her regal emblem now no longer
A bird of prey, with talons reeking,
Above the dying captive shrieking,
But, spreading out her ample wing —
A broad, impartial covering —
 The weaker sheltered by the stronger ! —
Oh ! then to Faith's anointed eyes
 The promised token shall be given ;
And on a nation's sacrifice,
 Atoning for the sin of years,
And wet with penitential tears —
The fire shall fall from Heaven !

1839.

NEW HAMPSHIRE.—1845.

God bless New Hampshire! — from her granite peaks
Once more the voice of Stark and Langdon speaks.
The long bound vassal of the exulting South
  For very shame her self-forged chain has broken —
Torn the black seal of slavery from her mouth,
  And in the clear tones of her old time spoken!
Oh, all undreamed of, all unhoped for changes! —
  The tyrant's ally proves his sternest foe;
To all his biddings, from her mountain ranges,
  New Hampshire thunders an indignant No!
Who is it now despairs? Oh, faint of heart,
  Look upward to those Northern mountains cold,
  Flouted by Freedom's victor-flag unrolled,
And gather strength to bear a manlier part!
All is not lost. The angel of God's blessing
  Encamps with Freedom on the field of fight;
Still to her banner, day by day, are pressing,
  Unlooked for allies, striking for the right!
Courage, then, Northern hearts! — Be firm, be true:
What one brave State hath done, can ye not also do?

THE NEW YEAR:

ADDRESSED TO THE PATRONS OF THE PENNSYLVANIA FREEMAN.

The wave is breaking on the shore —
  The echo fading from the chime —
Again the shadow moveth o'er
  The dial-plate of time !

Oh, seer-seen Angel ! waiting now
  With weary feet on sea and shore,
Impatient for the last dread vow
  That time shall be no more ! —

Once more across thy sleepless eye
  The semblance of a smile has passed ;
The year departing leaves more nigh
  Time's fearfullest and last.

Oh ! in that dying year hath been
  The sum of all since time began —
The birth and death, the joy and pain,
  Of Nature and of Man.

Spring, with her change of sun and shower,
  And streams released from winter's chain,
And bursting bud, and opening flower,
  And greenly growing grain ;

And Summer's shade, and sunshine warm,
  And rainbows o'er her hill-tops bowed,
And voices in her rising storm —
  God speaking from his cloud ! —

And Autumn's fruits and clustering sheaves,
 And soft, warm days of golden light,
The glory of her forest leaves,
 And harvest-moon at night;

And winter with her leafless grove,
 And prisoned stream, and drifting snow,
The brilliance of her heaven above
 And of her earth below: —

And man — in whom an angel's mind
 With earth's low instincts finds abode —
The highest of the links which bind
 Brute nature to her God;

His infant eye hath seen the light,
 His childhood's merriest laughter rung,
And active sports to manlier might
 The nerves of boyhood strung!

And quiet love, and passion's fires,
 Have soothed or burned in manhood's breast,
And lofty aims and low desires
 By turns disturbed his rest.

The wailing of the newly-born
 Has mingled with the funeral knell;
And o'er the dying's ear has gone
 The merry marriage-bell.

And Wealth has filled his halls with mirth,
 While Want, in many a humble shed,
Toiled, shivering by her cheerless hearth,
 The live-long night for bread.

And worse than all — the human slave —
 The sport of lust, and pride, and scorn!
Plucked off the crown his Maker gave —
 His regal manhood gone!

Oh! still my country! o'er thy plains,
  Blackened with slavery's blight and ban,
That human chattel drags his chains —
  An uncreated man!

And still, where'er to sun and breeze,
  My country, is thy flag unrolled,
With scorn, the gazing stranger sees
  A stain on every fold.

Oh, tear the gorgeous emblem down!
  It gathers scorn from every eye,
And despots smile, and good men frown,
  Whene'er it passes by.

Shame! shame! its starry splendors glow
  Above the slaver's loathsome jail —
Its folds are ruffling even now
  His crimson flag of sale.

Still round our country's proudest hall
  The trade in human flesh is driven,
And at each careless hammer-fall
  A human heart is riven.

And this, too, sanctioned by the men,
  Vested with power to shield the right,
And throw each vile and robber den
  Wide open to the light.

Yet shame upon them! — there they sit,
  Men of the North, subdued and still;
Meek, pliant poltroons, only fit
  To work a master's will.

Sold — bargained off for Southern votes —
  A passive herd of Northern mules,
Just braying through their purchased throats
  Whate'er their owner rules.

And he * — the basest of the base —
The vilest of the vile — whose name,
Embalmed in infinite disgrace,
Is deathless in its shame! —

A tool — to bolt the people's door
Against the people clamoring there, —
An ass — to trample on their floor
A people's right of prayer!

Nailed to his self-made gibbet fast,
Self-pilloried to the public view —
A mark for every passing blast
Of scorn to whistle through;

There let him hang, and hear the boast
Of Southrons o'er their pliant tool —
A St. Stylites on his post,
"Sacred to ridicule!"

Look we at home! — our noble hall,
To Freedom's holy purpose given,
Now rears its black and ruined wall,
Beneath the wintry heaven —

Telling the story of its doom —
The fiendish mob — the prostrate law —
The fiery jet through midnight's gloom,
Our gazing thousands saw.

Look to our State — the poor man's right
Torn from him: — and the sons of those
Whose blood in Freedom's sternest fight
Sprinkled the Jersey snows,

Outlawed within the land of Penn,
That Slavery's guilty fears might cease,
And those whom God created men,
Toil on as brutes in peace.

* The Northern author of the Congressional rule against receiving petitions of the people on the subject of Slavery.

Yet o'er the blackness of the storm,
  A bow of promise bends on high,
And gleams of sunshine, soft and warm,
  Break through our clouded sky.

East, West, and North, the shout is heard,
  Of freemen rising for the right:
Each valley hath its rallying word —
  Each hill its signal light.

O'er Massachusetts' rocks of grey,
  The strengthening light of freedom shines,
Rhode Island's Narragansett Bay —
  And Vermont's snow-hung pines!

From Hudson's frowning palisades
  To Alleghany's laureled crest,
O'er lakes and prairies, streams and glades,
  It shines upon the West.

Speed on the light to those who dwell
  In Slavery's land of woe and sin,
And through the blackness of that hell,
  Let Heaven's own light break in.

So shall the Southern conscience quake,
  Before that light poured full and strong,
So shall the Southern heart awake
  To all the bondman's wrong.

And from that rich and sunny land
  The song of grateful millions rise,
Like that of Israel's ransomed band
  Beneath Arabia's skies:

And all who now are bound beneath
  Our banner's shade — our eagle's wing,
From Slavery's night of moral death
  To light and life shall spring.

Broken the bondman's chain — and gone
The master's guilt, and hate, and fear,
And unto both alike shall dawn,
A New and Happy Year.

1839.

MASSACHUSETTS TO VIRGINIA.

[WRITTEN on reading an account of the proceedings of the citizens of Norfolk, Va., in reference to GEORGE LATIMER, the alleged fugitive slave, the result of whose case in Massachusetts will probably be similar to that of the negro SOMERSET in England, in 1772.]

THE blast from Freedom's Northern hills, upon its Southern way,
Bears greeting to Virginia from Massachusetts Bay : —
No word of haughty challenging, nor battle bugle's peal,
Nor steady tread of marching files, nor clang of horsemen's steel.

No trains of deep-mouthed cannon along our highways go —
Around our silent arsenals untrodden lies the snow ;
And to the land breeze of our ports, upon their errands far,
A thousand sails of commerce swell, but none are spread for war.

We hear thy threats, Virginia ! thy stormy words and high,
Swell harshly on the Southern winds which melt along our sky ;
Yet, not one brown, hard hand foregoes its honest labor here —
No hewer of our mountain oaks suspends his axe in fear.

Wild are the waves which lash the reefs along St. George's bank —
Cold on the shore of Labrador the fog lies white and dank ;
Through storm, and wave, and blinding mist, stout are the hearts which man
The fishing-smacks of Marblehead, the sea-boats of Cape Ann.

The cold north light and wintry sun glare on their icy forms,
Bent grimly o'er their straining lines or wrestling with the storms ;

Free as the winds they drive before, rough as the waves they roam,
They laugh to scorn the slaver's threat against their rocky home.

What means the Old Dominion? Hath she forgot the day
When o'er her conquered vallies swept the Briton's steel array?
How side by side, with sons of hers, the Massachusetts men
Encountered Tarleton's charge of fire, and stout Cornwallis, then?

Forgets she how the Bay State, in answer to the call
Of her old House of Burgesses, spoke out from Faneuil Hall?
When, echoing back her Henry's cry, came pulsing on each breath
Of Northern winds, the thrilling sounds of "LIBERTY OR DEATH!"

What asks the Old Dominion? If now her sons have proved
False to their fathers' memory — false to the faith they loved;
If she can scoff at Freedom, and its great charter spurn,
Must we of Massachusetts from truth and duty turn?

We hunt your bondmen, flying from Slavery's hateful hell —
Our voices, at your bidding, take up the bloodhound's yell —
We gather, at your summons, above our fathers' graves,
From Freedom's holy altar-horns to tear your wretched slaves!

Thank God! not yet so vilely can Massachusetts bow;
The spirit of her early time is with her even now;
Dream not because her Pilgrim blood moves slow, and calm, and cool,
She thus can stoop her chainless neck, a sister's slave and tool!

All that a *sister* State should do, all that a *free* State may,
Heart, hand, and purse we proffer, as in our early day;
But that one dark loathsome burden ye must stagger with alone,
And reap the bitter harvest which ye yourselves have sown!

Hold, while ye may, your struggling slaves, and burden God's free air
With woman's shriek beneath the lash, and manhood's wild despair;

Cling closer to the "cleaving curse" that writes upon your plains
The blasting of Almighty wrath against a land of chains.

Still shame your gallant ancestry, the cavaliers of old,
By watching round the shambles where human flesh is sold —
Gloat o'er the new-born child, and count his market value, when
The maddened mother's cry of woe shall pierce the slaver's den!

Lower than plummet soundeth, sink the Virginian name;
Plant, if ye will, your fathers' graves with rankest weeds of shame;
Be, if ye will, the scandal of God's fair universe —
We wash our hands forever, of your sin, and shame, and curse.

A voice from lips whereon the coal from Freedom's shrine hath been,
Thrilled, as but yesterday, the hearts of Berkshire's mountain men:
The echoes of that solemn voice are sadly lingering still
In all our sunny valleys, on every wind-swept hill.

And when the prowling man-thief came hunting for his prey
Beneath the very shadow of Bunker's shaft of grey,
How, through the free lips of the son, the father's warning spoke;
How, from its bonds of trade and sect, the Pilgrim city broke!

A hundred thousand right arms were lifted up on high, —
A hundred thousand voices sent back their loud reply;
Through the thronged towns of Essex the startling summons rang,
And up from bench and loom and wheel her young mechanics sprang!

The voice of free, broad Middlesex — of thousands as of one —
The shaft of Bunker calling to that of Lexington —
From Norfolk's ancient villages; from Plymouth's rocky bound
To where Nantucket feels the arms of ocean close her round; —

From rich and rural Worcester, where through the calm repose
Of cultured vales and fringing woods the gentle Nashua flows,
To where Wachuset's wintry blasts the mountain larches stir,
Swelled up to Heaven the thrilling cry of "God save Latimer!"

And sandy Barnstable rose up, wet with the salt sea spray —
And Bristol sent her answering shout down Narragansett Bay!
Along the broad Connecticut old Hampden felt the thrill,
And the cheer of Hampshire's woodmen swept down from Holyoke Hill.

The voice of Massachusetts! Of her free sons and daughters —
Deep calling unto deep aloud — the sound of many waters!
Against the burden of that voice what tyrant power shall stand?
No fetters in the Bay State! No slave upon her land!

Look to it well, Virginians! In calmness we have borne,
In answer to our faith and trust, your insult and your scorn;
You 've spurned our kindest counsels — you 've hunted for our lives —
And shaken round our hearths and homes your manacles and gyves!

We wage no war — we lift no arm — we fling no torch within
The fire-damps of the quaking mine beneath your soil of sin;
We leave ye with your bondmen, to wrestle, while ye can,
With the strong upward tendencies and God-like soul of man!

But for us and for our children, the vow which we have given
For freedom and humanity, is registered in Heaven;
No slave-hunt in our borders — no pirate on our strand!
No fetters in the Bay State — no slave upon our land!

THE RELIC.

[Pennsylvania Hall, dedicated to Free Discussion and the cause of human liberty, was destroyed by a mob in 1838. The following was written on receiving a cane wrought from a fragment of the wood-work which the fire had spared.]

Token of friendship true and tried,
  From one whose fiery heart of youth
With mine has beaten, side by side,
  For Liberty and Truth ;
With honest pride the gift I take,
And prize it for the giver's sake.

But not alone because it tells
  Of generous hand and heart sincere ;
Around that gift of friendship dwells
  A memory doubly dear —
Earth's noblest aim — man's holiest thought,
With that memorial frail inwrought !

Pure thoughts and sweet, like flowers unfold,
  And precious memories round it cling,
Even as the Prophet's rod of old
  In beauty blossoming :
And buds of feeling pure and good
Spring from its cold unconscious wood.

Relic of Freedom's shrine ! — a brand
  Plucked from its burning ! — let it be
Dear as a jewel from the hand
  Of a lost friend to me ! —
Flower of a perished garland left,
Of life and beauty unbereft !

Oh! if the young enthusiast bears,
O'er weary waste and sea, the stone
Which crumbled from the Forum's stairs,
Or round the Parthenon;
Or olive bough from some wild tree
Hung over old Thermopylæ:

If leaflets from some hero's tomb,
Or moss-wreath torn from ruins hoary,—
Or faded flowers whose sisters bloom
On fields renowned in story,—
Or fragment from the Alhambra's crest,
Or the grey rock by Druids blessed;

Sad Erin's shamrock greenly growing
Where Freedom led her stalwart kern,
Or Scotia's "rough bur thistle" blowing
On Bruce's Bannockburn—
Or Runnymede's wild English rose,
Or lichen plucked from Sempach's snows!—

If it be true that things like these
To heart and eye bright visions bring,
Shall not far holier memories
To this memorial cling?
Which needs no mellowing mist of time
To hide the crimson stains of crime!

Wreck of a temple, unprofaned—
Of courts where Peace with Freedom trod,
Lifting on high, with hands unstained,
Thanksgiving unto God;
Where Mercy's voice of love was pleading
For human hearts in bondage bleeding!—

Where midst the sound of rushing feet
And curses on the night air flung,
That pleading voice rose calm and sweet
From woman's earnest tongue;
And Riot turned his scowling glance,
Awed, from her tranquil countenance!

That temple now in ruin lies! —
  The fire-stain on its shattered wall,
And open to the changing skies
  Its black and roofless hall,
It stands before a nation's sight,
A grave-stone over buried Right!

But from that ruin, as of old,
  The fire-scorched stones themselves are crying,
And from their ashes white and cold
  Its timbers are replying!
A voice which slavery cannot kill
Speaks from the crumbling arches still!

And even this relic from thy shrine,
  Oh, holy Freedom! — hath to me
A potent power, a voice and sign
  To testify of thee;
And, grasping it, methinks I feel
A deeper faith, a stronger zeal.

And not unlike that mystic rod,
  Of old stretched o'er the Egyptian wave,
Which opened, in the strength of God,
  A pathway for the slave,
It yet may point the bondman's way,
And turn the spoiler from his prey.

STANZAS FOR THE TIMES—1844.

[WRITTEN on reading the sentence of JOHN L. BROWN, of South Carolina, to be executed on the 25th of Fourth month, 1844, for the crime of assisting a female slave to escape from bondage. The sentence was afterwards commuted.]

Ho! thou who seekest late and long
  A license from the Holy Book
For brutal lust and hell's red wrong,
  Man of the pulpit look! —
Lift up those cold and atheist eyes,
  This ripe fruit of thy teaching see;
And tell us how to Heaven will rise
The incense of this sacrifice —
  This blossom of the Gallows Tree! —

Search out for SLAVERY's hour of need
  Some fitting text of sacred writ; *
Give Heaven the credit of a deed
Which shames the nether pit.
Kneel, smooth blasphemer, unto Him
  Whose truth is on thy lips a lie,
Ask that His bright-winged cherubim
May bend around that scaffold grim
  To guard and bless and sanctify! —

Ho! champion of the people's cause —
  Suspend thy loud and vain rebuke
Of foreign wrong and Old World laws,
  Man of the Senate, look! —

* Three new publications, from the pens of Dr. Junkin, President of Miami College, Alexander McCaine of the Methodist Protestant church, and of a clergyman of the Cincinnati Synod, defending Slavery on Scriptural ground, have recently made their appearance.

Was this the promise of the free, —
  The great hope of our early time, —
That Slavery's poison vine should be
Upborne by Freedom's prayer-nursed tree,
  O'erclustered with such fruits of crime? —

Send out the summons, east and west,
  And south and north, let all be there,
Where he who pitied the oppressed
  Swings out in sun and air.
Let not a democratic hand
  The grisly hangman's task refuse;
There let each loyal patriot stand
Awaiting Slavery's command
  To twist the rope and draw the noose!

But vain is irony — unmeet
  Its cold rebuke for deeds which start
In fiery and indignant beat
  The pulses of the heart.
Leave studied wit, and guarded phrase;
  And all that kindled heart can feel
Speak out in earnest words which raise,
Where'er they fall, an answering blaze,
  Like flints which strike the fire from steel.

Still let a mousing priesthood ply
  Their garbled text and gloss of sin,
And make the lettered scroll deny
  Its living soul within;
Still let the place-fed titled knave
  Plead Robbery's right with purchased lips,
And tell us that our fathers gave
For Freedom's pedestal, a slave,
  For frieze and moulding, chains and whips! —

But ye who own that higher law
  Whose tables in the heart are set,
Speak out in words of power and awe
  That God is living yet!

Breathe forth once more those tones sublime
  Which thrilled the burthened prophet's lyre,
And in a dark and evil time
Smote down on Israel's fast of crime
  And gift of blood, a rain of fire!

Oh, not for us the graceful lay,
  To whose soft measures lightly move
The Dryad and the woodland Fay,
  O'erlooked by Mirth and Love;
But such a stern and startling strain
  As Britain's hunted bards flung down
From Snowden, to the conquered plain,
Where harshly clanked the Saxon chain
  On trampled field and smoking town.

By Liberty's dishonored name,
  By man's lost hope, and failing trust,
By words and deeds, which bow with shame
  Our foreheads to the dust, —
By the exulting tyrant's sneer,
  Borne to us from the Old World's thrones,
And by their grief, who pining hear,
In sunless mines and dungeons drear,
  How Freedom's land her faith disowns; —

Speak out in *acts*; the time for words
  Has passed, and deeds alone suffice;
In the loud clang of meeting swords
  The softer music dies!
Act — act, in God's name, while ye may,
  Smite from the church her leprous limb,
Throw open to the light of day
The bondman's cell, and break away
  The chains the State has bound on him.

Ho! every true and living soul,
  To Freedom's periled altar bear
The freeman's and the Christian's whole,
  Tongue, pen, and vote, and prayer!

One last great battle for the Right, —
  One short, sharp struggle to be free ! —
To do is to succeed — our fight
Is waged in Heaven's approving sight —
  The smile of God is Victory !

THE BRANDED HAND.

[Captain Jonathan Walker, of Harwich, Mass., was solicited by several fugitive slaves at Pensacola, Florida, to convey them in his vessel to the British West Indies. Although well aware of the hazard of the enterprize, he attempted to comply with their request. He was seized by an American vessel, consigned to the American authorities at Key West, and by them taken back to Florida — where, after a long and rigorous imprisonment, he was brought to trial. He was sentenced to be branded on the right hand with the letters "S. S." ("Slave Stealer") and amerced in a heavy fine. He was released on the payment of his fine in the Sixth month of 1845.]

Welcome home again, brave seaman ! with thy thoughtful brow and grey,
And the old heroic spirit of our earlier, better day —
With that front of calm endurance, on whose steady nerve, in vain
Pressed the iron of the prison, smote the fiery shafts of pain !

Is the tyrant's brand upon thee ? Did the brutal cravens aim
To make God's truth thy falsehood, His holiest work thy shame ?
When, all blood-quenched, from the torture the iron was withdrawn,
How laughed their evil angel the baffled fools to scorn !

They change to wrong, the duty which God hath written out
On the great heart of humanity too legible for doubt !
They, the loathsome moral lepers, blotched from footsole up to crown,
Give to shame what God hath given unto honor and renown !

Why, that brand is highest honor! — than its traces never yet
Upon old armorial hatchments was a prouder blazon set;
And thy unborn generations, as they tread our rocky strand,
Shall tell with pride the story of their father's BRANDED HAND!

As the Templar home was welcomed, bearing back from Syrian wars
The scars of Arab lances, and of Paynim scimetars.
The pallor of the prison and the shackle's crimson span,
So we meet thee, so we greet thee, truest friend of God and man!

He suffered for the ransom of the dear Redeemer's grave,
Thou for His living presence in the bound and bleeding slave;
He for a soil no longer by the feet of angels trod,
Thou for the true Shechinah, the present home of God!

For, while the jurist sitting with the slave-whip o'er him swung,
From the tortured truths of freedom the lie of slavery wrung,
And the solemn priest to Moloch, on each God-deserted shrine,
Broke the bondman's heart for bread, poured the bondman's blood for wine —

While the multitude in blindness to a far-off Saviour knelt,
And spurned, the while, the temple where a present Saviour dwelt;
Thou beheld'st Him in the task-field, in the prison shadows dim,
And thy mercy to the bondman, it was mercy unto Him!

In thy lone and long night watches, sky above and wave below,
Thou did'st learn a higher wisdom than the babbling school-men know;
God's stars and silence taught thee, as His angels only can,
That the one, sole sacred thing beneath the cope of heaven is Man!

That he who treads profanely on the scrolls of law and creed,
In the depth of God's great goodness may find mercy in his need;
But woe to him who crushes the SOUL with chain and rod,
And herds with lower natures the awful form of God!

Then lift that manly right hand, bold ploughman of the wave !
Its branded palm shall prophecy, " SALVATION TO THE SLAVE ! "
Hold up its fire-wrought language, that whoso reads may feel
His heart swell strong within him, his sinews change to steel.

Hold it up before our sunshine, up against our Northern air —
Ho ! men of Massachusetts, for the love of God look there !
Take it henceforth for your standard — like the Bruce's heart of yore,
In the dark strife closing round ye, let that hand be seen before !

And the tyrants of the slave-land shall tremble at that sign,
When it points its finger Southward along the Puritan line :
Woe to the State-gorged leeches, and the Church's locust band,
When they look from slavery's ramparts on the coming of that hand !

TEXAS.

VOICE OF NEW ENGLAND.

UP the hill-side, down the glen,
Rouse the sleeping citizen ;
Summon out the might of men !

Like a lion growling low —
Like a night-storm rising slow —
Like the tread of unseen foe —

It is coming — it is nigh !
Stand your homes and altars by ;
On your own free thresholds die.

Clang the bells in all your spires ;
On the grey hills of your sires
Fling to heaven your signal fires.

From Wachuset, lone and bleak,
Unto Berkshire's tallest peak,
Let the flame-tongued heralds speak.

O! for God and duty stand,
Heart to heart and hand to hand,
Round the old graves of the land.

Whoso shrinks or falters now,
Whoso to the yoke would bow,
Brand the craven on his brow!

Freedom's soil hath only place
For a free and fearless race —
None for traitors false and base.

Perish party — perish clan;
Strike together while ye can,
Like the arm of one strong man.

Like that angel's voice sublime,
Heard above a world of crime.
Crying of the end of time —

With one heart and with one mouth,
Let the North unto the South
Speak the word befitting both:

"What though Issachar be strong!
Ye may load his back with wrong
Overmuch and over long:

Patience with her cup o'errun,
With her weary thread outspun,
Murmurs that her work is done.

Make our Union-bond a chain,
Weak as tow in Freedom's strain
Link by link shall snap in twain.

Vainly shall your sand-wrought rope
Bind the starry cluster up,
Shattered over heaven's blue cope!

Give us bright though broken rays,
Rather than eternal haze,
Clouding o'er the full-orbed blaze.

Take your land of sun and bloom;
Only leave to Freedom room
For her plough, and forge, and loom;

Take your slavery-blackened vales;
Leave us but our own free gales,
Blowing on our thousand sails.

Boldly, or with treacherous art,
Strike the blood-wrought chain apart;
Break the Union's mighty heart;

Work the ruin, if ye will;
Pluck upon your heads an ill
Which shall grow and deepen still.

With your bondman's right arm bare,
With his heart of black despair,
Stand alone, if stand ye dare!

Onward with your fell design;
Dig the gulf and draw the line:
Fire beneath your feet the mine:

Deeply, when the wide abyss
Yawns between your land and this,
Shall ye feel your helplessness.

By the hearth, and in the bed,
Shaken by a look or tread,
Ye shall own a guilty dread.

And the curse of unpaid toil,
Downward through your generous soil
Like a fire shall burn and spoil.

Our bleak hills shall bud and blow,
Vines our rocks shall overgrow,
Plenty in our vallies flow;—

And when vengeance clouds your skies,
Hither shall ye turn your eyes,
As the lost on Paradise!

We but ask our rocky strand,
Freedom's true and brother band,
Freedom's strong and honest hand,—

Valleys by the slave untrod,
And the Pilgrim's mountain sod,
Blessed of our fathers' God!"

TO FANEUIL HALL.

[Written in 1844, on reading a call by "a Massachusetts Freeman" for a meeting in Faneuil Hall of the citizens of Massachusetts, without distinction of party, opposed to the annexation of Texas, and the aggressions of South Carolina, and in favor of decisive action against Slavery.]

Men!—if manhood still ye claim,
If the Northern pulse can thrill,
Roused by wrong or stung by shame,
Freely, strongly still:—
Let the sounds of traffic die:
Shut the mill-gate—leave the stall—
Fling the axe and hammer by—
Throng to Faneuil Hall!

Wrongs which freemen never brooked —
  Dangers grim and fierce as they,
Which, like couching lions, looked
  On your fathers' way ; —
These your instant zeal demand,
  Shaking with their earthquake-call
Every rood of Pilgrim land —
  Ho, to Faneuil Hall !

From your capes and sandy bars —
  From your mountain-ridges cold,
Through whose pines the westering stars
  Stoop their crowns of gold —
Come, and with your footsteps wake
  Echoes from that holy wall :
Once again, for Freedom's sake,
  Rock your fathers' hall !

Up, and tread beneath your feet
  Every cord by party spun ;
Let your hearts together beat
  As the heart of one.
Banks and tariffs, stocks and trade,
  Let them rise or let them fall :
Freedom asks your common aid —
  Up, to Faneuil Hall !

Up, and let each voice that speaks
  Ring from thence to Southern plains,
Sharply as the blow which breaks
  Prison-bolts and chains !
Speak as well becomes the free —
  Dreaded more than steel or ball,
Shall your calmest utterance be,
  Heard from Faneuil Hall !

Have they wronged us ? Let us then
  Render back nor threats nor prayers ;
Have they chained our free-born men ?
  Let us unchain theirs !

Up! your banner leads the van,
  Blazoned "Liberty for all!"
Finish what your sires began —
  Up, to Faneuil Hall!

TO MASSACHUSETTS.

WRITTEN DURING THE PENDING OF THE TEXAS QUESTION.

WHAT though around thee blazes
  No fiery rallying sign?
From all thy own high places,
  Give heaven the light of thine!
What though unthrilled, unmoving,
  The statesman stands apart,
And comes no warm approving
  From Mammon's crowded mart?

Still let the land be shaken
  By a summons of thine own!
By all save truth forsaken,
  Why, stand with that alone!
Shrink not from strife unequal!
  With the best is always hope;
And ever in the sequel
  God holds the right side up!

But when, with thine uniting,
  Come voices long and loud,
And far-off hills are writing
  Thy fire-words on the cloud:
When from Penobscot's fountains
  A deep response is heard,
And across the Western mountains
  Rolls back thy rallying word;

Shall thy line of battle falter,
  With its allies just in view?
Oh, by hearth and holy altar,
  My Father-land, be true!
Fling abroad thy scrolls of Freedom!
  Speed them onward far and fast!
Over hill and valley speed them,
  Like the Sybil's on the blast!

Lo! the Empire State is shaking
  The shackles from her hand;
With the rugged North is waking
  The level sunset land!
On they come — the free battalions!
  East and West and North they come,
And the heart-beat of the millions
  Is the beat of Freedom's drum.

"To the tyrant's plot no favor!
  No heed to place-fed knaves!
Bar and bolt the door forever
  Against the land of Slaves!"
Hear it, mother Earth, and hear it,
  The Heavens above us spread!
The land is roused — its spirit
  Was sleeping, but not dead!

THE PINE TREE.

Written on hearing that the Anti-Slavery Resolves of Stephen C. Phillips had been rejected by the Whig Convention in Faneuil Hall, in 1846.

Lift again the stately emblem on the Bay State's rusted shield,
Give to Northern winds the Pine Tree on our banner's tattered field,
Sons of men who sat in council with their Bibles round the board,
Answering England's royal missive with a firm, "Thus saith the Lord!"
Rise again for home and freedom! — set the battle in array! —
What the fathers did of old time we their sons must do to-day.

Tell us not of banks and tariffs — cease your paltry pedlar cries —
Shall the good State sink her honor that your gambling stocks may rise?
Would ye barter man for cotton? — That your gains may be the same,
Must we kiss the feet of Moloch, pass our children through the flame?
Is the dollar only real? — God and truth and right a dream?
Weighed against your lying ledgers must our manhood kick the beam?

Oh, my God! — for that free spirit, which of old in Boston town
Smote the Province House with terror, struck the crest of Andros down! —

For another strong-voiced Adams in the city's streets to cry:
"Up for God and Massachusetts! — Set your feet on Mammon's lie!
Perish banks and perish traffic — spin your cotton's latest pound —
But in Heaven's name keep your honor — keep the heart o' the Bay State sound!"

Where 's the MAN for Massachusetts? — Where 's the voice to speak her free? —
Where 's the hand to light up bonfires from her mountains to the sea?
Beats her Pilgrim pulse no longer? — Sits she dumb in her despair? —
Has she none to break the silence? — Has she none to do and dare?
Oh my God! for one right worthy to lift up her rusted shield,
And to plant again the Pine Tree in her banner's tattered field!

LINES,

SUGGESTED BY A VISIT TO THE CITY OF WASHINGTON IN THE 12TH MONTH OF 1845.

WITH a cold and wintry noon-light,
On its roofs and steeples shed,
Shadows weaving with the sun-light
From the grey sky overhead,
Broadly, vaguely, all around me, lies the half-built town outspread.

Through this broad street, restless ever,
Ebbs and flows a human tide,
Wave on wave a living river ;
Wealth and fashion side by side ;
Toiler, idler, slave and master, in the same quick current glide.

Underneath yon dome, whose coping
Springs above them, vast and tall,
Grave men in the dust are groping
For the largess, base and small,
Which the hand of Power is scattering, crumbs which from its table fall.

Base of heart ! They vilely barter
Honor's wealth for party's place :
Step by step on Freedom's charter
Leaving footprints of disgrace ;
For to-day's poor pittance turning from the great hope of their race.

Yet, where festal lamps are throwing
Glory round the dancer's hair,

Gold-tressed, like an angel's flowing
Backward on the sunset air;
And the low quick pulse of music beats its measures sweet and rare:

There to-night shall woman's glances,
Star-like, welcome give to them,
Fawning fools with shy advances
Seek to touch their garments' hem,
With the tongue of flattery glozing deeds which God and Truth condemn.

From this glittering lie my vision
Takes a broader, sadder range,
Full before me have arisen
Other pictures dark and strange;
From the parlor to the prison must the scene and witness change.

Hark! the heavy gate is swinging
On its hinges, harsh and slow;
One pale prison lamp is flinging
On a fearful group below
Such a light as leaves to terror whatsoe'er it does not show.

Pitying God! — Is that a WOMAN
On whose wrist the shackles clash?
Is that shriek she utters human,
Underneath the stinging lash?
Are they MEN whose eyes of madness from that sad procession flash?

Still the dance goes gaily onward!
What is it to Wealth and Pride?
That without the stars are looking
On a scene which earth should hide?
That the SLAVE-SHIP lies in waiting, rocking on Potomac's tide!

Vainly to that mean Ambition
Which, upon a rival's fall,

Winds above its old condition,
With a reptile's slimy crawl,
Shall the pleading voice of sorrow, shall the slave in anguish call.

Vainly to the child of Fashion,
Giving to ideal woe
Graceful luxury of compassion,
Shall the stricken mourner go;
Hateful seems the earnest sorrow, beautiful the hollow show!

Nay, my words are all too sweeping:
In this crowded human mart,
Feeling is not dead, but sleeping;
Man's strong will and woman's heart,
In the coming strife for Freedom, yet shall bear their generous part.

And from yonder sunny vallies,
Southward in the distance lost,
Freedom yet shall summon allies
Worthier than the North can boast,
With the Evil by their hearth-stones grappling at severer cost.

Now, the soul alone is willing:
Faint the heart and weak the knee;
And as yet no lip is thrilling
With the mighty words "Be Free!"
Tarrieth long the land's Good Angel, but his advent is to be!

Meanwhile, turning from the revel
To the prison-cell my sight,
For intenser hate of evil,
For a keener sense of right,
Shaking off thy dust, I thank thee, City of the Slaves, to-night!

"To thy duty now and ever!
Dream no more of rest or stay;
Give to Freedom's great endeavor
All thou art and hast to-day:"—
Thus, above the city's murmur, saith a Voice or seems to say.

Ye with heart and vision gifted
  To discern and love the right,
Whose worn faces have been lifted
  To the slowly-growing light,
Where from Freedom's sunrise drifted slowly back the murk of night! —

Ye who through long years of trial
  Still have held your purpose fast,
While a lengthening shade the dial
  From the westering sunshine cast,
And of hope each hour's denial seemed an echo of the last! —

Oh, my brothers! oh, my sisters!
  Would to God that ye were near,
Gazing with me down the vistas
  Of a sorrow strange and drear;
Would to God that ye were listening to the Voice I seem to hear!

With the storm above us driving,
  With the false earth mined below —
Who shall marvel if thus striving
  We have counted friend as foe;
Unto one another giving in the darkness blow for blow.

Well it may be that our natures
  Have grown sterner and more hard,
And the freshness of their features
  Somewhat harsh and battle-scarred,
And their harmonies of feeling overtasked and rudely jarred.

Be it so. It should not swerve us
  From a purpose true and brave;
Dearer Freedom's rugged service
  Than the pastime of the slave;
Better is the storm above it than the quiet of the grave.

Let us then, uniting, bury
  All our idle feuds in dust,

And to future conflicts carry
  Mutual faith and common trust;
Always he who most forgiveth in his brother is most just.

From the eternal shadow rounding
  All our sun and starlight here,
Voices of our lost ones sounding
  Bid us be of heart and cheer,
Through the silence, down the spaces, falling on the inward ear.

Know we not our dead are looking
  Downward with a sad surprise,
All our strife of words rebuking
  With their mild and loving eyes?
Shall we grieve the holy angels? Shall we cloud their blessed skies?

Let us draw their mantles o'er us
  Which have fallen in our way;
Let us do the work before us,
  Cheerly, bravely, while we may,
Ere the long night-silence cometh, and with us it is not day!

LINES,

FROM A LETTER TO A YOUNG CLERICAL FRIEND.

A STRENGTH Thy service cannot tire —
  A faith which doubt can never dim —
A heart of love, a lip of fire —
  Oh! Freedom's God! be Thou to him!

Speak through him words of power and fear,
  As through Thy prophet bards of old,
And let a scornful people hear
  Once more Thy Sinai-thunders rolled.

For lying lips Thy blessing seek,
  And hands of blood are raised to Thee,
And on Thy children, crushed and weak,
  The oppressor plants his kneeling knee.

Let then, oh, God! Thy servant dare
  Thy truth in all its power to tell,
Unmask the priestly thieves, and tear
  The Bible from the grasp of hell!

From hollow rite and narrow span
  Of law and sect by Thee released,
Oh! teach him that the Christian man
  Is holier than the Jewish priest.

Chase back the shadows, grey and old,
  Of the dead ages, from his way,
And let his hopeful eyes behold
  The dawn of Thy millenial day; —

That day when fettered limb and mind
  Shall know the truth which maketh free,
And he alone who loves his kind
  Shall, child-like, claim the love of Thee!

YORKTOWN.

[Dr. Thacher, surgeon in Scammel's regiment, in his description of the siege of Yorktown, says: "The labor on the Virginia plantations is performed altogether by a species of the human race cruelly wrested from their native country, and doomed to perpetual bondage, while their masters are manfully contending for freedom and the natural rights of man. Such is the inconsistency of human nature." Eighteen hundred slaves were found at Yorktown, after its surrender, and restored to their masters. Well was it said by Dr. Barnes, in his late work on Slavery: "No slave was any nearer his freedom after the surrender of Yorktown, than when Patrick Henry first taught the notes of liberty to echo among the hills and vales of Virginia."]

From Yorktown's ruins, ranked and still,
Two lines stretch far o'er vale and hill:
Who curbs his steed at head of one?
Hark! the low murmur: Washington!
Who bends his keen, approving glance
Where down the gorgeous line of France
Shine knightly star and plume of snow?
Thou too art victor, Rochambeau!

The earth which bears this calm array
Shook with the war charge yesterday,
Ploughed deep with hurrying hoof and wheel,
Shot-sown and bladed thick with steel;
October's clear and noonday sun
Paled in the breath-smoke of the gun.
And down night's double blackness fell,
Like a dropped star, the blazing shell.

Now all is hushed: the gleaming lines
Stand moveless as the neighboring pines;

While through them, sullen, grim, and slow,
The conquered hosts of England go:
O'Hara's brow belies his dress,
Gay Tarlton's troop ride bannerless:
Shout, from thy fired and wasted homes,
Thy scourge, Virginia, captive comes!

Nor thou alone: with one glad voice
Let all thy sister States rejoice;
Let Freedom, in whatever clime
She waits with sleepless eye her time,
Shouting from cave and mountain wood,
Make glad her desert solitude,
While they who hunt her quail with fear:
The New World's chain lies broken here!

But who are they, who, cowering, wait
Within the shattered fortress gate?
Dark tillers of Virginia's soil,
Classed with the battle's common spoil,
With household stuffs, and fowl, and swine,
With Indian weed and planters' wine,
With stolen beeves, and foraged corn —
Are they not men, Virginian born?

Oh! veil your faces, young and brave!
Sleep, Scammel, in thy soldier grave!
Sons of the North-land, ye who set
Stout hearts against the bayonet,
And pressed with steady footfall near
The moated battery's blazing tier,
Turn your scarred faces from the sight,
Let shame do homage to the right!

Lo! threescore years have passed; and where
The Gallic timbrel stirred the air,
With Northern drum-roll, and the clear,
Wild horn-blow of the mountaineer,
While Britain grounded on that plain
The arms she might not lift again,

As abject as in that old day
The slave still toils his life away.

Oh! fields still green and fresh in story,
Old days of pride, old names of glory,
Old marvels of the tongue and pen,
Old thoughts which stirred the hearts of men,
Ye spared the wrong; and over all
Behold the avenging shadow fall!
Your world-wide honor stained with shame—
Your freedom's self a hollow name!

Where's now the flag of that old war?
Where flows its stripe? Where burns its star?
Bear witness, Palo Alto's day,
Dark Vale of Palms, red Monterey,
Where Mexic Freedom, young and weak,
Fleshes the Northern eagle's beak:
Symbol of terror and despair,
Of chains and slaves, go seek it there!

Laugh, Prussia, midst thy iron ranks!
Laugh, Russia, from thy Neva's banks!
Brave sport to see the fledgling born
Of Freedom by its parent torn!
Safe now is Speilberg's dungeon cell,
Safe drear Siberia's frozen hell:
With Slavery's flag o'er both unrolled,
What of the New World fears the Old?

LINES,

WRITTEN IN THE BOOK OF A FRIEND.

On page of thine I cannot trace
The cold and heartless common-place —
A statue's fixed and marble grace.

For ever as these lines are penned,
Still with the thought of thee will blend
That of some loved and common friend —

Who in life's desert track has made
His pilgrim tent with mine, or strayed
Beneath the same remembered shade.

And hence my pen unfettered moves
In freedom which the heart approves —
The negligence which friendship loves.

And wilt thou prize my poor gift less
For simple air and rustic dress,
And sign of haste and carelessness ? —

Oh ! more than specious counterfeit
Of sentiment, or studied wit,
A heart like thine should value it.

Yet half I fear my gift will be
Unto thy book, if not to thee,
Of more than doubtful courtesy.

A banished name from Fashion's sphere,
A lay unheard of Beauty's ear,
Forbid, disowned, — what do they here ? —

Upon my ear not all in vain
Came the sad captive's clanking chain —
The groaning from his bed of pain.

And sadder still, I saw the woe
Which only wounded spirits know
When Pride's strong footsteps o'er them go.

Spurned not alone in walks abroad,
But from the "temples of the Lord"
Thrust out apart, like things abhorred.

Deep as I felt, and stern and strong,
In words which Prudence smothered long,
My soul spoke out against the wrong;

Not mine alone the task to speak
Of comfort to the poor and weak,
And dry the tear on Sorrow's cheek;

But, mingled in the conflict warm,
To pour the fiery breath of storm
Through the harsh trumpet of Reform;

To brave Opinion's settled frown,
From ermined robe and saintly gown,
While wrestling reverenced Error down.

Founts gushed beside my pilgrim way,
Cool shadows on the green sward lay,
Flowers swung upon the bending spray.

And, broad and bright, on either hand,
Stretched the green slopes of Fairy land,
With Hope's eternal sunbow spanned;

Whence voices called me like the flow,
Which on the listener's ear will grow,
Of forest streamlets soft and low.

And gentle eyes, which still retain
Their picture on the heart and brain,
Smiled, beckoning from that path of pain.

In vain! — nor dream, nor rest, nor pause
Remain for him who round him draws
The battered mail of Freedom's cause.

From youthful hopes — from each green spot
Of young Romance, and gentle Thought,
Where storm and tumult enter not —

From each fair altar, where belong
The offerings Love requires of Song
In homage to her bright-eyed throng —

With soul and strength, with heart and hand,
I turned to Freedom's struggling band —
To the sad Helots of our land.

What marvel then that Fame should turn
Her notes of praise to those of scorn —
Her gifts reclaimed — her smiles withdrawn?

What matters it! — a few years more,
Life's surge so restless heretofore
Shall break upon the unknown shore!

In that far land shall disappear
The shadows which we follow here —
The mist-wreaths of our atmosphere!

Before no work of mortal hand,
Of human will or strength expand
The pearl gates of the Better Land;

Alone in that great love which gave
Life to the sleeper of the grave,
Resteth the power to "seek and save."

Yet, if the spirit gazing through
The vista of the past can view
One deed to Heaven and virtue true —

If through the wreck of wasted powers,
Of garlands wreathed from Folly's bowers,
Of idle aims and misspent hours —

The eye can note one sacred spot
By Pride and Self profaned not —
A green place in the waste of thought —

Where deed or word hath rendered less
"The sum of human wretchedness,"
And Gratitude looks forth to bless —

The simple burst of tenderest feeling
From sad hearts worn by evil-dealing,
For blessing on the hand of healing, —

Better than Glory's pomp will be
That green and blessed spot to me —
A palm-shade in Eternity ! —

Something of Time which may invite
The purified and spiritual sight
To rest on with a calm delight.

And when the summer winds shall sweep
With their light wings my place of sleep,
And mosses round my head-stone creep —

If still, as Freedom's rallying sign,
Upon the young heart's altars shine
The very fires they caught from mine —

If words my lips once uttered still,
In the calm faith and steadfast will
Of other hearts, their work fulfill —

Perchance with joy the soul may learn
These tokens, and its eye discern
The fires which on those altars burn —

A marvellous joy that even then,
The spirit hath its life again,
In the strong hearts of mortal men.

Take, lady, then, the gift I bring,
No gay and graceful offering —
No flower-smile of the laughing spring.

Midst the green buds of Youth's fresh May,
With Fancy's leaf-enwoven bay,
My sad and sombre gift I lay.

And if it deepens in thy mind
A sense of suffering human kind —
The outcast and the spirit-blind:

Oppressed and spoiled on every side,
By Prejudice, and Scorn, and Pride,
Life's common courtesies denied;

Sad mothers mourning o'er their trust,
Children by want and misery nursed,
Tasting life's bitter cup at first;

If to their strong appeals which come
From fireless hearth, and crowded room,
And the close alley's noisome gloom —

Though dark the hands upraised to thee
In mute beseeching agony,
Thou lend'st thy woman's sympathy —

Not vainly on thy gentle shrine,
Where Love, and Mirth, and Friendship twine
Their varied gifts, I offer mine.

MISCELLANEOUS.

PALESTINE.

Blest land of Judea! thrice hallowed of song
Where the holiest of memories pilgrim-like throng;
In the shade of thy palms, by the shores of thy sea,
On the hills of thy beauty, my heart is with thee.

With the eye of a spirit I look on that shore,
Where pilgrim and prophet have lingered before;
With the glide of a spirit I traverse the sod
Made bright by the steps of the angels of God.

Blue sea of the hills! — in my spirit I hear
Thy waters, Genesaret, chime on my ear;
Where the Lowly and Just with the people sat down,
And thy spray on the dust of His sandals was thrown.

Beyond are Bethulia's mountains of green,
And the desolate hills of the wild Gadarene;
And I pause on the goat-crags of Tabor to see
The gleam of thy waters, O dark Galilee!

Hark, a sound in the valley! where, swollen and strong,
Thy river, O Kishon, is sweeping along;
Where the Canaanite strove with Jehovah in vain,
And thy torrent grew dark with the blood of the slain.

There down from his mountains stern Zebulon came,
And Napthali's stag, with his eye-balls of flame,
And the chariots of Jabin rolled harmlessly on,
For the arm of the Lord was Abinoam's son!

There sleep the still rocks and the caverns which rang
To the song which the beautiful prophetess sang,
When the princes of Issachar stood by her side,
And the shout of a host in its triumph replied.

Lo, Bethlehem's hill-site before me is seen,
With the mountains around, and the valleys between;
There rested the shepherds of Judah, and there
The song of the angels rose sweet on the air.

And Bethany's palm trees in beauty still throw
Their shadows at noon on the ruins below;
But where are the sisters who hastened to greet
The lowly Redeemer, and sit at His feet?

I tread where the TWELVE in their way-faring trod;
I stand where they stood with the CHOSEN OF GOD—
Where His blessing was heard and His lessons were taught,
Where the blind were restored and the healing was wrought.

Oh, here with His flock the sad Wanderer came—
These hills He toiled over in grief, are the same—
The founts where He drank by the wayside still flow,
And the same airs are blowing which breathed on His brow!

And throned on her hills sits Jerusalem yet,
But with dust on her forehead, and chains on her feet;
For the crown of her pride to the mocker hath gone,
And the holy Shechinah is dark where it shone.

But wherefore this dream of the earthly abode
Of Humanity clothed in the brightness of God?
Were my spirit but turned from the outward and dim,
It could gaze, even now, on the presence of Him!

Not in clouds and in terrors, but gentle as when,
In love and in meekness, He moved among men;
And the voice which breathed peace to the waves of the sea,
In the hush of my spirit would whisper to me!

And what if my feet may not tread where He stood,
Nor my ears hear the dashing of Galilee's flood,
Nor my eyes see the cross which He bowed him to bear,
Nor my knees press Gethsemane's garden of prayer.

Yet loved of the Father, Thy Spirit is near
To the meek, and the lowly, and penitent here;
And the voice of Thy love is the same even now,
As at Bethany's tomb, or on Olivet's brow.

Oh, the outward hath gone! — but in glory and power,
The SPIRIT surviveth the things of an hour;
Unchanged, undecaying, its Pentecost flame
On the hearts secret altar is burning the same!

EZEKIEL.

CHAPTER XXXIII. 30—33.

THEY hear thee not, O God! nor see:
Beneath Thy rod they mock at Thee;
The princes of our ancient line
Lie drunken with Assyrian wine;
The priests around Thy altar speak
The false words which their hearers seek;
And hymns which Chaldea's wanton maids
Have sung in Dura's idol-shades,
Are with the Levites' chant ascending,
With Zion's holiest anthems blending!

On Israel's bleeding bosom set,
The heathen heel is crushing yet;
The towers upon our holy hill
Echo Chaldean footsteps still.
Our wasted shrines — who weeps for them?
Who mourneth for Jerusalem?
Who turneth from his gains away?
Whose knee with mine is bowed to pray?
Who, leaving feast and purpling cup,
Takes Zion's lamentation up?

A sad and thoughtful youth, I went
With Israel's early banishment;
And where the sullen Chebar crept,
The ritual of my fathers kept.
The water for the trench I drew,
The firstling of the flock I slew,

And, standing at the altar's side,
I shared the Levites' lingering pride,
That still amidst her mocking foes,
The smoke of Zion's offering rose.

In sudden whirlwind, cloud and flame,
The Spirit of the Highest came!
Before mine eyes a vision passed,
A glory terrible and vast;
With dreadful eyes of living things,
And sounding sweep of angel wings,
With circling light and sapphire throne,
And flame-like form of One thereon,
And voice of that dread Likeness sent
Down from the crystal firmament!

The burden of a prophet's power
Fell on me in that fearful hour;
From off unutterable woes
The curtain of the future rose;
I saw far down the coming time
The fiery chastisement of crime;
With noise of mingling hosts, and jar
Of falling towers and shouts of war,
I saw the nations rise and fall,
Like fire-gleams on my tent's white wall.

In dream and trance, I saw the slain
Of Egypt heaped like harvest grain;
I saw the walls of sea-born Tyre
Swept over by the spoiler's fire;
And heard the low, expiring moan
Of Edom on his rocky throne;
And, woe is me! the wild lament
From Zion's desolation sent;
And felt within my heart each blow
Which laid her holy places low.

In bonds and sorrow, day by day,
Before the pictured tile I lay;

And there, as in a mirror, saw
The coming of Assyria's war, —
Her swarthy lines of spearmen pass
Like locusts through Bethhoron's grass;
I saw them draw their stormy hem
Of battle round Jerusalem;
And, listening, heard the Hebrew wail
Blend with the victor-trump of Baal!

Who trembled at my warning word?
Who owned the prophet of the Lord?
How mocked the rude — how scoffed the vile —
How stung the Levites scornful smile,
As o'er my spirit, dark and slow,
The shadow crept of Israel's woe,
As if the angel's mournful roll
Had left its record on my soul,
And traced in lines of darkness there
The picture of its great despair!

Yet ever at the hour I feel
My lips in prophecy unseal.
Prince, priest, and Levite, gather near,
And Salem's daughters haste to hear,
On Chebar's waste and alien shore,
The harp of Judah swept once more.
They listen, as in Babel's throng
The Chaldeans to the dancer's song,
Or wild sabbeka's nightly play,
As careless and as vain as they.

And thus, oh Prophet-bard of old,
Hast thou thy tale of sorrow told!
The same which earth's unwelcome seers
Have felt in all succeeding years.
Sport of the changeful multitude,
Nor calmly heard nor understood,

Their song has seemed a trick of art,
Their warnings but the actor's part.
With bonds, and scorn, and evil will,
The world requites its prophets still.

So was it when the Holy One
The garments of the flesh put on!
Men followed where the Highest led
For common gifts of daily bread,
And gross of ear, of vision dim,
Owned not the God-like power of Him.
Vain as a dreamer's words to them
His wail above Jerusalem,
And meaningless the watch He kept
Through which His weak disciples slept.

Yet shrink not thou, whoe'er thou art,
For God's great purpose set apart,
Before whose far discerning eyes,
The Future as the Present lies!
Beyond a narrow-bounded age
Stretches thy prophet-heritage,
Through Heaven's dim spaces angel-trod,
Through arches round the throne of God!
Thy audience, worlds! — all Time to be
The witness of the Truth in thee!

THE WIFE OF MANOAH TO HER HUSBAND.

Against the sunset's glowing wall
The city towers rise black and tall,
Where Zorah on its rocky height,
Stands like an armed man in the light.

Down Eshtaol's vales of ripened grain
Falls like a cloud the night amain,
And up the hill-sides climbing slow
The barley reapers homeward go.

Look, dearest! how our fair child's head
The sunset light hath hallowed,
Where at this olive's foot he lies,
Uplooking to the tranquil skies.

Oh! while beneath the fervent heat
Thy sickle swept the bearded wheat,
I've watched with mingled joy and dread,
Our child upon his grassy bed.

Joy, which the mother feels alone
Whose morning hope like mine had flown,
When to her bosom, over blessed,
A dearer life than hers is pressed.

Dread, for the future dark and still,
Which shapes our dear one to its will;
For ever in his large calm eyes,
I read a tale of sacrifice.—

The same foreboding awe I felt
When at the altar's side we knelt,
And he, who as a pilgrim came,
Rose, winged and glorious, through the flame!

I slept not, though the wild bees made
A dreamlike murmuring in the shade,
And on me the warm-fingered hours
Pressed with the drowsy smell of flowers.

Before me, in a vision, rose
The hosts of Israel's scornful foes, —
Rank over rank, helm, shield, and spear,
Glittered in noon's hot atmosphere.

I heard their boast, and bitter word,
Their mockery of the Hebrew's Lord,
I saw their hands His ark assail,
Their feet profane His holy veil.

No angel down the blue space spoke,
No thunder from the still sky broke,
But in their midst, in power and awe,
Like God's waked wrath, OUR CHILD I saw!

A child no more! — harsh-browed and strong,
He towered a giant in the throng,
And down his shoulders, broad and bare,
Swept the black terror of his hair.

He raised his arm — he smote amain,
As round the reaper falls the grain,
So the dark host around him fell,
So sank the foes of Israel!

Again I looked. In sunlight shone
The towers and domes of Askelon.
Priest, warrior, slave, a mighty crowd
Within her idol temple bowed.

Yet one knelt not; stark, gaunt, and blind,
His arms the massive pillars twined,—
An eyeless captive, strong with hate,
He stood there like an evil Fate.

The red shrines smoked — the trumpets pealed —
He stooped — the giant columns reeled —
Reeled tower and fane, sank arch and wall,
And the thick dust-cloud closed o'er all!

Above the shriek, the crash, the groan
Of the fallen pride of Askelon,
I heard, sheer down the echoing sky,
A voice as of an angel cry.—

The voice of him, who at our side
Sat through the golden eventide,
Of him, who on thy altar's blaze
Rose fire-winged, with his song of praise!

"Rejoice o'er Israel's broken chain,
Grey mother of the mighty slain!
Rejoice!" it cried, "He vanquisheth!
The strong in life is strong in death!

To him shall Zorah's daughters raise
Through coming years their hymns of praise,
And grey old men, at evening tell
Of all he wrought for Israel.

And they who sing and they who hear
Alike shall hold thy memory dear,
And pour their blessings on thy head,
Oh, mother of the mighty dead!"

It ceased: and though a sound I heard
As if great wings the still air stirred,
I only saw the barley sheaves,
And hills half hid by olive leaves.

I bowed my face, in awe and fear,
On the dear child who slumbered near,
"With me, as with my only son,
Oh God!" I said, "THY WILL BE DONE!"

THE CITIES OF THE PLAIN.

"GET ye up from the wrath of God's terrible day!
Ungirded, unsandalled, arise and away!
'T is the vintage of blood — 't is the fullness of time,
And vengeance shall gather the harvest of crime!

The warning was spoken — the righteous had gone,
And the proud ones of Sodom were feasting alone;
All gay was the banquet — the revel was long,
With the pouring of wine and the breathing of song.

'T was an evening of beauty; the air was perfume,
The earth was all greenness, the trees were all bloom;
And softly the delicate viol was heard,
Like the murmur of love or the notes of a bird.

And beautiful maidens moved down in the dance,
With the magic of motion and sunshine of glance;
And white arms wreathed lightly, and tresses fell free,
As the plumage of birds in some tropical tree.

Where the shrines of foul idols were lighted on high,
And wantonness tempted the lust of the eye;
Midst rites of obsceneness, strange, loathsome, abhorred,
The blasphemer scoffed at the name of the Lord.

Hark! the growl of the thunder — the quaking of earth!
Woe — woe to the worship, and woe to the mirth!
The black sky has opened — there 's flame in the air —
The red arm of vengeance is lifted and bare!

Then the shriek of the dying rose wild where the song
And the low tone of love had been whispered along;
For the fierce flames went lightly o'er palace and bower,
Like the red tongues of demons, to blast and devour!

Down — down, on the fallen, the red ruin rained,
And the reveller sank with his wine-cup undrained;
The foot of the dancer, the music's loved thrill,
And the shout and the laughter grew suddenly still.

The last throb of anguish was fearfully given;
The last eye glared forth in its madness on Heaven!
The last groan of horror rose wildly and vain,
And death brooded over the pride of the Plain!

THE CRUCIFIXION.

SUN-LIGHT upon Judea's hills!
  And on the waves of Galilee —
On Jordan's stream, and on the rills
  That feed the dead and sleeping sea!
Most freshly from the green wood springs
The light breeze on its scented wings;
And gaily quiver in the sun
The cedar tops of Lebanon!

A few more hours — a change hath come!
  The sky is dark without a cloud!
The shouts of wrath and joy are dumb,
  And proud knees unto earth are bowed.
A change is on the hill of Death,
The helmed watchers pant for breath,
And turn with wild and maniac eyes
From the dark scene of sacrifice!

That Sacrifice! — the death of Him —
  The High and ever Holy One!
Well may the conscious Heaven grow dim,
  And blacken the beholding Sun!
The wonted light hath fled away,
Night settles on the middle day,
And earthquake from his caverned bed
Is waking with a thrill of dread!

The dead are waking underneath!
  Their prison door is rent away!
And, ghastly with the seal of death,
  They wander in the eye of day!

The temple of the Cherubim,
The House of God is cold and dim;
A curse is on its trembling walls,
Its mighty veil asunder falls!

Well may the cavern-depths of Earth
  Be shaken, and her mountains nod;
Well may the sheeted dead come forth
  To gaze upon a suffering God!
Well may the temple-shrine grow dim,
And shadows veil the Cherubim,
When He, the chosen one of Heaven,
A sacrifice for guilt is given!

And shall the sinful heart, alone,
  Behold unmoved the atoning hour,
When Nature trembles on her throne,
  And Death resigns his iron power?
Oh, shall the heart — whose sinfulness
Gave keenness to His sore distress,
And added to His tears of blood —
Refuse its trembling gratitude!

THE STAR OF BETHLEHEM.

Where Time the measure of his hours
  By changeful bud and blossom keeps,
And like a young bride crowned with flowers,
  Fair Shiraz in her garden sleeps;

Where, to her poet's turban stone,
  The Spring her gift of flowers imparts,
Less sweet than those his thoughts have sown
  In the warm soil of Persian hearts:

There sat the stranger, where the shade
  Of scattered date-trees thinly lay,
While in the hot clear heaven delayed
  The long, and still, and weary day.

Strange trees and fruits above him hung,
  Strange odors filled the sultry air,
Strange birds upon the branches swung,
  Strange insect voices murmured there.

And strange bright blossoms shone around,
  Turned sunward from the shadowy bowers,
As if the Gheber's soul had found
  A fitting home in Iran's flowers.

Whate'er he saw, whate'er he heard,
  Awakened feelings new and sad,—
No Christian garb, nor Christian word,
  Nor church with Sabbath bell chimes glad,

But Moslem graves, with turban stones,
  And mosque-spires gleaming white, in view,
And grey-beard Mollahs in low tones
  Chanting their Koran service through.

The flowers which smiled on either hand
  Like tempting fiends, were such as they
Which once, o'er all that Eastern land,
  As gifts on demon altars lay.

As if the burning eye of Baal
  The servant of his Conqueror knew,
From skies which knew no cloudy veil,
  The Sun's hot glances smote him through.

"Ah me!" the lonely stranger said,
  "The hope which led my footsteps on,
And light from Heaven around them shed,
  O'er weary wave and waste, is gone!

"Where are the harvest fields all white,
  For Truth to thrust her sickle in?
Where flock the souls, like doves in flight,
  From the dark hiding place of sin?

"A silent horror broods o'er all —
  The burden of a hateful spell —
The very flowers around recall
  The hoary magi's rites of hell!

"And what am I, o'er such a land
  The banner of the Cross to bear?
Dear Lord uphold me with thy hand,
  Thy strength with human weakness share!"

He ceased; for at his very feet
  In mild rebuke a floweret smiled —
How thrilled his sinking heart to greet
  The Star-flower of the Virgin's child!

H. Billings del. A. C. Warren Sc.

Each Moslem tomb and Cypress old
Looked holy through the sunset air.
&c.

Page 229

Sown by some wandering Frank, it drew
  Its life from alien air and earth,
And told to Paynim sun and dew
  The story of the Saviour's birth.

From scorching beams, in kindly mood,
  The Persian plants its beauty screened;
And on its pagan sisterhood,
  In love, the Christian floweret leaned.

With tears of joy the wanderer felt
  The darkness of his long despair
Before that hallowed symbol melt,
  Which God's dear love had nurtured there.

From Nature's face, that simple flower
  The lines of sin and sadness swept;
And Magian pile and Paynim bower
  In peace like that of Eden slept.

Each Moslem tomb, and cypress old,
  Looked holy through the sunset air;
And angel-like, the Muezzin told
  From tower and mosque the hour of prayer.

With cheerful steps, the morrow's dawn
  From Shiraz saw the stranger part;
The Star-flower of the Virgin-Born
  Still blooming in his hopeful heart!

HYMNS.

FROM THE FRENCH OF LEMARTINE.

ONE hymn more, O my lyre!
Praise to the God above,
Of joy and life and love,
Sweeping its strings of fire!

Oh! who the speed of bird and wind
And sunbeam's glance will lend to me,
That, soaring upward, I may find
My resting place and home in Thee?—
Thou, whom my soul, midst doubt and gloom,
Adoreth with a fervent flame—
Mysterious spirit! unto whom
Pertain nor sign nor name!

Swiftly my lyre's soft murmurs go,
Up from the cold and joyless earth,
Back to the God who bade them flow,
Whose moving spirit sent them forth.
But as for me, O God! for me,
The lowly creature of Thy will,
Lingering and sad, I sigh to Thee,
An earth-bound pilgrim still!

Was not my spirit born to shine
Where yonder stars and suns are glowing?
To breathe with them the light divine,
From God's own holy altar flowing?

To be, indeed, whate'er the soul
  In dreams hath thirsted for so long —
A portion of Heaven's glorious whole
  Of loveliness and song?

Oh! watchers of the stars at night,
  Who breathe their fire, as we the air —
Suns, thunders, stars, and rays of light,
  Oh! say, is He, the Eternal, there?
Bend there around His awful throne
  The seraph's glance, the angel's knee?
Or are thy inmost depths his own,
  O wild and mighty sea?

Thoughts of my soul, how swift ye go!
  Swift as the eagle's glance of fire,
Or arrows from the archer's bow,
  To the far aim of your desire!
Thought after thought, ye thronging rise,
  Like spring-doves from the startled wood,
Bearing like them your sacrifice
  Of music unto God!

And shall these thoughts of joy and love
  Come back again no more to me? —
Returning like the Patriarch's dove
  Wing-weary from the eternal sea,
To bear within my longing arms
  The promise-bough of kindlier skies,
Plucked from the green, immortal palms
  Which shadow Paradise?

All-moving spirit! — freely forth
  At Thy command the strong wind goes;
Its errand to the passive earth,
  Nor art can stay, nor strength oppose,
Until it folds its weary wing
  Once more within the hand divine;
So, weary from its wandering,
  My spirit turns to Thine!

Child of the sea, the mountain stream,
  From its dark caverns, hurries on,
Ceaseless, by night and morning's beam,
  By evening's star and noontide's sun,
Until at last it sinks to rest,
  O'erwearied, in the waiting sea,
And moans upon its mother's breast —
  So turns my soul to Thee!

O Thou who bidst the torrent flow,
  Who lendest wings unto the wind —
Mover of all things! where art Thou?
  Oh, whither shall I go to find
The secret of Thy resting place?
  Is there no holy wing for me,
That, soaring, I may search the space
  Of highest Heaven for Thee?

Oh, would I were as free to rise
  As leaves on Autumn's whirlwind borne —
The arrowy light of sunset skies,
  Or sound, or ray, or star of morn
Which melts in heaven at twilight's close,
  Or aught which soars unchecked and free
Through Earth and Heaven; that I might lose
  Myself in finding Thee!

When the BREATH DIVINE is flowing,
Zephyr-like o'er all things going,
And as the touch of viewless fingers,
Softly on my soul it lingers,
Open to a breath the lightest,
Conscious of a touch the slightest —
As some calm still lake, whereon
Sinks the snowy-bosomed swan,
And the glistening water-rings
Circle round her moving wings:

When my upward gaze is turning
Where the stars of heaven are burning
Through the deep and dark abyss —
Flowers of midnight's wilderness,
Blowing with the evening's breath
Sweetly in their Maker's path :

When the breaking day is flushing
All the East, and light is gushing
Upward through the horizon's haze,
Sheaf-like, with its thousand rays
Spreading, until all above
Overflows with joy and love,
And below, on earth's green bosom,
All is changed to light and blossom :

When my waking fancies over
Forms of brightness flit and hover,
Holy as the seraphs are,
Who by Zion's fountains wear
On their foreheads, white and broad,
"HOLINESS UNTO THE LORD!"
When, inspired with rapture high,
It would seem a single sigh
Could a world of love create —
That my life could know no date,
And my eager thoughts could fill
Heaven and Earth, o'erflowing still! —

Then, O Father! — Thou alone,
From the shadow of Thy throne,
To the sighing of my breast
And its rapture answerest.
All my thoughts, which, upward winging,
Bathe where Thy own light is springing —
All my yearnings to be free
Are as echoes answering Thee!

Seldom upon lips of mine
Father! rests that name of Thine —

Deep within my inmost breast,
  In the secret place of mind,
  Like an awful presence shrined,
Doth the dread idea rest!
Hushed and holy dwells it there —
Prompter of the silent prayer,
Lifting up my spirit's eye
And its faint, but earnest cry,
From its dark and cold abode,
Unto Thee, my Guide and God!

THE FEMALE MARTYR.

[Mary G——, aged 18, a "Sister of Charity," died in one of our Atlantic cities, during the prevalence of the Indian Cholera, while in voluntary attendance upon the sick.]

"Bring out your dead!" the midnight street
  Heard and gave back the hoarse, low call;
Harsh fell the tread of hasty feet —
Glanced through the dark the coarse white sheet —
  Her coffin and her pall.
  "What — only one!" The brutal hackman said,
  As, with an oath, he spurned away the dead.

How sunk the inmost hearts of all,
  As rolled that dead-cart slowly by,
With creaking wheel and harsh hoof-fall!
The dying turned him to the wall,
  To hear it and to die! —
Onward it rolled; while oft its driver stayed,
And hoarsely clamored, "Ho! — bring out your dead."

It paused beside the burial-place;
  "Toss in your load!". — and it was done. —

With quick hand and averted face,
Hastily to the grave's embrace
  They cast them, one by one —
Stranger and friend — the evil and the just,
Together trodden in the church-yard dust!

And thou, young martyr! — thou wast there —
  No white-robed sisters round thee trod —
Nor holy hymn, nor funeral prayer
Rose through the damp and noisome air,
  Giving thee to thy God;
Nor flower, nor cross, nor hallowed taper gave
Grace to the dead, and beauty to the grave!

Yet, gentle sufferer! — there shall be,
  In every heart of kindly feeling,
A rite as holy paid to thee
As if beneath the convent-tree
  Thy sisterhood were kneeling,
At vesper hours, like sorrowing angels, keeping
Their tearful watch around thy place of sleeping.

For thou wast one in whom the light
  Of Heaven's own love was kindled well,
Enduring with a martyr's might,
Through weary day and wakeful night,
  Far more than words may tell:
Gentle, and meek, and lowly, and unknown —
Thy mercies measured by thy God alone!

Where manly hearts were failing, — where
  The throngful street grew foul with death,
O high souled martyr! — thou wast there,
Inhaling from the loathsome air,
  Poison with every breath.
Yet shrinking not from offices of dread
For the wrung dying, and the unconscious dead.

And, where the sickly taper shed
  Its light through vapors, damp, confined,

Hushed as a seraph's fell thy tread —
A new Electra by the bed
  Of suffering human-kind!
Pointing the spirit, in its dark dismay,
To that pure hope which fadeth not away.

Innocent teacher of the high
  And holy mysteries of Heaven!
How turned to thee each glazing eye,
In mute and awful sympathy,
  As thy low prayers were given;
And the o'er-hovering Spoiler wore, the while,
An angel's features — a deliverer's smile!

A blessed task! — and worthy one
  Who, turning from the world, as thou,
Before life's pathway had begun
To leave its spring-time flower and sun,
  Had sealed her early vow;
Giving to God her beauty and her youth,
Her pure affections and her guileless truth.

Earth may not claim thee. Nothing here
  Could be for thee a meet reward;
Thine is a treasure far more dear —
Eye hath not seen it, nor the ear
  Of living mortal heard, —
The joys prepared — the promised bliss above —
The holy presence of Eternal Love!

Sleep on in peace. The earth has not
  A nobler name than thine shall be.
The deeds by martial manhood wrought,
The lofty energies of thought,
  The fire of poesy —
These have but frail and fading honors; — thine
Shall Time unto Eternity consign.

Yea, and when thrones shall crumble down,
  And human pride and grandeur fall, —

The herald's line of long renown —
The mitre and the kingly crown —
  Perishing glories all !
The pure devotion of thy generous heart
Shall live in Heaven, of which it was a part !

THE FROST SPIRIT.

He comes — he comes — the Frost Spirit comes ! You may trace his footsteps now
On the naked woods and the blasted fields and the brown hill's withered brow.
He has smitten the leaves of the grey old trees where their pleasant green came forth,
And the winds, which follow wherever he goes, have shaken them down to earth.

He comes — he comes — the Frost Spirit comes ! — from the frozen Labrador —
From the icy bridge of the Northern seas, which the white bear wanders o'er —
Where the fisherman's sail is stiff with ice, and the luckless forms below
In the sunless cold of the lingering night into marble statues grow !

He comes — he comes — the Frost Spirit comes ! — on the rushing Northern blast,
And the dark Norwegian pines have bowed as his fearful breath went past.
With an unscorched wing he has hurried on, where the fires of Hecla glow
On the darkly beautiful sky above and the ancient ice below.

He comes — he comes — the Frost Spirit comes! — and the quiet lake shall feel
The torpid touch of his glazing breath, and ring to the skater's heel;
And the streams which danced on the broken rocks, or sang to the leaning grass,
Shall bow again to their winter chain, and in mournful silence pass.

He comes — he comes — the Frost Spirit comes! — let us meet him as we may,
And turn with the light of the parlor-fire his evil power away;
And gather closer the circle round, when that firelight dances high,
And laugh at the shriek of the baffled Fiend as his sounding wing goes bv!

THE VAUDOIS TEACHER.

[" The manner in which the Waldenses and heretics disseminated their principles among the Catholic gentry, was by carrying with them a box of trinkets, or articles of dress. Having entered the houses of the gentry, and disposed of some of their goods, they cautiously intimated that they had commodities far more valuable than these — inestimable jewels, which they would show if they could be protected from the clergy. They would then give their purchasers a bible or testament; and thereby many were deluded into heresy." — *R. Saccho.*]

" Oh, lady fair, these silks of mine are beautiful and rare —
The richest web of the Indian loom, which beauty's queen might wear ;
And my pearls are pure as thy own fair neck, with whose radiant light they vie ;
I have brought them with me a weary way, — will my gentle lady buy ? "

And the lady smiled on the worn old man through the dark and clustering curls,
Which veiled her brow as she bent to view his silks and glittering pearls ;
And she placed their price in the old man's hand, and lightly turned away,
But she paused at the wanderer's earnest call — " My gentle lady, stay ! "

" Oh, lady fair, I have yet a gem which a purer lustre flings,
Than the diamond flash of the jewelled crown on the lofty brow of kings —
A wonderful pearl of exceeding price, whose virtue shall not decay,
Whose light shall be as a spell to thee and a blessing on thy way ! "

The lady glanced at the mirroring steel where her form of grace
was seen,
Where her eye shone clear, and her dark locks waved their
clasping pearls between ; —
Bring forth thy pearl of exceeding worth, thou traveller grey
and old —
And name the price of thy precious gem, and my page shall
count thy gold.

The cloud went off from the pilgrim's brow, as a small and
meagre book,
Unchased with gold or gem of cost, from his folding robe he
took !
" Here, lady fair, is the pearl of price, may it prove as such to
thee !
Nay — deep thy gold — I ask it not, for the word of God is
free ! "

The hoary traveller went his way, but the gift he left behind
Hath had its pure and perfect work on that high-born maiden's
mind,
And she hath turned from the pride of sin to the lowliness of
truth,
And given her human heart to God in its beautiful hour of
youth !

And she hath left the grey old halls, where an evil faith had
power,
The courtly knights of her father's train, and the maidens of
her bower ;
And she hath gone to the Vaudois vales by lordly feet untrod,
Where the poor and needy of earth are rich in the perfect love
of God !

THE CALL OF THE CHRISTIAN.

Not always as the whirlwind's rush
  On Horeb's mount of fear,
Not always as the burning bush
  To Midian's shepherd seer,
Nor as the awful voice which came
  To Israel's prophet bards,
Nor as the tongues of cloven flame,
  Nor gift of fearful words —

Not always thus, with outward sign
  Of fire or voice from Heaven,
The message of a truth divine,
  The call of God is given!
Awaking in the human heart
  Love for the true and right —
Zeal for the Christian's "better part,"
  Strength for the Christian's fight.

Nor unto manhood's heart alone
  The holy influence steals:
Warm with a rapture not its own,
  The heart of woman feels!
As she who by Samaria's wall
  The Saviour's errand sought —
As those who with the fervent Paul
  And meek Aquila wrought:

Or those meek ones whose martyrdom
  Rome's gathered grandeur saw:
Or those who in their Alpine home
  Braved the Crusader's war,

When the green Vaudois, trembling, heard,
  Through all its vales of death,
The martyr's song of triumph poured
  From woman's failing breath.

And gently, by a thousand things
  Which o'er our spirits pass,
Like breezes o'er the harp's fine strings,
  Or vapors o'er a glass,
Leaving their token strange and new
  Of music or of shade,
The summons to the right and true
  And merciful is made.

Oh, then, if gleams of truth and light
  Flash o'er thy waiting mind,
Unfolding to thy mental sight
  The wants of human kind;
If brooding over human grief,
  The earnest wish is known
To soothe and gladden with relief
  An anguish not thine own:

Though heralded with nought of fear,
  Or outward sign, or show:
Though only to the inward ear
  It whispers soft and low;
Though dropping, as the manna fell,
  Unseen, yet from above,
Noiseless as dew-fall, heed it well—
  Thy Father's call of love!

MY SOUL AND I.

STAND still, my soul, in the silent dark
I would question thee,
Alone in the shadow drear and stark
With God and me!

What, my soul, was thy errand here?
Was it mirth or ease,
Or heaping up dust from year to year?
"Nay, none of these!"

Speak, soul, aright in His holy sight
Whose eye looks still
And steadily on thee through the night:
"To do his will!"

What hast thou done, oh soul of mine
That thou tremblest so?—
Hast thou wrought His task, and kept the line
He bade thee go?

What, silent all!—art sad of cheer?
Art fearful now?
When God seemed far and men were near
How brave wert thou?

Aha! thou tremblest!—well I see
Thou 'rt craven grown.
Is it so hard with God and me
To stand alone?—

Summon thy sunshine bravery back,
Oh, wretched sprite!
Let me hear thy voice through this deep and black
Abysmal night.

What hast thou wrought for Right and Truth,
For God and Man,
From the golden hours of bright-eyed youth
To life's mid span?

Ah, soul of mine, thy tones I hear,
But weak and low,
Like far sad murmurs on my ear
They come and go.

"I have wrestled stoutly with the Wrong,
And borne the Right
From beneath the footfall of the throng
To life and light.

"Wherever Freedom shivered a chain,
God speed, quoth I;
To Error amidst her shouting train
I gave the lie."

Ah, soul of mine! ah, soul of mine!
Thy deeds are well:
Were they wrought for Truth's sake or for thine?
My soul, pray tell.

"Of all the work my hand hath wrought
Beneath the sky,
Save a place in kindly human thought,
No gain have I."

Go to, go to! — for thy very self
Thy deeds were done:
Thou for fame, the miser for pelf,
Your end is one!

And where art thou going, soul of mine?
    Canst see the end?
And whither this troubled life of thine
    Evermore doth tend?

What daunts thee now? — what shakes thee so?
    My sad soul say.
"I see a cloud like a curtain low
    Hang o'er my way.

"Whither I go I cannot tell:
    That cloud hangs black,
High as the heaven and deep as hell,
    Across my track.

"I see its shadow coldly enwrap
    The souls before.
Sadly they enter it, step by step,
    To return no more.

"They shrink, they shudder, dear God! they kneel
    To thee in prayer.
They shut their eyes on the cloud, but feel
    That it still is there.

"In vain they turn from the dread Before
    To the Known and Gone;
For while gazing behind them evermore
    Their feet glide on.

"Yet, at times, I see upon sweet pale faces
    A light begin
To tremble, as if from holy places
    And shrines within.

"And at times methinks their cold lips move
    With hymn and prayer,
As if somewhat of awe, but more of love
    And hope were there.

"I call on the souls who have left the light
  To reveal their lot;
I bend mine ear to that wall of night,
  And they answer not.

"But I hear around me sighs of pain
  And the cry of fear,
And a sound like the slow sad dropping of rain,
  Each drop a tear!

"Ah, the cloud is dark, and day by day,
  I am moving thither:
I must pass beneath it on my way —
  God pity me! — WHITHER?"

Ah soul of mine! so brave and wise
  In the life-storm loud,
Fronting so calmly all human eyes
  In the sun-lit crowd!

Now standing apart with God and me
  Thou art weakness all,
Gazing vainly after the things to be
  Through Death's dread wall.

But never for this, never for this
  Was thy being lent;
For the craven's fear is but selfishness,
  Like his merriment.

Folly and Fear are sisters twain:
  One closing her eyes,
The other peopling the dark inane
  With spectral lies.

Know well, my soul, God's hand controls
  Whate'er thou fearest;
Round Him in calmest music rolls
  Whate'er thou hearest.

What to thee is shadow, to Him is day,
And the end He knoweth,
And not on a blind and aimless way
The spirit goeth.

Man sees no future — a phantom show
Is alone before him ;
Past Time is dead, and the grasses grow,
And flowers bloom o'er him.

Nothing before, nothing behind :
The steps of Faith
Fall on the seeming void, and find
The rock beneath.

The Present, the Present is all thou hast
For thy sure possessing ;
Like the patriarch's angel hold it fast
Till it gives its blessing.

Why fear the night? why shrink from Death,
That phantom wan ?
There is nothing in Heaven or earth beneath
Save God and man.

Peopling the shadows we turn from Him
And from one another ;
All is spectral and vague and dim
Save God and our brother !

Like warp and woof all destinies
Are woven fast,
Linked in sympathy like the keys
Of an organ vast.

Pluck one thread, and the web ye mar ;
Break but one
Of a thousand keys, and the paining jar
Through all will run.

Oh, restless spirit! wherefore strain
Beyond thy sphere?—
Heaven and hell, with their joy and pain
Are now and here.

Back to thyself is measured well
All thou hast given;
Thy neighbor's wrong is thy present hell,
His bliss thy heaven.

And in life, in death, in dark and light
All are in God's care;
Sound the black abyss, pierce the deep of night,
And He is there!

All which is real now remaineth,
And fadeth never:
The hand which upholds it now, sustaineth
The soul forever

Leaning on Him, make with reverent meekness
His own thy will,
And with strength from Him shall thy utter weakness
Life's task fulfill;

And that cloud itself, which now before thee
Lies dark in view,
Shall with beams of light from the inner glory
Be stricken through.

And like meadow mist through Autumn's dawn
Uprolling thin,
Its thickest folds when about thee drawn
Let sun-light in.

Then of what is to be, and of what is done
Why queriest thou?—
The past and the time to be are one,
And both are NOW!

TO A FRIEND,

ON HER RETURN FROM EUROPE.

How smiled the land of France
Under thy blue eye's glance,
    Light hearted rover!
Old walls of chateaux grey,
Towers of an early day,
Which the Three Colors play
    Flauntingly over.

Now midst the brilliant train
Thronging the banks of Seine:
    Now midst the splendor
Of the wild Alpine range,
Waking with change on change
Thoughts in thy young heart strange,
    Lovely, and tender.

Vales, soft Elysian,
Like those in the vision
    Of Mirza, when, dreaming,
He saw the long hollow dell,
Touched by the prophet's spell,
Into an ocean swell
    With its isles teeming.

Cliffs wrapped in snows of years,
Splintering with icy spears
    Autumn's blue heaven:
Loose rock and frozen slide,

Hung on the mountain side,
Waiting their hour to glide
Downward, storm-driven!

Rhine stream, by castle old,
Baron's and robber's hold,
Peacefully flowing;
Sweeping through vineyards green,
Or where the cliffs are seen
O'er the broad wave between
Grim shadows throwing.

Or, where St. Peter's dome
Swells o'er eternal Rome,
Vast, dim, and solemn,—
Hymns ever chanting low—
Censers swung to and fro—
Sable stoles sweeping slow
Cornice and column!

Oh, as from each and all
Will there not voices call
Evermore back again?
In the mind's gallery
Wilt thou not always see
Dim phantoms beckon thee
O'er that old track again?

New forms thy presence haunt—
New voices softly chant—
New faces greet thee!—
Pilgrims from many a shrine
Hallowed by poet's line,
At memory's magic sign,
Rising to meet thee.

And when such visions come
Unto thy olden home,
Will they not waken
Deep thoughts of Him whose hand

Led thee o'er sea and land
Back to the household band
    Whence thou wast taken?

While, at the sunset time,
Swells the cathedral's chime,
    Yet, in thy dreaming,
While to thy spirit's eye
Yet the vast mountain's lie
Piled in the Switzer's sky,
    Icy and gleaming:

Prompter of silent prayer,
Be the wild picture there
    In the mind's chamber,
And, through each coming day
Him, who, as staff and stay,
Watched o'er thy wandering way,
    Freshly remember.

So, when the call shall be
Soon or late unto thee,
    As to all given,
Still may that picture live,
All its fair forms survive,
And to thy spirit give
    Gladness in Heaven!

THE ANGEL OF PATIENCE.

A FREE PARAPHRASE OF THE GERMAN.

To weary hearts, to mourning homes,
God's meekest Angel gently comes:
No power has he to banish pain,
Or give us back our lost again;
And yet in tenderest love, our dear
And Heavenly Father sends him here.

There 's quiet in that Angel's glance,
There 's rest in his still countenance!
He mocks no grief with idle cheer,
Nor wounds with words the mourner's ear;
But ills and woes he may not cure
He kindly trains us to endure.

Angel of Patience! sent to calm
Our feverish brows with cooling palm;
To lay the storms of hope and fear,
And reconcile life's smile and tear;
The throbs of wounded pride to still,
And make our own our Father's will!

Oh! thou who mournest on thy way,
With longings for the close of day;
He walks with thee, that Angel kind,
And gently whispers "Be resigned:
Bear up, bear on, the end shall tell
The dear Lord ordereth all things well!"

FOLLEN.

ON READING HIS ESSAY ON THE "FUTURE STATE."

Friend of my soul! — as with moist eye
  I look up from this page of thine,
Is it a dream that thou art nigh,
  Thy mild face gazing into mine?

That presence seems before me now,
  A placid heaven of sweet moonrise,
When dew-like, on the earth below
  Descends the quiet of the skies.

The calm brow through the parted hair,
  The gentle lips which knew no guile,
Softening the blue eye's thoughtful care
  With the bland beauty of their smile.

Ah me! — at times that last dread scene
  Of Frost and Fire and moaning Sea,
Will cast its shade of doubt between
  The failing eyes of Faith and thee.

Yet, lingering o'er thy charmed page,
  Where through the twilight air of earth,
Alike enthusiast and sage,
  Prophet and bard, thou gazest forth;

Lifting the Future's solemn veil;
  The reaching of a mortal hand
To put aside the cold and pale
  Cloud-curtains of the Unseen Land;

In thoughts which answer to my own,
  In words which reach my inward ear,
Like whispers from the void Unknown,
  I feel thy living presence here.

The waves which lull thy body's rest,
  The dust thy pilgrim footsteps trod,
Unwasted, through each change, attest
  The fixed economy of God.

Shall these poor elements outlive
  The mind whose kingly will they wrought?
Their gross unconsciousness survive
  Thy Godlike energy of thought?

THOU LIVEST, FOLLEN! — not in vain
  Hath thy fine spirit meekly borne
The burden of Life's cross of pain,
  And the thorned crown of suffering worn.

Oh! while Life's solemn mystery glooms
  Around us like a dungeon's wall —
Silent earth's pale and crowded tombs,
  Silent the heaven which bends o'er all! —

While day by day our loved ones glide
  In spectral silence, hushed and lone,
To the cold shadows which divide
  The living from the dread Unknown;

While even on the closing eye,
  And on the lip which moves in vain,
The seals of that stern mystery
  Their undiscovered trust retain; —

And only midst the gloom of death,
  Its mournful doubts and haunting fears,
Two pale, sweet angels, Hope and Faith,
  Smile dimly on us through their tears;

'T is something to a heart like mine
  To think of thee as living yet;
To feel that such a light as thine
  Could not in utter darkness set.

Less dreary seems the untried way
  Since thou hast left thy footprints there,
And beams of mournful beauty play
  Round the sad Angel's sable hair.

Oh! — at this hour when half the sky
  Is glorious with its evening light,
And fair broad fields of summer lie
  Hung o'er with greenness in my sight;

While through these elm boughs wet with rain
  The sunset's golden walls are seen,
With clover bloom and yellow grain
  And wood-draped hill and stream between;

I long to know if scenes like this
  Are hidden from an angel's eyes;
If earth's familiar loveliness
  Haunts not thy heaven's serener skies.

For sweetly here upon thee grew
  The lesson which that beauty gave,
The ideal of the Pure and True
  In earth and sky and gliding wave.

And it may be that all which lends
  The soul an upward impulse here,
With a diviner beauty blends,
  And greets us in a holier sphere.

Through groves where blighting never fell
  The humbler flowers of earth may twine;
And simple draughts from childhood's well
  Blend with the angel-tasted wine.

But be the prying vision veiled,
  And let the seeking lips be dumb, —
Where even seraph eyes have failed
  Shall mortal blindness seek to come?

We only know that thou hast gone,
  And that the same returnless tide
Which bore thee from us still glides on,
  And we who mourn thee with it glide.

On all thou lookest we shall look,
  And to our gaze ere long shall turn
That page of God's mysterious book
  We so much wish, yet dread to learn.

With Him, before whose awful power
  Thy spirit bent its trembling knee, —
Who, in the silent greeting flower,
  And forest leaf, looked out on thee, —

We leave thee, with a trust serene,
  Which Time, nor Change, nor Death can move,
While with thy childlike faith we lean
  On Him whose dearest name is Love!

TO THE REFORMERS OF ENGLAND.*

God bless ye, brothers! — in the fight
  Ye 're waging now, ye cannot fail,
For better is your sense of right
  Than kingcraft's triple mail.

Than tyrant's law, or bigot's ban
  More mighty is your simplest word;
The free heart of an honest man
  Than crosier or the sword.

Go — let your bloated Church rehearse
  The lesson it has learned so well;
It moves not with its prayer or curse
  The gates of Heaven or hell.

Let the State scaffold rise again —
  Did Freedom die when Russel died?
Forget ye how the blood of Vane
  From earth's green bosom cried?

The great hearts of your olden time
  Are beating with you, full and strong;
All holy memories and sublime
  And glorious round ye throng.

*It can scarcely be necessary to say that the author refers to those who are seeking the reform of political evils in Great Britain, by peaceful and Christian means.

The bluff, bold men of Runnymede
  Are with ye still in times like these;
The shades of England's mighty dead,
  Your cloud of witnesses!

The truths ye urge are borne abroad
  By every wind and every tide;
The voice of Nature and of God
  Speaks out upon your side.

The weapons which your hands have found
  Are those which Heaven itself has wrought,
Light, Truth, and Love; — your battle ground
  The free, broad field of Thought.

No partial, selfish purpose breaks
  The simple beauty of your plan,
Nor lie from throne or altar shakes
  Your steady faith in man.

The languid pulse of England starts
  And bounds beneath your words of power;
The beating of her million hearts
  Is with you at this hour!

Oh, ye who, with undoubting eyes,
  Through present cloud and gathering storm,
Behold the span of Freedom's skies,
  And sunshine soft and warm, —

Press bravely onward! — not in vain
  Your generous trust in human kind;
The good which bloodshed could not gain
  Your peaceful zeal shall find.

Press on! — the triumph shall be won
  Of common rights and equal laws,
The glorious dream of Harrington,
  And Sidney's good old cause.

Blessing the cotter and the crown,
  Sweetening worn Labor's bitter cup;
And, plucking not the highest down,
  Lifting the lowest up.

Press on! — and we who may not share
  The toil or glory of your fight,
May ask, at least, in earnest prayer,
  God's blessing on the right!

THE QUAKER OF THE OLDEN TIME.

The Quaker of the olden time! —
  How calm and firm and true,
Unspotted by its wrong and crime,
  He walked the dark earth through!
The lust of power, the love of gain,
  The thousand lures of sin
Around him, had no power to stain
  The purity within.

With that deep insight which detects
  All great things in the small,
And knows how each man's life affects
  The spiritual life of all,
He walked by faith and not by sight,
  By love and not by law;
The presence of the wrong or right
  He rather felt than saw.

He felt that wrong with wrong partakes,
  That nothing stands alone,
That whoso gives the motive, makes
  His brother's sin his own.

And, pausing not for doubtful choice
  Of evils great or small,
He listened to that inward voice
  Which called away from all.

Oh ! Spirit of that early day,
  So pure and strong and true,
Be with us in the narrow way
  Our faithful fathers knew.
Give strength the evil to forsake,
  The cross of Truth to bear,
And love and reverent fear to make
  Our daily lives a prayer !

THE REFORMER.

ALL grim and soiled and brown with tan,
I saw a Strong One, in his wrath,
Smiting the godless shrines of man
Along his path.

The Church beneath her trembling dome
Essayed in vain her ghostly charm:
Wealth shook within his gilded home
With strange alarm.

Fraud from his secret chambers fled
Before the sunlight bursting in:
Sloth drew her pillow o'er her head
To drown the din.

"Spare," Art implored, "yon holy pile;
That grand, old, time-worn turret spare;"
Meek Reverence, kneeling in the aisle,
Cried out, "Forbear!"

Grey-bearded Use, who, deaf and blind,
Groped for his old accustomed stone,
Leaned on his staff, and wept, to find
His seat o'erthrown.

Young Romance raised his dreamy eyes,
O'erhung with paly locks of gold:
"Why smite," he asked in sad surprise,
"The fair, the old?"

Yet louder rang the Strong One's stroke,
  Yet nearer flashed his axe's gleam ;
Shuddering and sick of heart I woke,
    As from a dream.

I looked : aside the dust cloud rolled —
  The Waster seemed the Builder too ;
Up springing from the ruined Old
    I saw the New.

'T was but the ruin of the bad —
  The wasting of the wrong and ill ;
Whate'er of good the old time had
    Was living still.

Calm grew the brows of him I feared ;
  The frown which awed me passed away,
And left behind a smile which cheered
    Like breaking day.

The grain grew green on battle-plains,
  O'er swarded war-mounds grazed the cow ;
The slave stood forging from his chains
    The spade and plough.

Where frowned the fort, pavilions gay
  And cottage windows, flower-entwined,
Looked out upon the peaceful bay
    And hills behind.

Through vine-wreathed cups with wine once red,
  The lights on brimming crystal fell,
Drawn, sparkling, from the rivulet head
    And mossy well.

Through prison walls, like Heaven-sent hope,
  Fresh breezes blew, and sunbeams strayed,
And with the idle gallows-rope
    The young child played.

Where the doomed victim in his cell
  Had counted o'er the weary hours,
Glad school-girls, answering to the bell,
    Came crowned with flowers.

Grown wiser for the lesson given,
  I fear no longer, for I know
That, where the share is deepest driven,
    The best fruits grow.

The outworn rite, the old abuse,
  The pious fraud transparent grown,
The good held captive in the use
    Of wrong alone —

These wait their doom, from that great law
  Which makes the past time serve to-day;
And fresher life the world shall draw
    From their decay.

Oh! backward-looking son of time! —
  The new is old, the old is new,
The cycle of a change sublime
    Still sweeping through.

So wisely taught the Indian seer;
  Destroying Seva, forming Brahm,
Who wake by turns Earth's love and fear,
    Are one, the same.

As idly as, in that old day,
  Thou mournest, did thy sires repine,
So, in his time, thy child grown grey,
    Shall sigh for thine.

Yet, not the less for them or thou
  The eternal step of Progress beats
To that great anthem, calm and slow,
    Which God repeats!

Take heart! — the Waster builds again —
  A charmed life old goodness hath;
The tares may perish — but the grain
    Is not for death.

God works in all things; all obey
  His first propulsion from the night:
Ho, wake and watch! — the world is grey
    With morning light!

THE PRISONER FOR DEBT.

Look on him! — through his dungeon grate
  Feebly and cold, the morning light
Comes stealing round him, dim and late,
  As if it loathed the sight.
Reclining on his strawy bed,
His hand upholds his drooping head —
His bloodless cheek is seamed and hard,
Unshorn his grey, neglected beard;
And o'er his bony fingers flow
His long, dishevelled locks of snow.

No grateful fire before him glows,
  And yet the winter's breath is chill;
And o'er his half-clad person goes
  The frequent ague thrill!
Silent, save ever and anon,
A sound, half murmur and half groan,
Forces apart the painful grip
Of the old sufferer's bearded lip;
O sad and crushing is the fate
Of old age chained and desolate!

Just God! why lies that old man there?
  A murderer shares his prison bed,
Whose eye-balls, through his horrid hair,
  Gleam on him, fierce and red;
And the rude oath and heartless jeer
Fall ever on his loathing ear,
And, or in wakefulness or sleep,
Nerve, flesh, and pulses thrill and creep
Whene'er that ruffian's tossing limb,
Crimson with murder, touches him!

What has the grey-haired prisoner done?
  Has murder stained his hands with gore?
Not so; his crime 's a fouler one;
  GOD MADE THE OLD MAN POOR!
For this he shares a felon's cell —
The fittest earthly type of hell!
For this, the boon for which he poured
His young blood on the invader's sword,
And counted light the fearful cost —
His blood-gained liberty is lost!

And so, for such a place of rest,
  Old prisoner, dropped thy blood as rain
On Concord's field, and Bunker's crest,
  And Saratoga's plain?
Look forth, thou man of many scars,
Through thy dim dungeon's iron bars;
It must be joy, in sooth, to see
Yon monument upreared to thee —
Piled granite and a prison cell —
The land repays thy service well!

Go, ring the bells and fire the guns,
  And fling the starry banner out;
Shout "Freedom!" till your lisping ones
  Give back their cradle-shout:
Let boastful eloquence declaim
Of honor, liberty, and fame;

Still let the poet's strain be heard,
With glory for each second word,
And every thing with breath agree
To praise "our glorious liberty!"

But when the patriot cannon jars,
  That prison's cold and gloomy wall
And through its grates the stripes and stars
  Rise on the wind and fall —
Think ye that prisoner's aged ear
Rejoices in the general cheer?
Think ye his dim and failing eye
Is kindled at your pageantry?
Sorrowing of soul, and chained of limb,
What is your carnival to him?

Down with the LAW that binds him thus!
  Unworthy freemen, let it find
No refuge from the withering curse
  Of God and human kind!
Open the prison's living tomb,
And usher from its brooding gloom
The victims of your savage code,
To the free sun and air of God;
No longer dare as crime to brand
The chastening of the Almighty's hand.

LINES,

WRITTEN ON READING SEVERAL PAMPHLETS PUBLISHED BY CLERGYMEN AGAINST THE ABOLITION OF THE GALLOWS.

I.

THE suns of eighteen centuries have shone
Since the Redeemer walked with man, and made
The fisher's boat, the cavern's floor of stone,
And mountain moss, a pillow for his head;
And He, who wandered with the peasant Jew,
And broke with publicans the bread of shame,
And drank, with blessings in His Father's name,
The water which Samaria's outcast drew,
Hath now His temples upon every shore,
Altar and shrine and priest, — and incense dim
Evermore rising, with low prayer and hymn,
From lips which press the temple's marble floor,
Or kiss the gilded sign of the dread Cross He bore!

II.

Yet as of old, when, meekly "doing good,"
He fed a blind and selfish multitude,
And even the poor companions of His lot
With their dim earthly vision knew Him not,
How ill are His high teachings understood!
Where He hath spoken Liberty, the priest
At His own altar binds the chain anew;
Where He hath bidden to Life's equal feast,
The starving many wait upon the few;

Where He hath spoken Peace, His name hath been
The loudest war-cry of contending men;
Priests, pale with vigils, in His name have blessed
The unsheathed sword, and laid the spear in rest,
Wet the war-banner with their sacred wine,
And crossed its blazon with the holy sign;
Yea, in His name who bade the erring live,
And daily taught His lesson — to forgive! —
  Twisted the cord and edged the murderous steel;
And, with His words of mercy on their lips,
Hung gloating o'er the pincer's burning grips,
  And the grim horror of the straining wheel;
Fed the slow flame which gnawed the victim's limb,
Who saw before his searing eye-balls swim
  The image of *their* Christ, in cruel zeal,
Through the black torment-smoke, held mockingly to him!

III.

The blood which mingled with the desert sand,
  And beaded with its red and ghastly dew
The vines and olives of the Holy Land —
  The shrieking curses of the hunted Jew —
The white-sown bones of heretics, where'er
They sank beneath the Crusade's holy spear —
Goa's dark dungeons — Malta's sea-washed cell,
  Where with the hymns the ghostly fathers sung
  Mingled the groans by subtle torture wrung,
Heaven's anthem blending with the shriek of hell!
The midnight of Bartholomew — the stake
  Of Smithfield, and that thrice-accursed flame
Which Calvin kindled by Geneva's lake —
New England's scaffold, and the priestly sneer
Which mocked its victims in that hour of fear,
  When guilt itself a human tear might claim, —
Bear witness, O Thou wronged and merciful One!
That Earth's most hateful crimes have in Thy name been done!

IV.

Thank God! that I have lived to see the time
When the great truth begins at last to find
An utterance from the deep heart of mankind,
Earnest and clear, that ALL REVENGE IS CRIME!
That man is holier than a creed, — that all
Restraint upon him must consult his good,
Hope's sunshine linger on his prison wall,
And Love look in upon his solitude.
The beautiful lesson which our Saviour taught
Through long, dark centuries its way hath wrought
Into the common mind and popular thought;
And words, to which by Galilee's lake shore
The humble fishers listened with hushed oar,
Have found an echo in the general heart,
And of the public faith become a living part.

V.

Who shall arrest this tendency? — Bring back
The cells of Venice and the bigot's rack?
Harden the softening human heart again
To cold indifference to a brother's pain?
Ye most unhappy men! — who, turned away
From the mild sunshine of the Gospel day,
Grope in the shadows of Man's twilight time,
What mean ye, that with ghoul-like zest ye brood
O'er those foul altars streaming with warm blood,
Permitted in another age and clime?
Why cite that law with which the bigot Jew
Rebuked the Pagan's mercy, when he knew
No evil in the Just One? — Wherefore turn
To the dark cruel past? — Can ye not learn
From the pure Teacher's life, how mildly free
Is the great Gospel of Humanity?
The Flamen's knife is bloodless, and no more
Mexitli's altars soak with human gore,

No more the ghastly sacrifices smoke
Through the green arches of the Druid's oak;
And ye of milder faith, with your high claim
Of prophet-utterance in the Holiest name,
Will ye become the Druids of *our* time?
  Set up your scaffold-altars in *our* land,
And, consecrators of Law's darkest crime,
  Urge to its loathsome work the hangman's hand?
Beware — lest human nature, roused at last,
From its peeled shoulder your incumbrance cast,
  And, sick to loathing of your cry for blood,
Rank ye with those who led their victims round
The Celt's red altar and the Indian's mound,
  Abhorred of Earth and Heaven — a pagan brotherhood!

THE HUMAN SACRIFICE.*

I.

Far from his close and noisome cell,
  By grassy lane and sunny stream,
Blown clover field and strawberry dell,
And green and meadow freshness, fell
  The footsteps of his dream.
Again from careless feet the dew
  Of summer's misty morn he shook;
Again with merry heart he threw
  His light line in the rippling brook.
Back crowded all his school-day joys —
  He urged the ball and quoit again,
And heard the shout of laughing boys
  Come ringing down the walnut glen.
Again he felt the western breeze,
  With scent of flowers and crisping hay;
And down again through wind-stirred trees
  He saw the quivering sunlight play.
An angel in home's vine-hung door,
He saw his sister smile once more;

* Some of the leading sectarian papers have lately published the letter of a clergyman, giving an account of his attendance upon a criminal (who had committed murder during a fit of intoxication), at the time of his execution, in Western New York. The writer describes the agony of the wretched being — his abortive attempts at prayer — his appeal for life — his fear of a violent death; and, after declaring his belief that the poor victim died without hope of salvation, concludes with a warm eulogy upon the Gallows, being more than ever convinced of its utility by the awful dread and horror which it inspired.

Once more the truant's brown-locked head
Upon his mother's knee was laid,
And sweetly lulled to slumber there,
With evening's holy hymn and prayer!

II.

He woke. At once on heart and brain
The present Terror rushed again —
Clanked on his limbs the felon's chain!
He woke, to hear the church-tower tell
Time's footfall on the conscious bell,
And, shuddering, feel that clanging din
His life's LAST HOUR had ushered in;
To see within his prison yard,
Through the small window, iron barred,
The gallows shadow rising dim
Between the sunrise heaven and him, —
A horror in God's blessed air —
  A blackness in His morning light —
Like some foul devil-altar there
  Built up by demon hands at night.
  And, maddened by that evil sight,
Dark, horrible, confused, and strange,
A chaos of wild, weltering change,
All power of check and guidance gone,
Dizzy and blind, his mind swept on.
In vain he strove to breathe a prayer,
  In vain he turned the Holy Book,
He only heard the gallows-stair
  Creak as the wind its timbers shook.
No dream for him of sin forgiven,
  While still that baleful spectre stood,
  With its hoarse murmur, "*Blood for Blood!*"
Between him and the pitying Heaven!

III.

Low on his dungeon floor he knelt,
  And smote his breast, and on his chain,

Whose iron clasp he always felt,
  His hot tears fell like rain;
And near him, with the cold, calm look
  And tone of one whose formal part,
  Unwarmed, unsoftened of the heart,
Is measured out by rule and book,
With placid lip and tranquil blood,
The hangman's ghostly ally stood,
Blessing with solemn text and word
The gallows-drop and strangling cord;
Lending the sacred Gospel's awe
And sanction to the crime of Law.

IV.

He saw the victim's tortured brow —
  The sweat of anguish starting there —
The record of a nameless woe
  In the dim eye's imploring stare,
  Seen hideous through the long, damp hair —
Fingers of ghastly skin and bone
Working and writhing on the stone! —
And heard, by mortal terror wrung
From heaving breast and stiffened tongue,
  The choking sob and low hoarse prayer;
As o'er his half-crazed fancy came
A vision of the eternal flame —
Its smoking cloud of agonies —
Its demon-worm that never dies —
The everlasting rise and fall
Of fire-waves round the infernal wall;
While high above that dark red flood,
Black, giant-like, the gallows stood:
Two busy fiends attending there;
One with cold mocking rite and prayer,
The other, with impatient grasp,
Tightening the death-rope's strangling clasp!

V.

The unfelt rite at length was done —
  The prayer unheard at length was said —
An hour had passed: — the noon-day sun
  Smote on the features of the dead!
And he who stood the doomed beside,
Calm gauger of the swelling tide
Of mortal agony and fear,
Heeding with curious eye and ear
Whate'er revealed the keen excess
Of man's extremest wretchedness:
And who in that dark anguish saw
  An earnest of the victim's fate,
The vengeful terrors of God's law,
  The kindlings of Eternal hate —
The first drops of that fiery rain
Which beats the dark red realm of pain, —
Did he uplift his earnest cries
  Against the crime of Law, which gave
  His brother to that fearful grave,
Whereon Hope's moonlight never lies,
  And Faith's white blossoms never wave
To the soft breath of Memory's sighs; —
Which sent a spirit marred and stained,
By fiends of sin possessed, profaned,
In madness and in blindness stark,
Into the silent, unknown dark?
No — from the wild and shrinking dread
With which he saw the victim led
  Beneath the dark veil which divides
Ever the living from the dead,
  And Nature's solemn secret hides,
The man of prayer can only draw
New reasons for his bloody law;
New faith in staying Murder's hand
By murder at that Law's command;
New reverence for the gallows-rope,
As human nature's latest hope;

Last relic of the good old time,
When Power found license for its crime,
And held a writhing world in check
By that fell cord about its neck;
Stifled Sedition's rising shout,
Choked the young breath of Freedom out,
And timely checked the words which sprung
From Heresy's forbidden tongue;
While in its noose of terror bound,
The Church its cherished union found,
Conforming, on the Moslem plan,
The motley-colored mind of man,
Not by the Koran and the Sword,
But by the Bible and the Cord!

VI.

Oh, Thou! at whose rebuke the grave
Back to warm life its sleeper gave,
Beneath whose sad and tearful glance
The cold and changed countenance
Broke the still horror of its trance,
And waking, saw with joy above,
A brother's face of tenderest love;
Thou, unto whom the blind and lame,
The sorrowing and the sin-sick came,
And from thy very garment's hem
Drew life and healing unto them,
The burden of Thy holy faith
Was love and life, not hate and death,
Man's demon ministers of pain,
  The fiends of his revenge were sent
  From Thy pure Gospel's element
To their dark home again.
Thy name is Love! What, then, is he,
  Who in that name the gallows rears,
An awful altar built to Thee,
  With sacrifice of blood and tears?
Oh, once again Thy healing lay
  On the blind eyes which know Thee not;

And let the light of Thy pure day
  Melt in upon his darkened thought.
Soften his hard, cold heart, and show
  The power which in forbearance lies,
And let him feel that mercy now
  Is better than old sacrifice !

VII.

As on the White Sea's* charmed shore,
  The Parsee sees his holy hill
With dunnest smoke-clouds curtained o'er,
Yet knows beneath them, evermore,
  The low, pale fire is quivering still ;
So underneath its clouds of sin,
  The heart of man retaineth yet
Gleams of its holy origin ;
  And half-quenched stars that never set,
Dim colors of its faded bow,
  And early beauty, linger there,
And o'er its wasted desert blow
  Faint breathings of its morning air.
Oh ! never yet upon the scroll
Of the sin-stained, but priceless soul,
  Hath Heaven inscribed " DESPAIR ! "
Cast not the clouded gem away,
Quench not the dim but living ray —
  My brother man, Beware !
With that deep voice which from the skies
Forbade the Patriarch's sacrifice,
  God's angel cries, FORBEAR !

* Among the Tartars, the Caspian is known as *Akdingis*, that is, White Sea. Baku, on its Persian side, is remarkable for its perpetual fire, scarcely discoverable under the pitchy clouds of smoke from the bitumen which feeds it. It is the natural fire-altar of the old Persian worship.

RANDOLPH OF ROANOKE.

OH, Mother Earth! upon thy lap
  Thy weary ones receiving,
And o'er them, silent as a dream,
  Thy grassy mantle weaving,
Fold softly in thy long embrace
  That heart so worn and broken,
And cool its pulse of fire beneath
  Thy shadows old and oaken.

Shut out from him the bitter word
  And serpent hiss of scorning;
Nor let the storms of yesterday
  Disturb his quiet morning.
Breathe over him forgetfulness
  Of all save deeds of kindness,
And, save to smiles of grateful eyes,
  Press down his lids in blindness.

There, where with living ear and eye
  He heard Potomac's flowing,
And, through his tall ancestral trees,
  Saw Autumn's sunset glowing,
He sleeps — still looking to the West,
  Beneath the dark wood shadow,
As if he still would see the sun
  Sink down on wave and meadow.

Bard, Sage, and Tribune! — in himself
  All moods of mind contrasting —
The tenderest wail of human wo,
  The scorn like lightning blasting;

The pathos which from rival eyes
 Unwilling tears could summon,
The stinging taunt, the fiery burst
 Of hatred scarcely human!

Mirth, sparkling like a diamond shower,
 From lips of life-long sadness;
Clear picturings of majestic thought
 Upon a ground of madness;
And over all Romance and Song
 A classic beauty throwing,
And laurelled Clio at his side
 Her storied pages showing.

All parties feared him: each in turn
 Beheld its schemes disjointed,
As right or left his fatal glance
 And spectral finger pointed.
Sworn foe of Cant, he smote it down
 With trenchant wit unsparing,
And, mocking, rent with ruthless hand
 The robe Pretence was wearing.

Too honest or too proud to feign
 A love he never cherished,
Beyond Virginia's border line
 His patriotism perished.
While others hailed in distant skies
 Our eagle's dusky pinion,
He only saw the mountain bird
 Stoop o'er his Old Dominion!

Still through each change of fortune strange,
 Racked nerve, and brain all burning,
His loving faith in Mother-land
 Knew never shade of turning;
By Britain's lakes, by Neva's wave,
 Whatever sky was o'er him,
He heard her rivers' rushing sound,
 Her blue peaks rose before him.

He held his slaves, yet made withal
  No false and vain pretences,
Nor paid a lying priest to seek
  For scriptural defences.
His harshest words of proud rebuke,
  His bitterest taunt and scorning,
Fell fire-like on the Northern brow
  That bent to him in fawning.

He held his slaves: yet kept the while
  His reverence for the Human;
In the dark vassals of his will
  He saw but Man and Woman!
No hunter of God's outraged poor
  His Roanoke valley entered;
No trader in the souls of men
  Across his threshhold ventured.*

And when the old and wearied man
  Laid down for his last sleeping,
And at his side, a slave no more,
  His brother man stood weeping,
His latest thought, his latest breath,
  To Freedom's duty giving,
With failing tongue and trembling hand
  The dying blest the living.

Oh! never bore his ancient State
  A truer son or braver!
None trampling with a calmer scorn
  On foreign hate or favor.
He knew her faults, yet never stooped
  His proud and manly feeling
To poor excuses of the wrong
  Or meanness of concealing.

But none beheld with clearer eye
  The plague-spot o'er her spreading,

* Randolph had a hearty hatred of slave traders, and it is said treated some of them quite roughly, who ventured to cheapen his "chattels personal."

None heard more sure the steps of Doom
  Along her future treading.
For her as for himself he spake,
  When, his gaunt frame upbracing,
He traced with dying hand "REMORSE!" †
  And perished in the tracing.

As from the grave where Henry sleeps,
  From Vernon's weeping willow,
And from the grassy pall which hides
  The Sage of Monticello,
So from the leaf-strewn burial-stone
  Of Randolph's lowly dwelling,
Virginia! o'er thy land of slaves
  A warning voice is swelling!

And hark! from thy deserted fields
  Are sadder warnings spoken,
From quenched hearths, where thy exiled sons
  Their household gods have broken.
The curse is on thee — wolves for men,
  And briars for corn-sheaves giving!
Oh! more than all thy dead renown
  Were now one hero living!

* See the remarkable statement of Dr. Parish, his medical attendant.

DEMOCRACY.

[All things whatsoever ye would that men should do to you, do ye even so to them."—*Matthew* vii. 12.]

Bearer of Freedom's holy light,
  Breaker of Slavery's chain and rod,
The foe of all which pains the light,
  Or wounds the generous ear of God!

Beautiful yet thy temples rise,
  Though there profaning gifts are thrown;
And fires unkindled of the skies
  Are glaring round thy altar-stone.

Still sacred — though thy name be breathed
  By those whose hearts thy truth deride;
And garlands, plucked from thee, are wreathed
  Around the haughty brows of Pride.

O, ideal of my boyhood's time!
  The faith in which my father stood,
Even when the sons of Lust and Crime
  Had stained thy peaceful courts with blood!

Still to those courts my footsteps turn,
  For through the mists which darken there,
I see the flame of Freedom burn —
  The Kebla of the patriot's prayer!

The generous feeling, pure and warm,
  Which owns the rights of *all* divine —
The pitying heart — the helping arm —
  The prompt self-sacrifice — are thine.

Beneath thy broad, impartial eye,
  How fade the lines of caste and birth!
How equal in their suffering lie
  The groaning multitudes of earth!

Still to a stricken brother true,
  Whatever clime hath nurtured him;
As stooped to heal the wounded Jew
  The worshipper of Gerizim.

By misery unrepelled, unawed
  By pomp or power, thou see'st a MAN
In prince or peasant — slave or lord —
  Pale priest, or swarthy artisan.

Through all disguise, form, place, or name,
  Beneath the flaunting robes of sin,
Through poverty and squalid shame,
  Thou lookest on *the man* within.

On man, as man, retaining yet,
  Howe'er debased, and soiled, and dim,
The crown upon his forehead set —
  The immortal gift of God to him.

And there is reverence in thy look;
  For that frail form which mortals wear
The Spirit of the Holiest took,
  And veiled His perfect brightness there.

Not from the shallow babbling fount
  Of vain philosophy thou art;
He who of old on Syria's mount
  Thrilled, warmed, by turns, the listener's heart,

In holy words which cannot die,
  In thoughts which angels leaned to know,
Proclaimed thy message from on high —
  Thy mission to a world of woe.

That voice's echo hath not died!
  From the blue lake of Galilee,
And Tabor's lonely mountain side,
  It calls a struggling world to thee.

Thy name and watchword o'er this land
  I hear in every breeze that stirs,
And round a thousand altars stand
  Thy banded party worshippers.

Not to these altars of a day,
  At party's call, my gift I bring;
But on thy olden shrine I lay
  A freeman's dearest offering: —

The voiceless utterance of his will —
  His pledge to Freedom and to Truth,
That manhood's heart remembers still
  The homage of his generous youth.

Election Day, 1843.

TO RONGE.

Strike home, strong-hearted man! Down to the root
Of old oppression sink the Saxon steel.
Thy work is to hew down. In God's name then
Put nerve into thy task. Let other men
Plant, as they may, that better tree, whose fruit
The wounded bosom of the Church shall heal.
Be thou the image-breaker. Let thy blows
Fall heavy as the Suabian's iron hand,
On crown or crosier, which shall interpose
Between thee and the weal of Father-land.
Leave creeds to closet idlers. First of all,
Shake thou all German dream-land with the fall
Of that accursed tree, whose evil trunk
Was spared of old by Erfurt's stalwart monk.
Fight not with ghosts and shadows. Let us hear
The snap of chain-links. Let our gladdened ear
Catch the pale prisoner's welcome, as the light
Follows thy axe-stroke, through his cell of night.
Be faithful to both worlds; nor think to feed
Earth's starving millions with the husks of creed.
Servant of Him whose mission high and holy
Was to the wronged, the sorrowing, and the lowly,
Thrust not His Eden promise from our sphere,
Distant and dim beyond the blue sky's span;
Like him of Patmos, see it, now and here,—
The New Jerusalem comes down to man!
Be warned by Luther's error. Nor like him,
When the roused Tenton dashes from his limb
The rusted chain of ages, help to bind
His hands, for whom thou claim'st the freedom of the mind!

CHALKLEY HALL.*

How bland and sweet the greeting of this breeze
    To him who flies
From crowded street and red wall's weary gleam,
Till far behind him like a hideous dream
    The close dark city lies! —

Here, while the market murmurs, while men throng
    The marble floor
Of Mammon's altar, from the crush and din
Of the world's madness let me gather in
    My better thoughts once more.

Oh! once again revive, while on my ear
    The cry of Gain
And low hoarse hum of Traffic dies away,
Ye blessed memories of my early day
    Like sere grass wet with rain! —

Once more let God's green earth and sunset air
    Old feelings waken;
Through weary years of toil and strife and ill,
Oh, let me feel that my good angel still
    Hath not his trust forsaken.

* Chalkley Hall, near Frankford, Pa., the residence of THOMAS CHALKLEY, an eminent minister of the "Friends" denomination. He was one of the early settlers of the Colony, and his Journal, which was published in 1749, presents a quaint but beautiful picture of a life of unostentatious and simple goodness. He was the master of a merchant vessel, and, in his visits to the West Indies and Great Britain, omitted no opportunity to labor for the highest interests of his fellow men. During a temporary residence in Philadelphia, in the summer of 1838, the quiet and beautiful scenery around the ancient village of Frankford, frequently attracted me from the heat and bustle of the city.

And well do time and place befit my mood:
    Beneath the arms
Of this embracing wood, a good man made
His home, like Abraham resting in the shade
    Of Mamre's lonely palms.

Here, rich with autumn gifts of countless years,
    The virgin soil
Turned from the share he guided, and in rain
And summer sunshine throve the fruits and grain
    Which blessed his honest toil.

Here, from his voyages on the stormy seas,
    Weary and worn,
He came to meet his children, and to bless
The Giver of all good in thankfulness
    And praise for his return.

And here his neighbors gathered in to greet
    Their friend again,
Safe from the wave and the destroying gales,
Which reap untimely green Bermuda's vales,
    And vex the Carrib main.

To hear the good man tell of simple truth,
    Sown in an hour
Of weakness in some far-off Indian isle,
From the parched bosom of a barren soil,
    Raised up in life and power:

How at those gatherings in Barbadian vales,
    A tendering love
Came o'er him, like the gentle rain from heaven,
And words of fitness to his lips were given,
    And strength as from above:

How the sad captive listened to the Word,
    Until his chain
Grew lighter, and his wounded spirit felt
The healing balm of consolation melt
    Upon its life-long pain:

How the armed warrior sate him down to hear
Of Peace and Truth,
And the proud ruler and his Creole dame,
Jewelled and gorgeous in her beauty came,
And fair and bright-eyed youth.

Oh, far away beneath New England's sky,
Even when a boy,
Following my plough by Merrimack's green shore,
His simple record I have pondered o'er
With deep and quiet joy.

And hence this scene, in sunset glory warm —
Its woods around,
Its still stream winding on in light and shade,
Its soft, green meadows and its upland glade —
To me is holy ground.

And dearer far than haunts where Genius keeps
His vigils still;
Than that where Avon's son of song is laid,
Or Vaucluse hallowed by its Petrarch's shade,
Or Virgil's laurelled hill.

To the grey walls of fallen Paraclete,
To Juliet's urn,
Fair Arno and Sorrento's orange grove,
Where Tasso sang, let young Romance and Love
Like brother pilgrims turn.

But here a deeper and serener charm
To all is given;
And blessed memories of the faithful dead
O'er wood and vale and meadow-stream have shed
The holy hues of Heaven!

TO JOHN PIERPONT.

Not as a poor requital of the joy
  With which my childhood heard that lay of thine,
  Which, like an echo of the song divine
At Bethlelem breathed above the Holy Boy,
  Bore to my ear the airs of Palestine, —
Not to the poet, but the man I bring
In friendship's fearless trust my offering:
How much it lacks I feel, and thou wilt see,
Yet well I know that thou hast deemed with me
Life all too earnest, and its time too short
For dreamy ease and Fancy's graceful sport;
  And girded for thy constant strife with wrong,
Like Nehemiah fighting while he wrought
  The broken walls of Zion, even thy song
Hath a rude martial tone, a blow in every thought!

THE CYPRESS TREE OF CEYLON.

[IBN BATUTA, the celebrated Mussulman traveller of the fourteenth century, speaks of a Cypress tree in Ceylon, universally held sacred by the natives, the leaves of which were said to fall only at certain intervals, and he who had the happiness to find and eat one of them, was restored, at once, to youth and vigor. The traveller saw several venerable JOGEES, or saints, sitting silent and motionless under the tree, patiently awaiting the falling of a leaf.]

THEY sat in silent watchfulness
  The sacred cypress tree about,
And, from beneath old wrinkled brows
  Their failing eyes looked out.

Grey Age and Sickness waiting there
  Through weary night and lingering day —
Grim as the idols at their side
  And motionless as they.

Unheeded in the boughs above
  The song of Ceylon's birds was sweet;
Unseen of them the island flowers
  Bloomed brightly at their feet.

O'er them the tropic night-storm swept,
  The thunder crashed on rock and hill;
The cloud-fire on their eye-balls blazed,
  Yet there they waited still!

What was the world without to them?
  The Moslem's sunset-call — the dance
Of Ceylon's maids — the passing gleam
  Of battle-flag and lance?

They waited for that falling leaf,
  Of which the wandering Jogees sing:
Which lends once more to wintry age
  The greenness of its spring.

Oh! — if these poor and blinded ones
  In trustful patience wait to feel
O'er torpid pulse and failing limb
  A youthful freshness steal;

Shall we, who sit beneath that Tree,
  Whose healing leaves of life are shed
In answer to the breath of prayer
  Upon the waiting head:

Not to restore our failing forms,
  And build the spirit's broken shrine,
But, on the fainting SOUL to shed
  A light and life divine:

Shall we grow weary in our watch,
  And murmur at the long delay?
Impatient of our Father's time
  And His appointed way?

Or, shall the stir of outward things
  Allure and claim the Christian's eye,
When on the heathen watcher's ear
  Their powerless murmurs die?

Alas! a deeper test of faith
  Than prison cell or martyr's stake,
The self-abasing watchfulness
  Of silent prayer may make.

We gird us bravely to rebuke
  Our erring brother in the wrong:
And in the ear of Pride and Power
  Our warning voice is strong.

Easier to smite with Peter's sword,
  Than "watch one hour" in humbling prayer:
Life's "great things," like the Syrian lord
  Our hearts can do and dare.

But oh! we shrink from Jordan's side,
  From waters which alone can save:
And murmur for Abana's banks
  And Pharpar's brighter wave.

Oh, Thou, who in the garden's shade
  Didst wake Thy weary ones again,
Who slumbered at that fearful hour
  Forgetful of thy pain;

Bend o'er us now, as over them,
  And set our sleep-bound spirits free,
Nor leave us slumbering in the watch
  Our souls should keep with Thee!

A DREAM OF SUMMER.

Bland as the morning breath of June
  The southwest breezes play;
And, through its haze, the winter noon
  Seems warm as summer's day.
The snow-plumed Angel of the North
  Has dropped his icy spear;
Again the mossy earth looks forth,
  Again the streams gush clear.

The fox his hill-side cell forsakes,
  The muskrat leaves his nook,
The bluebird in the meadow brakes
  Is singing with the brook.

"Bear up, oh mother Nature!" cry
  Bird, breeze, and streamlet free;
"Our winter voices prophesy
  Of summer days to thee!"

So, in those winters of the soul,
  By bitter blasts and drear
O'erswept from Memory's frozen pole,
  Will sunny days appear.
Reviving Hope and Faith, they show
  The soul its living powers,
And how beneath the winter's snow
  Lie germs of summer flowers!

The Night is mother of the Day,
  The Winter of the Spring,
And ever upon old Decay
  The greenest mosses cling.
Behind the cloud the star-light lurks,
  Through showers the sunbeams fall;
For God, who loveth all His works,
  Has left His Hope with all!

4th 1st month, 1847.

TO ——,

WITH A COPY OF WOOLMAN'S JOURNAL.*

MAIDEN! with the fair brown tresses
  Shading o'er thy dreamy eye,
Floating on thy thoughtful forehead
  Cloud wreaths of its sky.

Youthful years and maiden beauty,
  Joy with them should still abide —
Instinct take the place of Duty —
  Love, not Reason, guide.

Ever in the New rejoicing,
  Kindly beckoning back the Old,
Turning, with a power like Midas,
  All things into gold.

And the passing shades of sadness
  Wearing even a welcome guise,
As when some bright lake lies open
  To the sunny skies;

Every wing of bird above it,
  Every light cloud floating on,
Glitters like that flashing mirror
  In the self-same sun.

* "Get the writings of John Woolman by heart." — *Essays of Elia.*

But, upon thy youthful forehead
  Something like a shadow lies ;
And a serious soul is looking
  From thy earnest eyes.

With an early introversion,
  Through the forms of outward things,
Seeking for the subtle essence,
  And the hidden springs.

Deeper than the gilded surface
  Hath thy wakeful vision seen,
Farther than the narrow present
  Have thy journeyings been.

Thou hast midst Life's empty noises
  Heard the solemn steps of Time,
And the low mysterious voices
  Of another clime.

All the mystery of Being
  Hath upon thy spirit pressed —
Thoughts which, like the Deluge wanderer,
  Find no place of rest :

That which mystic Plato pondered,
  That which Zeno heard with awe,
And the star-rapt Zoroaster
  In his night-watch saw.

From the doubt and darkness springing
  Of the dim, uncertain Past,
Moving to the dark still shadows
  O'er the Future cast,

Early hath Life's mighty question
  Thrilled within thy heart of youth
With a deep and strong beseeching :
  WHAT and WHERE IS TRUTH ?

Hollow creed and ceremonial,
  Whence the ancient life hath fled,
Idle faith unknown to action,
  Dull and cold and dead.

Oracles, whose wire-worked meanings
  Only wake a quiet scorn, —
Not from these thy seeking spirit
  Hath its answer drawn.

But, like some tired child at even,
  On thy mother Nature's breast,
Thou methinks, art vainly seeking
  Truth, and peace, and rest.

O'er that mother's rugged features
  Thou art throwing Fancy's veil,
Light and soft as woven moonbeams,
  Beautiful and frail!

O'er the rough chart of Existence,
  Rocks of sin and wastes of woe,
Soft airs breathe, and green leaves tremble,
  And cool fountains flow.

And to thee an answer cometh
  From the earth and from the sky,
And to thee the hills and waters
  And the stars reply.

But a soul-sufficing answer
  Hath no outward origin;
More than Nature's many voices
  May be heard within.

Even as the great Augustine
  Questioned earth and sea and sky,*
And the dusty tomes of learning
  And old poesy.

*August. Sililoq. cap. xxxi. "Interrogavi Terram," &c.

But his earnest spirit needed
  More than outward Nature taught —
More than blest the poet's vision
  Or the sage's thought.

Only in the gathered silence
  Of a calm and waiting frame
Light and wisdom as from Heaven
  To the seeker came.

Not to ease and aimless quiet
  Doth that inward answer tend,
But to works of love and duty
  As our being's end, —

Not to idle dreams and trances,
  Length of face, and solemn tone,
But to Faith, in daily striving
  And performance shown.

Earnest toil and strong endeavor
  Of a spirit which within
Wrestles with familiar evil
  And besetting sin ;

And without, with tireless vigor,
  Steady heart, and weapon strong,
In the power of truth assailing
  Every form of wrong.

Guided thus, how passing lovely
  Is the track of WOOLMAN'S feet !
And his brief and simple record
  How serenely sweet !

O'er life's humblest duties throwing
  Light the earthling never knew,
Freshening all its dark waste places
  As with Hermon's dew.

All which glows in Pascal's pages —
  All which sainted Guion sought,
Or the blue-eyed German Rahel
  Half-unconscious taught: —

Beauty, such as Goethe pictured,
  Such as Shelly dreamed of, shed
Living warmth and starry brightness
  Round that poor man's head.

Not a vain and cold ideal,
  Not a poet's dream alone,
But a presence warm and real,
  Seen and felt and known.

When the red right hand of slaughter
  Moulders with the steel it swung,
When the name of seer and poet
  Dies on Memory's tongue,

All bright thoughts and pure shall gather
  Round that meek and suffering one —
Glorious, like the seer-seen angel
  Standing in the sun!

Take the good man's book and ponder
  What its pages say to thee —
Blessed as the hand of healing
  May its lesson be.

If it only serves to strengthen
  Yearnings for a higher good,
For the fount of living waters
  And diviner food;

If the pride of human reason
  Feels its meek and still rebuke,
Quailing like the eye of Peter
  From the Just One's look! —

If with readier ear thou heedest
What the Inward Teacher saith,
Listening with a willing spirit
And a child-like faith, —

Thou mayest live to bless the giver,
Who himself but frail and weak,
Would at least the highest welfare
Of another seek ;

And his gift, though poor and lowly
It may seem to other eyes,
Yet may prove an angel holy
In a pilgrim's guise.

LEGGETT'S MONUMENT.

"Ye build the tombs of the prophets." — Holy Writ.

Yes — pile the marble o'er him! It is well
That ye who mocked him in his long stern strife,
And planted in the pathway of his life
The plowshares of your hatred hot from hell,
Who clamored down the bold reformer when
He pleaded for his captive fellow men,
Who spurned him in the market-place, and sought
Within thy walls, St. Tammany, to bind
In party chains the free and honest thought,
The angel utterance of an upright mind, —
Well is it now that o'er his grave ye raise
The stony tribute of your tardy praise,
For not alone that pile shall tell to Fame
Of the brave heart beneath, but of the builders' shame!

THE ANGELS OF BUENA VISTA.

[A LETTER-WRITER from Mexico states that at the terrible fight of Buena Vista, MEXICAN women were seen hovering near the field of death, for the purpose of giving aid and succor to the wounded. One poor woman was found surrounded by the maimed and suffering of both armies, ministering to the wants of AMERICANS as well as MEXICANS, with impartial tenderness.]

SPEAK and tell us, our Ximena, looking northward far away,
O'er the camp of the invaders, o'er the Mexican array,
Who is losing? who is winning? are they far or come they near?
Look abroad, and tell us, sister, whither rolls the storm we hear.

"Down the hills of Angostura still the storm of battle rolls;
Blood is flowing, men are dying; God have mercy on their souls!"
Who is losing? who is winning? — "Over hill and over plain,
I see but smoke of cannon clouding through the mountain rain."

Holy Mother! keep our brothers! Look, Ximena, look once more:
"Still I see the fearful whirlwind rolling darkly as before,
Bearing on, in strange confusion, friend and foeman, foot and horse,
Like some wild and troubled torrent sweeping down its mountain course."

Look forth once more, Ximena! "Ah! the smoke has rolled away;
And I see the Northern rifles gleaming down the ranks of grey.
Hark! that sudden blast of bugles! there the troop of Minon wheels;
There the Northern horses thunder, with the cannon at their heels.

"Jesu, pity! how it thickens! now retreat and now advance!
Right against the blazing cannon shivers Puebla's charging lance!
Down they go, the brave young riders; horse and foot together fall;
Like a plowshare in the fallow, through them plows the Northern ball."

Nearer came the storm and nearer, rolling fast and frightful on:
Speak, Ximena, speak and tell us, who has lost, and who has won?
"Alas! alas! I know not; friend and foe together fall,
O'er the dying rush the living: pray, my sisters, for them all!"

"Lo! the wind the smoke is lifting: Blessed Mother, save my brain!
I can see the wounded crawling slowly out from heaps of slain.
Now they stagger, blind and bleeding; now they fall, and strive to rise;
Hasten, sisters, haste and save them, lest they die before our eyes!"

"Oh my heart's love! oh my dear one! lay thy poor head on my knee;
Dost thou know the lips that kiss thee? Canst thou hear me? canst thou see?
Oh, my husband, brave and gentle! oh, my Bernal, look once more
On the blessed cross before thee! mercy! mercy! all is o'er!"

Dry thy tears, my poor Ximena; lay thy dear one down to rest;
Let his hands be meekly folded, lay the cross upon his breast;
Let his dirge be sung hereafter, and his funeral masses said;
To-day, thou poor bereaved one, the living ask thy aid.

Close beside her, faintly moaning, fair and young, a soldier lay,
Torn with shot and pierced with lances, bleeding slow his life away;
But, as tenderly before him, the lorn Ximena knelt,
She saw the Northern eagle shining on his pistol belt.

With a stifled cry of horror straight she turned away her head;
With a sad and bitter feeling looked she back upon her dead;

H. Billings Del.

BUENA VISTA.

But, as tenderly before him, the lorn Ximena knelt,
She saw the Northern eagle shining on his pistol belt.

But she heard the youth's low moaning, and his struggling breath of pain,
And she raised the cooling water to his parching lips again.

Whispered low the dying soldier, pressed her hand and faintly smiled :
Was that pitying face his mother's ? did she watch beside her child ?
All his stranger words with meaning her woman's heart supplied;
With her kiss upon his forehead, "Mother!" murmured he, and died !

"A bitter curse upon them, poor boy, who led thee forth,
From some gentle, sad-eyed mother, weeping, lonely, in the North !"
Spake the mournful Mexic woman, as she laid him with her dead,
And turned to soothe the living, and bind the wounds which bled.

Look forth once more, Ximena ! "Like a cloud before the wind
Rolls the battle down the mountains, leaving blood and death behind ;
Ah ! they plead in vain for mercy ; in the dust the wounded strive ;
Hide your faces, holy angels ! oh, thou Christ of God, forgive !"

Sink, oh Night, among thy mountains ! let the cool, grey shadows fall ;
Dying brothers, fighting demons, drop thy curtain over all !
Through the thickening winter twilight, wide apart the battle rolled,
In its sheath the sabre rested, and the cannon's lips grew cold.

But the noble Mexic women still their holy task pursued,
Through that long, dark night of sorrow, worn and faint and lacking food ;
Over weak and suffering brothers, with a tender care they hung,
And the dying foeman blessed them in a strange and Northern tongue.

Not wholly lost, oh Father! is this evil world of ours;
Upward, through its blood and ashes, spring afresh the Eden
flowers;
From its smoking hell of battle, Love and Pity send their
prayer,
And still thy white-winged angels hover dimly in our air!

FORGIVENESS.

My heart was heavy, for its trust had been
Abused, its kindness answered with foul wrong;
So, turning gloomily from my fellow men,
One summer Sabbath day I strolled among
The green mounds of the village burial place;
Where, pondering how all human love and hate
Find one sad level — and how, soon or late,
Wronged and wrong-doer, each with meekened face,
And cold hands folded over a still heart,
Pass the green threshhold of our common grave,
Whither all footsteps tend, whence none depart,
Awed for myself, and pitying my race,
Our common sorrow, like a mighty wave,
Swept all my pride away, and trembling I forgave!

BARCLAY OF URY.

[AMONG the earliest converts to the doctrines of FRIENDS, in Scotland, was BARCLAY, of Ury, an old and distinguished soldier, who had fought under GUSTAVUS ADOLPHUS, in Germany. As a Quaker, he became the object of persecution and abuse at the hands of the magistrates and the populace. None bore the indignities of the mob with greater patience and nobleness of soul than this once proud gentleman and soldier. One of his friends, on an occasion of uncommon rudeness, lamented that he should be treated so harshly in his old age, who had been so honored before. "I find more satisfaction," said BARCLAY, "as well as honor, in being thus insulted for my religious principles, than when, a few years ago, it was usual for the magistrates, as I passed the city of Aberdeen, to meet me on the road and conduct me to public entertainment in their hall, and then escort me out again, to gain my favor."]

UP the streets of Aberdeen,
By the kirk and college green,
Rode the Laird of Ury;
Close behind him, close beside,
Foul of mouth and evil-eyed,
Pressed the mob in fury.

Flouted him the drunken churl,
Jeered at him the serving girl,
Prompt to please her master;
And the begging carlin, late
Fed and clothed at Ury's gate,
Cursed him as he passed her.

Yet, with calm and stately mien,
Up the streets of Aberdeen
Came he slowly riding;
And, to all he saw and heard
Answering not with bitter word,
Turning not for chiding.

Came a troop with broadswords swinging,
Bits and bridles sharply ringing,
    Loose and free and froward;
Quoth the foremost, "Ride him down!
Push him! prick him! through the town
    Drive the Quaker coward!"

But from out the thickening crowd
Cried a sudden voice and loud:
    "Barclay! Ho! a Barclay!"
And the old man at his side,
Saw a comrade, battle tried,
    Scarred and sunburned darkly;

Who with ready weapon bare,
Fronting to the troopers there,
    Cried aloud: "God save us!
Call ye coward him who stood
Ankle deep in Lutzen's blood,
    With the brave Gustavus?"

"Nay, I do not need thy sword,
Comrade mine," said Ury's lord;
    "Put it up I pray thee:
Passive to His holy will,
Trust I in my Master still,
    Even though he slay me."

"Pledges of thy love and faith,
Proved on many a field of death,
    Not by me are needed."
Marvelled much that henchman bold,
That his laird, so stout of old,
    Now so meekly pleaded.

"Wo 's the day," he sadly said,
With a slowly-shaking head,
    And a look of pity;
"Ury's honest lord reviled,
Mock of knave and sport of child,
    In his own good city!

H. Billings del. D. L. Glover Sc.

"Nay I do not need thy sword,
Comrade mine" said Ury's lord,
"Put it up I pray thee:

Page. 314.

"Speak the word, and, master mine,
As we charged on Tilly's line,
And his Walloon lancers,
Smiting through their midst we 'll teach
Civil look and decent speech
To these boyish prancers!"

"Marvel not, mine ancient friend,
Like beginning, like the end:"
Quoth the Laird of Ury,
"Is the sinful servant more
Than his gracious Lord who bore
Bonds and stripes in Jewry?

"Give me joy that in His name
I can bear, with patient frame,
All these vain ones offer;
While for them He suffereth long,
Shall I answer wrong with wrong,
Scoffing with the scoffer?

"Happier I, with loss of all,
Hunted, outlawed, held in thrall,
With few friends to greet me,
Than when reeve and squire were seen,
Riding out from Aberdeen,
With bared heads, to meet me.

"When each good wife, o'er and o'er,
Blessed me as I passed her door;
And the snooded daughter,
Through her casement glancing down,
Smiled on him who bore renown
From red fields of slaughter.

"Hard to feel the stranger's scoff,
Hard the old friend's falling off,
Hard to learn forgiving:
But the Lord His own rewards,
And His love with theirs accords,
Warm and fresh and living.

"Through this dark and stormy night
Faith beholds a feeble light
    Up the blackness streaking;
Knowing God's own time is best,
In a patient hope I rest
    For the full day-breaking!"

So the Laird of Ury said,
Turning slow his horse's head
    Towards the Tolbooth prison,
Where, through iron grates, he heard
Poor disciples of the Word
    Preach of Christ arisen!

Not in vain, Confessor old,
Unto us the tale is told
    Of thy day of trial;
Every age on him, who strays
From its broad and beaten ways,
    Pours its seven-fold vial.

Happy he whose inward ear
Angel comfortings can hear,
    O'er the rabble's laughter;
And, while Hatred's fagots burn,
Glimpses through the smoke discern
    Of the good hereafter.

Knowing this, that never yet
Share of Truth was vainly set
    In the world's wide fallow;
After hands shall sow the seed,
After hands from hill and mead
    Reap the harvests yellow.

Thus, with somewhat of the Seer,
Must the moral pioneer
    From the Future borrow;
Clothe the waste with dreams of grain,
And, on midnight's sky of rain,
    Paint the golden morrow!

WHAT THE VOICE SAID.

Maddened by Earth's wrong and evil,
"Lord!" I cried in sudden ire,
"From thy right hand, clothed with thunder,
Shake the bolted fire!

"Love is lost, and Faith is dying;
With the brute the man is sold;
And the dropping blood of labor
Hardens into gold.

"Here the dying wail of Famine,
There the battle's groan of pain;
And, in silence, smooth-faced Mammon
Reaping men like grain.

"'Where is God, that we should fear Him?'
Thus the earth-born Titans say;
'God! if thou art living, hear us!'
Thus the weak ones pray.

"Thou, the patient Heaven upbraiding,"
Spake a solemn Voice within;
"Weary of our Lord's forbearance,
Art thou free from sin?

"Fearless brow to Him uplifting,
Canst thou for His thunders call,
Knowing that to guilt's attraction
Evermore they fall?

"Know'st thou not all germs of evil
In thy heart await their time?
Not thyself, but God's restraining,
Stays their growth of crime.

"Could'st thou boast, oh child of weakness!
O'er the sons of wrong and strife,
Were their strong temptations planted
In thy path of life?

"Thou hast seen two streamlets gushing
From one fountain, clear and free,
But by widely varying channels
Searching for the sea.

"Glideth one through greenest valleys,
Kissing them with lips still sweet;
One, mad roaring down the mountains,
Stagnates at their feet.

"Is it choice whereby the Parsee
Kneels before his mother's fire?
In his black tent did the Tartar
Choose his wandering sire?

"He alone, whose hand is bounding
Human power and human will,
Looking through each soul's surrounding,
Knows its good or ill.

"For thyself, while wrong and sorrow
Make to thee their strong appeal,
Coward wert thou not to utter
What the heart must feel.

"Earnest words must needs be spoken
When the warm heart bleeds or burns
With its scorn of wrong, or pity
For the wronged, by turns.

"But, by all thy nature's weakness,
  Hidden faults and follies known,
Be thou, in rebuking evil,
  Conscious of thine own.

"Not the less shall stern-eyed Duty
  To thy lips her trumpet set,
But with harsher blasts shall mingle
  Wailings of regret."

Cease not, Voice of holy speaking,
  Teacher sent of God, be near,
Whispering through the day's cool silence,
  Let my spirit hear!

So, when thoughts of evil doers
  Waken scorn or hatred move,
Shall a mournful fellow-feeling
  Temper all with love.

TO DELAWARE.

WRITTEN during the discussion in the Legislature of that State in the winter of 1846–7, of a bill for the abolition of Slavery.

Thrice welcome to thy sisters of the East,
To the strong tillers of a rugged home,
With spray-wet locks to Northern winds released,
And hardy feet o'er-swept by ocean's foam;
And to the young nymphs of the golden West,
Whose harvest mantles, fringed with prairie bloom,
Trail in the sunset, — oh, redeemed and blest,
To the warm welcome of thy sisters come!
Broad Pennsylvania, down her sail-white bay
Shall give thee joy, and Jersey from her plains,
And the great lakes, where echoes free alway
Moaned never shoreward with the clank of chains,
Shall weave new sun-bows in their tossing spray,
And all their waves keep grateful holiday.
And, smiling on thee through her mountain rains,
Vermont shall bless thee; and the Granite peaks,
And vast Katahdin o'er his woods, shall wear
Their snow-crowns brighter in the cold keen air;
And Massachusetts, with her rugged cheeks
O'errun with grateful tears, shall turn to thee,
When, at thy bidding, the electric wire
Shall tremble northward with its words of fire:
Glory and praise to God! another State is free!

WORSHIP.

["PURE religion, and undefiled, before God and the Father, is this: To visit the widows and the fatherless in their affliction, and to keep himself unspotted from the world." — *James* i. 27.]

THE Pagan's myths through marble lips are spoken,
  And ghosts of old Beliefs still flit and moan
Round fane and altar overthrown and broken,
  O'er tree-grown barrow and grey ring of stone.

Blind Faith had martyrs in those old high places,
  The Syrian hill grove and the Druid's wood,
With mothers' offering, to the Fiend's embraces,
  Bone of their bone, and blood of their own blood.

Red altars, kindling through that night of error,
  Smoked with warm blood beneath the cruel eye
Of lawless Power and sanguinary Terror,
  Throned on the circle of a pitiless sky;

Beneath whose baleful shadow, overcasting
  All heaven above, and blighting earth below,
The scourge grew red, the lip grew pale with fasting,
  And man's oblation was his fear and woe!

Then through great temples swelled the dismal moaning
  Of dirge-like music and sepulchral prayer;
Pale wizard priests, o'er occult symbols droning,
  Swung their white censers in the burdened air:

As if the pomp of rituals, and the savor
  Of gums and spices, could the Unseen One please;
As if His ear could bend, with childish favor,
  To the poor flattery of the organ keys!

Feet red from war fields trod the church aisles holy,
  With trembling reverence; and the oppressor there,
Kneeling before his priest, abased and lowly,
  Crushed human hearts beneath his knee of prayer.

Not such the service the benignant Father
  Requireth at his earthly children's hands:
Not the poor offering of vain rites, but rather
  The simple duty man from man demands.

For Earth he asks it: the full joy of Heaven
  Knoweth no change of waning or increase;
The great heart of the Infinite beats even,
  Untroubled flows the river of His peace.

He asks no taper lights, on high surrounding
  The priestly altar and the saintly grave,
No dolorous chant nor organ music sounding,
  Nor incense clouding up the twilight nave.

For he whom Jesus loved hath truly spoken:
  The holier worship which he deigns to bless
Restores the lost, and binds the spirit broken,
  And feeds the widow and the fatherless!

Types of our human weakness and our sorrow!
  Who lives unhaunted by his loved ones dead?
Who, with vain longing, seeketh not to borrow
  From stranger eyes the home lights which have fled?

Oh, brother man! fold to thy heart thy brother;
  Where pity dwells, the peace of God is there;
To worship rightly is to love each other,
  Each smile a hymn, each kindly deed a prayer.

Follow with reverent steps the great example
  Of Him whose holy work was "doing good;"
So shall the wide earth seem our Father's temple,
  Each loving life a psalm of gratitude.

Then shall all shackles fall; the stormy clangor
  Of wild war music o'er the earth shall cease;
Love shall tread out the baleful fire of anger,
  And in its ashes plant the tree of peace!

THE ALBUM.

The dark-eyed daughters of the Sun,
  At morn and evening hours,
O'er-hung their graceful shrines alone
  With wreaths of dewy flowers.

Not vainly did those fair ones cull
  Their gifts by stream and wood;
The Good is always beautiful,
  The Beautiful is good!

We live not in their simple day,
  Our Northern blood is cold,
And few the offerings which we lay
  On other shrines than Gold.

With scripture texts to chill and ban
  The heart's fresh morning hours,
The heavy-footed Puritan
  Goes trampling down the flowers;

Nor thinks of Him who sat of old
  Where Syrian lilies grew,

And from their mingling shade and gold
  A holy lesson drew.

Yet lady, shall this book of thine,
  Where Love his gifts has brought,
Become to thee a Persian shrine,
  O'er-hung with flowers of thought.

THE DEMON OF THE STUDY.

THE Brownie sits in the Scotchman's room,
  And eats his meat and drinks his ale,
And beats the maid with her unused broom,
  And the lazy lout with his idle flail,
But he sweeps the floor and threshes the corn,
And hies him away ere the break of dawn.

The shade of Denmark fled from the sun,
  And the Cocklane ghost from the barn loft cheer,
The fiend of Faust was a faithful one,
  Agrippa's demon wrought in fear,
And the devil of Martin Luther sat
By the stout monk's side in social chat.

The Old Man of the Sea, on the neck of him
  Who seven times crossed the deep,
Twined closely each lean and withered limb,
  Like the night-mare in one's sleep.
But he drank of the wine, and Sinbad cast
The evil weight from his back at last.

But the demon that cometh day by day
  To my quiet room and fire-side nook,
Where the casement light falls dim and grey
  On faded painting and ancient book,
Is a sorrier one than any whose names
Are chronicled well by good king James.

No bearer of burdens like Caliban,
  No runner of errands like Ariel,
He comes in the shape of a fat old man,
  Without rap of knuckle or pull of bell:
And whence he comes, or whither he goes,
I know as I do of the wind which blows.

A stout old man with a greasy hat
  Slouched heavily down to his dark, red nose,
And two grey eyes enveloped in fat,
  Looking through glasses with iron bows.
Read ye, and heed ye, and ye who can,
Guard well your doors from that old man!

He comes with a careless "how d' ye do,"
  And seats himself in my elbow chair;
And my morning paper and pamphlet new
  Fall forthwith under his special care,
And he wipes his glasses and clears his throat,
And, button by button, unfolds his coat.

And then he reads from paper and book,
  In a low and husky asthmatic tone,
With the stolid sameness of posture and look
  Of one who reads to himself alone;
And hour after hour on my senses come
That husky wheeze and that dolorous hum.

The price of stocks, the auction sales,
  The poet's song and the lover's glee,
The horrible murders, the seaboard gales,
  The marriage list, and the *jeu d' esprit*,
All reach my ear in the self-same tone,—
I shudder at each, but the fiend reads on!

Oh! sweet as the lapse of water at noon
  O'er the mossy roots of some forest tree,
The sigh of the wind in the woods of June,
  Or sound of flutes o'er a moonlight sea,
Or the low soft music, perchance which seems
To float through the slumbering singer's dreams.

So sweet, so dear is the silvery tone
  Of her in whose features I sometimes look,
As I sit at eve by her side alone,
  And we read by turns from the self-same book —
Some tale perhaps of the olden time,
Some lover's romance or quaint old rhyme.

Then when the story is one of woe, —
  Some prisoner's plaint through his dungeon-bar,
Her blue eye glistens with tears, and low
  Her voice sinks down like a moan afar;
And I seem to hear that prisoner's wail,
And his face looks on me worn and pale.

And when she reads some merrier song,
  Her voice is glad as an April bird's,
And when the tale is of war and wrong,
  A trumpet's summons is in her words,
And the rush of the hosts I seem to hear,
And see the tossing of plume and spear! —

Oh, pity me then, when, day by day,
  The stout fiend darkens my parlor door;
And reads me perchance the self-same lay
  Which melted in music the night before,
From lips as the lips of Hylas sweet,
And moved like twin roses which zephyrs meet!

I cross my floor with a nervous tread,
  I whistle and laugh and sing and shout,
I flourish my cane above his head,
  And stir up the fire to roast him out;
I topple the chairs, and drum on the pane,
And press my hands on my ears, in vain!

I 've studied Glanville and James the wise,
  And wizard black-letter tomes which treat
Of demons of every name and size,
  Which a Christian man is presumed to meet,
But never a hint and never a line
Can I find of a reading fiend like mine.

I 've crossed the Psalter with Brady and Tate,
  And laid the Primer above them all,
I 've nailed a horse shoe over the grate,
  And hung a wig to my parlor wall
Once worn by a learned Judge, they say,
  At Salem court in the witchcraft day !

" *Conjuro te, sceleratissime,*
  Abire ad tuum locum !" — still
Like a visible nightmare he sits by me —
  The exorcism has lost its skill ;
And I hear again in my haunted room
The husky wheeze and the dolorous hum !

Ah ! — commend me to Mary Magdalen
  With her seven-fold plagues — to the wandering Jew,
To the terrors which haunted Orestes when
  The furies his midnight curtains drew,
But charm him off, ye who charm him can,
  That reading demon, that fat old man ! —

THE PUMPKIN.

Oh! greenly and fair in the lands of the sun,
The vines of the gourd and the rich melon run,
And the rock and the tree and the cottage enfold,
With broad leaves all greenness and blossoms all gold,
Like that which o'er Nineveh's prophet once grew,
While he waited to know that his warning was true,
And longed for the storm-cloud, and listened in vain
For the rush of the whirlwind and red fire-rain.

On the banks of the Xenil the dark Spanish maiden
Comes up with the fruit of the tangled vine laden;
And the Creole of Cuba laughs out to behold
Through orange-leaves shining the broad spheres of gold;
Yet with dearer delight from his home in the North,
On the fields of his harvest the Yankee looks forth,
Where crook-necks are coiling and yellow fruit shines,
And the sun of September melts down on his vines.

Ah! — on Thanksgiving Day, when from East and from West,
From North and from South come the pilgrim and guest,
When the grey-haired New Englander sees round his board
The old broken links of affection restored,
When the care-wearied man seeks his mother once more,
And the worn matron smiles where the girl smiled before,
What moistens the lip and what brightens the eye?
What calls back the past, like the rich Pumpkin pie?

Oh! — fruit loved of boyhood! — the old days recalling,
When wood-grapes were purpling and brown nuts were falling!

When wild, ugly faces we carved in its skin,
Glaring out through the dark with a candle within!
When we laughed round the corn-heap, with hearts all in tune,
Our chair a broad pumpkin — our lantern the moon,
Telling tales of the fairy who travelled like steam,
In a pumpkin-shell coach, with two rats for her team!

Then thanks for thy present! — none sweeter or better
E'er smoked from an oven or circled a platter!
Fairer hands never wrought at a pastry more fine,
Brighter eyes never watched o'er its baking than thine!
And the prayer, which my mouth is too full to express,
Swells my heart that thy shadow may never be less;
That the days of thy lot may be lengthened below,
And the fame of thy worth like a pumpkin-vine grow,
And thy life be as sweet, and its last sunset sky
Golden-tinted and fair as thy own Pumpkin Pie!

EXTRACT FROM "A NEW ENGLAND LEGEND."

How has New England's romance fled,
  Even as a vision of the morning!
Its rites fordone — its guardians dead —
Its priestesses, bereft of dread,
  Waking the veriest urchin's scorning! —
Gone like the Indian wizard's yell
  And fire-dance round the magic rock,
Forgotten like the Druid's spell
  At moonrise by his holy oak!
No more along the shadowy glen,
Glide the dim ghosts of murdered men;
No more the unquiet church-yard dead
Glimpse upward from their turfy bed,
  Startling the traveller, late and lone;
As, on some night of starless weather,
They silently commune together,
  Each sitting on his own head-stone!
The roofless house, decayed, deserted,
Its living tenants all departed,
No longer rings with midnight revel
Of witch, or ghost, or goblin evil;
No pale, blue flame sends out its flashes
Through creviced roof and shattered sashes! —
The witch-grass round the hazel spring
May sharply to the night-air sing,
But there no more shall withered hags
Refresh at ease their broom-stick nags,
Or taste those hazel-shadowed waters
As beverage meet for Satan's daughters;

No more their mimic tones be heard —
The mew of cat — the chirp of bird,
Shrill blending with the hoarser laughter
Of the fell demon following after!

The cautious good-man nails no more
A horse-shoe on his outer door,
Lest some unseemly hag should fit
To his own mouth her bridle-bit —
The good-wife's churn no more refuses
Its wonted culinary uses
Until, with heated needle burned,
The witch has to her place returned!
Our witches are no longer old
And wrinkled beldames, Satan-sold,
But young and gay and laughing creatures,
With the heart's sunshine on their features —
Their sorcery — the light which dances
Where the raised lid unveils its glances;
Or that low breathed and gentle tone,
  The music of Love's twilight hours,
Soft, dream-like, as a fairy's moan
  Above her nightly closing flowers,
Sweeter than that which sighed of yore,
Along the charmed Ausonian shore!
Even she, our own weird heroine,
Sole Pythoness of ancient Lynn,
  Sleeps calmly where the living laid her;
And the wide realm of sorcery,
Left by its latest mistress free,
  Hath found no grey and skilled invader:
So perished Albion's "glammarye,"
  With him in Melrose Abbey sleeping,
His charmed torch beside his knee,
That even the dead himself might see
  The magic scroll within his keeping.
And now our modern Yankee sees
Nor omens, spells, nor mysteries;

And nought above, below, around,
Of life or death, of sight or sound,
  Whate'er its nature, form, or look,
Excites his terror or surprise —
All seeming to his knowing eyes
Familiar as his "catechize,"
  Or "Webster's Spelling Book."

HAMPTON BEACH.

THE sunlight glitters keen and bright,
    Where, miles away,
Lies stretching to my dazzled sight
A luminous belt, a misty light,
Beyond the dark pine bluffs and wastes of sandy grey.

The tremulous shadow of the Sea!
    Against its ground
Of silvery light, rock, hill, and tree,
Still as a picture, clear and free,
With varying outline mark the coast for miles around.

On — on — we tread with loose-flung rein
    Our seaward way,
Through dark-green fields and blossoming grain,
Where the wild brier-rose skirts the lane,
And bends above our heads the flowering locust spray.

Ha! like a kind hand on my brow
    Comes this fresh breeze,
Cooling its dull and feverish glow,
While through my being seems to flow
The breath of a new life — the healing of the seas!

Now rest we, where this grassy mound
His feet hath set
In the great waters, which have bound
His granite ancles greenly round
With long and tangled moss, and weeds with cool spray wet.

Good-bye to Pain and Care! I take
Mine ease to-day;
Here where these sunny waters break,
And ripples this keen breeze, I shake
All burdens from the heart, all weary thoughts away.

I draw a freer breath — I seem
Like all I see —
Waves in the sun — the white-winged gleam
Of sea-birds in the slanting beam —
And far-off sails which flit before the South wind free.

So when Time's veil shall fall asunder,
The soul may know
No fearful change, nor sudden wonder,
Nor sink the weight of mystery under,
But with the upward rise, and with the vastness grow.

And all we shrink from now may seem
No new revealing;
Familiar as our childhood's stream,
Or pleasant memory of a dream
The loved and cherished Past upon the new life stealing.

Serene and mild the untried light
May have its dawning;
And, as in Summer's northern night
The evening and the dawn unite,
The sunset hues of Time blend with the soul's new morning.

I sit alone: in foam and spray
Wave after wave
Breaks on the rocks which, stern and grey,
Beneath like fallen Titans lay,
Or murmurs hoarse and strong through mossy cleft and cave.

What heed I of the dusty land
And noisy town?
I see the mighty deep expand
From its white line of glimmering sand
To where the blue of heaven on bluer waves shuts down!

In listless quietude of mind,
I yield to all
The change of cloud and wave and wind,
And passive on the flood reclined,
I wander with the waves, and with them rise and fall.

But look, thou dreamer! — wave and shore
In shadow lie;
The night-wind warns me back once more
To where my native hill-tops o'er
Bends like an arch of fire the glowing sunset sky!

So then, beach, bluff, and wave, farewell!
I bear with me
No token stone nor glittering shell,
But long and oft shall Memory tell
Of this brief thoughtful hour of musing by the Sea.

LINES,

WRITTEN ON HEARING OF THE DEATH OF SILAS WRIGHT, OF NEW YORK.

As they who, tossing midst the storm at night,
While turning shoreward, where a beacon shone,
Meet the walled blackness of the heaven alone,
So, on the turbulent waves of party tossed,
In gloom and tempest, men have seen thy light
Quenched in the darkness. At thy hour of noon,
While life was pleasant to thy undimmed sight,
And, day by day, within thy spirit grew
A holier hope than young Ambition knew,
As through thy rural quiet, not in vain,
Pierced the sharp thrill of Freedom's cry of pain,
Man of the millions, thou art lost too soon!
Portents at which the bravest stand aghast—
The birth-throes of a Future, strange and vast,
Alarm the land; yet thou, so wise and strong,
Suddenly summoned to the burial bed,
Lapped in its slumbers deep and ever long,
Hear'st not the tumult surging overhead.
Who now shall rally Freedom's scattering host?
Who wear the mantle of the leader lost?
Who stay the march of slavery? He, whose voice
Hath called thee from thy task-field, shall not lack
Yet bolder champions, to beat bravely back
The wrong which, through His poor ones, reaches Him:
Yet firmer hands shall Freedom's torch-lights trim,
And wave them high across the abysmal black,
Till bound, dumb millions there shall see them and rejoice.

10th mo., 1847.

LINES,

ACCOMPANYING MANUSCRIPTS PRESENTED TO A FRIEND.

'T IS said that in the Holy Land
  The angels of the place have blessed
The pilgrim's bed of desert sand,
  Like Jacob's stone of rest.

That down the hush of Syrian skies
  Some sweet-voiced saint at twilight sings
The song whose holy symphonies
  Are beat by unseen wings ;

Still starting from his sandy bed,
  The way-worn wanderer looks to see
The halo of an angel's head
  Shine through the tamarisk tree.

So through the shadows of my way
  Thy smile hath fallen soft and clear,
So at the weary close of day
  Hath seemed thy voice of cheer.

That pilgrim pressing to his goal
  May pause not for the vision's sake,
Yet all fair things within his soul
  The thought of it shall wake ;

The graceful palm tree by the well,
  Seen on the far horizon's rim ;
The dark eyes of the fleet gazelle,
  Bent timidly on him ;

Each pictured saint, whose golden hair
  Streams sunlike through the convent's gloom ;
Pale shrines of martyrs young and fair,
  And loving Mary's tomb ;

And thus each tint or shade which falls
  From sunset cloud or waving tree,
Along my pilgrim path recalls
  The pleasant thought of thee.

Of one, in sun and shade the same,
  In weal and woe my steady friend,
Whatever by that holy name
  The angels comprehend.

Not blind to faults and follies, thou
  Hast never failed the good to see,
Nor judged by one unseemly bough
  The upward-struggling tree.

These light leaves at thy feet I lay —
  Poor common thoughts on common things,
Which time is shaking, day by day,
  Like feathers from his wings —

Chance shootings from a frail life-tree,
  To nurturing care but little known,
Their good was partly learned of thee,
  Their folly is my own.

That tree still clasps the kindly mould,
  Its leaves still drink the twilight dew,
And weaving its pale green with gold,
  Still shines the sunlight through.

There still the morning zephyrs play,
  And there at times the spring bird sings,
And mossy trunk and fading spray
  Are flowered with glossy wings.

Yet, even in genial sun and rain,
  Root, branch, and leaflet fail and fade;
The wanderer on its lonely plain
  Ere long shall miss its shade.

Oh, friend beloved, whose curious skill
  Keeps bright the last year's leaves and flowers,
With warm, glad summer thoughts to fill
  The cold, dark, winter hours!

Pressed on thy heart, the leaves I bring
  May well defy the wintry cold,
Until, in Heaven's eternal spring,
  Life's fairer ones unfold.

THE REWARD.

Who, looking backward from his manhood's prime,
Sees not the spectre of his misspent time?
    And, through the shade
Of funeral cypress planted thick behind,
Hears no reproachful whisper on the wind
    From his loved dead?

Who bears no trace of passion's evil force?
Who shuns thy sting, oh terrible Remorse?—
    Who does not cast
On the thronged pages of his memory's book,
At times, a sad and half reluctant look,
    Regretful of the Past?

Alas!—the evil which we fain would shun
We do, and leave the wished for good undone:
    Our strength to day

Is but to-morrow's weakness, prone to fall;
Poor, blind, unprofitable servants all
Are we alway.

Yet, who, thus looking backward o'er his years,
Feels not his eye-lids wet with grateful tears,
If he hath been
Permitted, weak and sinful as he was,
To cheer and aid, in some ennobling cause,
His fellow-men?

If he hath hidden the outcast, or let in
A ray of sunshine to the cell of sin, —
If he hath lent
Strength to the weak, and, in an hour of need,
Over the suffering, mindless of his creed
Or home, hath bent.

He has not lived in vain, and while he gives
The praise to Him, in whom he moves and lives,
With thankful heart;
He gazes backward, and with hope before,
Knowing that from his works he never more
Can henceforth part.

RAPHAEL.*

I SHALL not soon forget that sight:
  The glow of Autumn's westering day,
A hazy warmth, a dreamy light,
  On Raphael's picture lay.

It was a simple print I saw,
  The fair face of a musing boy;
Yet while I gazed a sense of awe
  Seemed blending with my joy.

A simple print: — the graceful flow
  Of boyhood's soft and wavy hair,
And fresh young lip and cheek, and brow
  Unmarked and clear, were there.

Yet through its sweet and calm repose
  I saw the inward spirit shine;
It was as if before me rose
  The white veil of a shrine.

As if, as Gothland's sage has told,
  The hidden life, the man within,
Dissevered from its frame and mould,
  By mortal eye were seen.

* Suggested by a portrait of Raphael, at the age of fifteen, in the possession of Thomas Tracy, of Newburyport.

Was it the lifting of that eye,
The waving of that pictured hand?
Loose as a cloud-wreath on the sky,
I saw the walls expand.

The narrow room had vanished, — space
Broad, luminous, remained alone,
Through which all hues and shapes of grace
And beauty looked or shone.

Around the mighty master came
The marvels which his pencil wrought,
Those miracles of power whose fame
Is wide as human thought.

There drooped thy more than mortal face,
Oh Mother, beautiful and mild!
Enfolding in one dear embrace
Thy Saviour and Thy Child!

The rapt brow of the Desert John;
The awful glory of that day,
When all the Father's brightness shone
Through manhood's veil of clay.

And, midst grey prophet forms, and wild
Dark visions of the days of old,
How sweetly woman's beauty smiled
Through locks of brown and gold!

There Fornarina's fair young face
Once more upon her lover shone,
Whose model of an angel's grace
He borrowed from her own.

Slow passed that vision from my view,
But not the lesson which it taught;
The soft, calm shadows which it threw
Still rested on my thought:

The truth, that painter, bard, and sage,
  Even in Earth's cold and changeful clime,
Plant for their deathless heritage
  The fruits and flowers of time.

We shape ourselves the joy or fear
  Of which the coming life is made,
And fill our Future's atmosphere
  With sunshine or with shade.

The tissue of the Life to be
  We weave with colors all our own,
And in the field of Destiny
  We reap as we have sown.

Still shall the soul around it call
  The shadows which it gathered here,
And painted on the eternal wall
  The Past shall reappear.

Think ye the notes of holy song
  On Milton's tuneful ear have died?
Think ye that Raphael's angel throng
  Has vanished from his side?

Oh no! — We live our life again:
  Or warmly touched or coldly dim
The pictures of the Past remain, —
  Man's works shall follow him!

MEMORIALS.

LUCY HOOPER.*

THEY tell me, Lucy, thou art dead —
That all of thee we loved and cherished,
Has with thy summer roses perished :
And left, as its young beauty fled,
An ashen memory in its stead —
The twilight of a parted day
Whose fading light is cold and vain :
The heart's faint echo of a strain
Of low, sweet music passed away.
That true and loving heart — that gift
Of a mind, earnest, clear, profound,
Bestowing, with a glad unthrift,
Its sunny light on all around,
Affinities which only could
Cleave to the pure, the true, and good ;
And sympathies which found no rest,
Save with the loveliest and best.
Of them — of thee remains there nought
But sorrow in the mourner's breast ? —
A shadow in the land of thought ?

* Died at Brooklyn, L. I., on the 1st of 8th mo., 1841, aged 24 years.

No ! — Even *my* weak and trembling faith
  Can lift for thee the veil which doubt
  And human fear have drawn about
The all-awaiting scene of death.
Even as thou wast I see thee still ;
And, save the absence of all ill,
And pain and weariness, which here
Summoned the sigh or wrung the tear,
The same as when, two summers back,
Beside our childhood's Merrimack,
I saw thy dark eye wander o'er
Stream, sunny upland, rocky shore,
And heard thy low, soft voice alone
'Midst lapse of waters, and the tone
Of pine leaves by the west-wind blown,
There's not a charm of soul or brow —
  Of all we knew and loved in thee —
But lives in holier beauty now,
  Baptized in immortality !
Not mine the sad and freezing dream
  Of souls that, with their earthly mould,
  Cast off the loves and joys of old —
Unbodied — like a pale moonbeam,
  As pure, as passionless, and cold ;
Nor mine the hope of Indra's son,
  Of slumbering in oblivion's rest,
Life's myriads blending into one —
  In blank annihilation blest ;
Dust-atoms of the infinite —
Sparks scattered from the central light,
And winning back through mortal pain
Their old unconsciousness again.
No ! — I have FRIENDS in Spirit Land —
Not shadows in a shadowy band,
  Not *others*, but *themselves* are they.
And still I think of them the same
As when the Master's summons came ;
Their change — the holy morn-light breaking

Upon the dream-worn sleeper, waking —
  A change from twilight into day.

They 've laid thee midst the household graves,
  Where father, brother, sister lie ;
Below thee sweep the dark blue waves,
  Above thee bends the summer sky.
Thy own loved church in sadness read
Her solemn ritual o'er thy head,
And blessed and hallowed with her prayer
The turf laid lightly o'er thee there.
That church, whose rites and liturgy,
Sublime and old, were truth to thee,
Undoubted to thy bosom taken,
As symbols of a faith unshaken.
Even I, of simpler views, could feel
The beauty of thy trust and zeal ;
And, owning not thy creed, could see
How deep a truth it seemed to thee,
And how thy fervent heart had thrown
O'er all, a coloring of its own,
And kindled up, intense and warm,
A life in every rite and form,
As, when on Chebar's banks of old,
The Hebrew's gorgeous vision rolled,
A spirit filled the vast machine —
A life "within the wheels" was seen.

Farewell ! A little time, and we
  Who knew thee well, and loved thee here,
One after one shall follow thee
  As pilgrims through the gate of fear,
Which opens on eternity.
Yet shall we cherish not the less
  All that is left our hearts meanwhile ;
The memory of thy loveliness
  Shall round our weary pathway smile,
Like moonlight when the sun has set —
A sweet and tender radiance yet.

Thoughts of thy clear-eyed sense of duty,
  Thy generous scorn of all things wrong —
The truth, the strength, the graceful beauty
  Which blended in thy song.
All lovely things by thee beloved,
  Shall whisper to our hearts of thee ;
These green hills, where thy childhood roved —
  Yon river winding to the sea —
The sunset light of autumn eves
  Reflecting on the deep, still floods,
Cloud, crimson sky, and trembling leaves
  Of rainbow-tinted woods, —
These, in our view, shall henceforth take
A tenderer meaning for thy sake ;
And all thou loved'st of earth and sky,
Seem sacred to thy memory.

CHANNING.*

Not vainly did old poets tell,
  Nor vainly did old genius paint
God's great and crowning miracle —
  The hero and the saint!

For even in a faithless day
  Can we our sainted ones discern;
And feel, while with them on the way,
  Our hearts within us burn.

And thus the common tongue and pen
  Which, world-wide, echo Channing's fame,
As one of Heaven's anointed men,
  Have sanctified his name.

In vain shall Rome her portals bar,
  And shut from him her saintly prize,
Whom, in the world's great calendar,
  All men shall canonize.

* The last time I saw Dr. Channing was in the summer of 1841, when, in company with my English friend, Joseph Sturge, so well known for his philanthropic labors and liberal political opinions, I visited him at his summer residence on Rhode Island. In recalling the impressions of that visit, it can scarcely be necessary to say that I have no reference to the peculiar religious opinions of a man, whose life, beautifully and truly manifested above the atmosphere of sect, is now the world's common legacy.

By Narragansett's sunny bay,
  Beneath his green embowering wood,
To me it seems but yesterday
  Since at his side I stood.

The slopes lay green with summer rains,
  The western wind blew fresh and free,
And glimmered down the orchard lanes
  The white surf of the sea.

With us was one, who, calm and true,
  Life's highest purpose understood,
And like his blessed Master knew
  The joy of doing good.

Unlearned, unknown to lettered fame,
  Yet on the lips of England's poor
And toiling millions dwelt his name,
  With blessings evermore.

Unknown to power or place, yet where
  The sun looks o'er the Carib sea,
It blended with the freeman's prayer
  And song of jubilee.

He told of England's sin and wrong —
  The ills her suffering children know —
The squalor of the city's throng —
  The green field's want and wo.

O'er Channing's face the tenderness
  Of sympathetic sorrow stole
Like a still shadow, passionless,
  The sorrow of the soul.

But, when the generous Briton told
  How hearts were answering to his own,
And Freedom's rising murmur rolled
  Up to the dull-eared throne,

I saw, methought, a glad surprise
  Thrill through that frail and pain-worn frame,
And kindling in those deep, calm eyes
  A still and earnest flame.

His few, brief words were such as move
  The human heart — the Faith-sown seeds
Which ripen in the soil of love
  To high heroic deeds.

No bars of sect or clime were felt —
  The Babel strife of tongues had ceased, —
And at one common altar knelt
  The Quaker and the priest.

And not in vain: with strength renewed,
  And zeal refreshed, and hope less dim,
For that brief meeting, each pursued
  The path allotted him.

How echoes yet each Western hill
  And vale with Channing's dying word!
How are the hearts of freemen still
  By that great warning stirred!

The stranger treads his native soil,
  And pleads with zeal unfelt before
The honest right of British toil,
  The claim of England's poor.

Before him time-wrought barriers fall,
  Old fears subside, old hatreds melt,
And, stretching o'er the sea's blue wall,
  The Saxon greets the Celt.

The yeoman on the Scottish lines,
  The Sheffield grinder, worn and grim,
The delver in the Cornwall mines,
  Look up with hope to him.

Swart smiters of the glowing steel,
  Dark feeders of the forge's flame,
Pale watchers at the loom and wheel,
  Repeat his honored name.

And thus the influence of that hour
  Of converse on Rhode Island's strand,
Lives in the calm, resistless power
  Which moves our father-land.

God blesses still the generous thought,
  And still the fitting word He speeds,
And Truth, at His requiring taught,
  He quickens into deeds.

Where is the victory of the grave?
  What dust upon the spirit lies?
God keeps the sacred life He gave —
  The prophet never dies!

TO THE MEMORY OF CHARLES B. STORRS,

LATE PRESIDENT OF WESTERN RESERVE COLLEGE.

[" He fell a martyr to the interests of his colored brethren. For many months did that mighty man of God apply his discriminating and gigantic mind to the subject of Slavery and its remedy; and, when his soul could no longer contain his holy indignation against the upholders and apologists of this unrighteous system, he gave vent to his aching heart, and poured forth his clear thoughts and holy feelings in such deep and soul-entrancing eloquence, that other men, whom he would fain in his humble modesty acknowledge his superiors, sat at his feet and looked up as children to a parent." — *Correspondent of the "Liberator,"* 16th of 11th mo., 1833.]

Thou hast fallen in thine armor,
  Thou martyr of the Lord!
With thy last breath crying — "Onward!"
  And thy hand upon the sword.
The haughty heart derideth,
  And the sinful lip reviles,
But the blessing of the perishing
  Around thy pillow smiles!

When to our cup of trembling
  The added drop is given,
And the long suspended thunder
  Falls terribly from Heaven, —
When a new and fearful freedom
  Is proffered of the Lord
To the slow consuming Famine —
  The Pestilence and Sword! —

When the refuges of Falsehood
  Shall be swept away in wrath,
And the temple shall be shaken,
  With its idol, to the earth, —

Shall not thy words of warning
  Be all remembered then?
And thy now unheeded message
  Burn in the hearts of men?

Oppression's hand may scatter
  Its nettles on thy tomb,
And even Christian bosoms
  Deny thy memory room;
For lying lips shall torture
  Thy mercy into crime,
And the slanderer shall flourish
  As the bay-tree for a time.

But, where the south wind lingers
  On Carolina's pines,
Or, falls the careless sunbeam
  Down Georgia's golden mines,—
Where now beneath his burthen
  The toiling slave is driven,—
Where now a tyrant's mockery
  Is offered unto Heaven,—

Where Mammon hath its altars
  Wet o'er with human blood,
And pride and lust debases
  The workmanship of God—
There shall thy praise be spoken,
  Redeemed from Falsehood's ban,
When the fetters shall be broken,
  And the *slave* shall be a *man!*

Joy to thy spirit, brother!
  A thousand hearts are warm—
A thousand kindred bosoms
  Are baring to the storm.
What though red-handed Violence
  With secret Fraud combine,
The wall of fire is round us—
  Our Present Help was thine!

Lo — the waking up of nations,
  From Slavery's fatal sleep —
The murmur of a Universe —
  Deep calling unto Deep!
Joy to thy spirit, brother!
  On every wind of heaven
The onward cheer and summons
  Of FREEDOM'S VOICE is given!

Glory to God for ever!
  Beyond the despot's will
The soul of Freedom liveth
  Imperishable still.
The words which thou hast uttered
  Are of that soul a part,
And the good seed thou hast scattered
  Is springing from the heart.

In the evil days before us,
  And the trials yet to come —
In the shadow of the prison,
  Or the cruel martyrdom —
We will think of thee, O brother!
  And thy sainted name shall be
In the blessing of the captive,
  And the anthem of the free.

LINES,

ON THE DEATH OF S. OLIVER TORREY, SECRETARY OF THE BOSTON YOUNG MEN'S ANTI-SLAVERY SOCIETY.

Gone before us, O our brother,
To the spirit-land!
Vainly look we for another
In thy place to stand.
Who shall offer youth and beauty
On the wasting shrine
Of a stern and lofty duty,
With a faith like thine?

Oh! thy gentle smile of greeting
Who again shall see?
Who amidst the solemn meeting
Gaze again on thee?—
Who, when peril gathers o'er us,
Wear so calm a brow?
Who, with evil men before us,
So serene as thou?

Early hath the spoiler found thee,
Brother of our love!
Autumn's faded earth around thee,
And its storms above!
Evermore that turf lie lightly,
And, with future showers,
O'er thy slumbers fresh and brightly
Blow the summer flowers!

In the locks thy forehead gracing,
Not a silvery streak;

Nor a line of sorrow's tracing
  On thy fair young cheek;
Eyes of light and lips of roses,
  Such as Hylas wore —
Over all that curtain closes,
  Which shall rise no more!

Will the vigil Love is keeping
  Round that grave of thine,
Mournfully, like Jazer weeping
  Over Sibmah's vine * —
Will the pleasant memories, swelling
  Gentle hearts, of thee,
In the spirit's distant dwelling
  All unheeded be?

If the spirit ever gazes,
  From its journeyings, back;
If the immortal ever traces
  O'er its mortal track;
Wilt thou not, O brother, meet us
  Sometimes on our way,
And, in hours of sadness, greet us
  As a spirit may?

Peace be with thee, O our brother,
  In the spirit-land!
Vainly look we for another
  In thy place to stand.
Unto Truth and Freedom giving
  All thy early powers,
Be thy virtues with the living,
  And thy spirit ours!

* "O vine of Sibmah! I will weep for thee with the weeping of Jazer!" — *Jeremiah* xlviii. 32.

A LAMENT.

——— "The parted spirit,
Knoweth it not our sorrow? Answereth not
Its blessing to our tears?"

THE circle is broken — one seat is forsaken, —
One bud from the tree of our friendship is shaken —
One heart from among us no longer shall thrill
With joy in our gladness, or grief in our ill,

Weep! — lonely and lowly, are slumbering now
The light of her glances, the pride of her brow,
Weep! — sadly and long shall we listen in vain
To hear the soft tones of her welcome again.

Give our tears to the dead! For humanity's claim
From its silence and darkness is ever the same;
The hope of that World whose existence is bliss
May not stifle the tears of the mourners of this.

For, oh! if one glance the freed spirit can throw
On the scene of its troubled probation below,
Than the pride of the marble — the pomp of the dead —
To that glance will be dearer the tears which we shed.

Oh, who can forget the mild light of her smile,
Over lips moved with music and feeling the while —
The eye's deep enchantment, dark, dream-like, and clear,
In the glow of its gladness — the shade of its tear.

And the charm of her features, while over the whole
Played the hues of the heart and the sunshine of soul, —

And the tones of her voice, like the music which seems
Murmured low in our ears by the Angel of dreams!

But holier and dearer our memories hold
Those treasures of feeling, more precious than gold—
The love and the kindness and pity which gave
Fresh flowers for the bridal, green wreaths for the grave!

The heart ever open to Charity's claim,
Unmoved from its purpose by censure and blame,
While vainly alike on her eye and her ear
Fell the scorn of the heartless, the jesting and jeer.

How true to our hearts was that beautiful sleeper!
With smiles for the joyful, with tears for the weeper!—
Yet, evermore prompt, whether mournful or gay,
With warnings in love to the passing astray.

For, though spotless herself, she could sorrow for them
Who sullied with evil the spirits pure gem;
And a sigh or a tear could the erring reprove,
And the sting of reproof was still tempered by love.

As a cloud of the sunset, slow melting in heaven,
As a star that is lost when the day-light is given,
As a glad dream of slumber, which wakens in bliss,
She hath passed to the world of the holy from this.

DANIEL WHEELER.

[Daniel Wheeler, a minister of the Society of Friends, and who had labored in the cause of his Divine Master in Great Britain, Russia, and the islands of the Pacific, died in New York, in the spring of 1840, while on a religious visit to this country.]

Oh, dearly loved!
And worthy of our love! — No more
Thy aged form shall rise before
The hushed and waiting worshipper,
In meek obedience utterance giving
To words of truth, so fresh and living,
That, even to the inward sense,
They bore unquestioned evidence
Of an anointed Messenger!
Or, bowing down thy silver hair
In reverent awfulness of prayer —
The world, its time and sense, shut out —
The brightness of Faith's holy trance
Gathered upon thy countenance,
As if each lingering cloud of doubt —
The cold, dark shadows resting here
In Time's unluminous atmosphere —
Were lifted by an angel's hand,
And through them on thy spiritual eye
Shone down the blessedness on high,
The glory of the Better Land!

The oak has fallen!
While, meet for no good work, the vine
May yet its worthless branches twine.
Who knoweth not that with thee fell

A great man in our Israel?
Fallen, while thy loins were girded still,
  Thy feet with Zion's dews still wet,
  And in thy hand retaining yet
The pilgrim's staff and scallop-shell!
Unharmed and safe, where, wild and free,
  Across the Neva's cold morass
The breezes from the Frozen Sea
  With winter's arrowy keenness pass;
Or, where the unwarning tropic gale
Smote to the waves thy tattered sail,
Or, where the noon-hour's fervid heat
Against Tahiti's mountains beat;
  The same mysterious hand which gave
  Deliverance upon land and wave,
Tempered for thee the blasts which blew
  Ladaga's frozen surface o'er,
And blessed for thee the baleful dew
  Of evening upon Eimeo's shore,
Beneath this sunny heaven of ours,
Midst our soft airs and opening flowers
  Hath given thee a grave!

His will be done,
Who seeth not as man, whose way
  Is not as ours! — 'T is well with thee!
Nor anxious doubt nor dark dismay
Disquieted thy closing day,
But, evermore, thy soul could say,
  "My Father careth still for me!"
Called from thy hearth and home — from her,
  The last bud on thy household tree,
The last dear one to minister
  In duty and in love to thee,
From all which nature holdeth dear,
  Feeble with years and worn with pain,
  To seek our distant land again,
Bound in the spirit, yet unknowing
  The things which should befall thee here,

Whether for labor or for death,
In child-like trust serenely going
To that last trial of thy faith!

Oh, far away,
Where never shines our Northern star
On that dark waste which Balboa saw
From Darien's mountains stretching far,
So strange, heaven-broad, and lone, that there
With forehead to its damp wind bare
He bent his mailed knee in awe;
In many an isle whose coral feet
The surges of that ocean beat,
In thy palm shadows, Oahu,
And Honolulu's silver bay,
Amidst Owhyhee's hills of blue,
And taro-plains of Tooboonai,
Are gentle hearts, which long shall be
Sad as our own at thought of thee, —
Worn sowers of Truth's holy seed,
Whose souls in weariness and need
Were strengthened and refreshed by thine,
For, blessed by our Father's hand,
Was thy deep love and tender care,
Thy ministry and fervent prayer —
Grateful as Eschol's clustered vine
To Israel in a weary land!

And they who drew
By thousands round thee, in the hour
Of prayerful waiting, hushed and deep,
That He who bade the islands keep
Silence before Him, might renew
Their strength with His unslumbering power,
They too shall mourn that thou art gone,
That never more thy aged lip
Shall soothe the weak, the erring warn,
Of those who first, rejoicing, heard
Through thee the Gospel's glorious word —

Seals of thy true apostleship.
And, if the brightest diadem,
Whose gems of glory purely burn
Around the ransomed ones in bliss,
Be evermore reserved for them
Who here, through toil and sorrow, turn
Many to righteousness, —
May we not think of thee, as wearing
That star-like crown of light, and bearing,
Amidst Heaven's white and blissful band,
The fadeless palm-branch in thy hand;
And joining with a seraph's tongue
In that new song the elders sung,
Ascribing to its blessed Giver
Thanksgiving, love, and praise forever!

Farewell!
And though the ways of Zion mourn
When her strong ones are called away,
Who like thyself have calmly borne
The heat and burden of the day,
Yet He who slumbereth not nor sleepeth
His ancient watch around us keepeth;
Still sent from His creating hand,
New witnesses for Truth shall stand —
New instruments to sound abroad
The Gospel of a risen Lord;
To gather to the fold once more,
The desolate and gone astray,
The scattered of a cloudy day,
And Zion's broken walls restore!
And, through the travail and the toil
Of true obedience, minister
Beauty for ashes, and the oil
Of joy for mourning, unto her!
So shall her holy bounds increase
With walls of praise and gates of peace:
So shall the Vine, which martyr tears
And blood sustained in other years,

With fresher life be clothed upon;
And to the world in beauty show
Like the rose-plant of Jericho,
And glorious as Lebanon!

DANIEL NEALL.

I.

FRIEND of the Slave, and yet the friend of all;
Lover of peace, yet ever foremost, when
The need of battling Freedom called for men
To plant the banner on the outer wall;
Gentle and kindly, ever at distress
Melted to more than woman's tenderness,
Yet firm and steadfast, at his duty's post
Fronting the violence of a maddened host,
Like some grey rock from which the waves are tossed!
Knowing his deeds of love, men questioned not
The faith of one whose walk and word were right—
Who tranquilly in Life's great task-field wrought,
And, side by side with evil, scarcely caught
A stain upon his pilgrim garb of white:
Prompt to redress another's wrong, his own
Leaving to Time and Truth and Penitence alone.

II.

Such was our friend. Formed on the good old plan,
A true and brave and downright honest man!—
He blew no trumpet in the market-place,
Nor in the church with hypocritic face
Supplied with cant the lack of Christian grace;
Loathing pretence, he did with cheerful will
What others talked of while their hands were still:

And, while "Lord, Lord!" the pious tyrants cried,
Who, in the poor, their Master crucified,
His daily prayer, far better understood
In acts than words, was simply DOING GOOD.
So calm, so constant was his rectitude,
That, by his loss alone we know its worth,
And feel how true a man has walked with us on earth.

Sixth month 6th, 1846.

TO MY FRIEND ON THE DEATH OF HIS SISTER.*

THINE is a grief, the depth of which another
May never know;
Yet, o'er the waters, O, my stricken brother!
To thee I go.

I lean my heart unto thee, sadly folding
Thy hand in mine;
With even the weakness of my soul upholding
The strength of thine.

I never knew, like thee, the dear departed;
I stood not by
When, in calm trust, the pure and tranquil-hearted
Lay down to die.

And on thy ears my words of weak condoling
Must vainly fall:
The funeral bell which in thy heart is tolling,
Sounds over all!

---

* SOPHIA STURGE, sister of JOSEPH STURGE, of Birmingham, the President of the British Complete Suffrage Association, died in the 6th mo. 1845. She was the colleague, counsellor, and ever ready helpmate of her brother in all his vast designs of beneficence. The Birmingham Pilot says of her: "Never, perhaps, were the active and passive virtues of the human character more harmoniously and beautifully blended, than in this excellent woman."

I will not mock thee with the poor world's common
And heartless phrase,
Nor wrong the memory of a sainted woman
With idle praise.

With silence only as their benediction,
God's angels come
Where, in the shadow of a great affliction,
The soul sits dumb!

Yet, would I say what thy own heart approveth:
Our Father's will,
Calling to Him the dear one whom He loveth,
Is mercy still.

Not upon thee or thine the solemn angel
Hath evil wrought:
Her funeral anthem is a glad evangel —
The good die not!

God calls our loved ones, but we lose not wholly
What He hath given;
They live on earth, in thought and deed, as truly
As in His heaven.

And she is with thee; in thy path of trial
She walketh yet;
Still with the baptism of thy self-denial
Her locks are wet.

Up, then, my brother! Lo, the fields of harvest
Lie white in view!
She lives and loves thee, and the God thou servest
To both is true.

Thrust in thy sickle! — England's toil-worn peasants
Thy call abide;
And she thou mourn'st, a pure and holy presence,
Shall glean beside!

GONE.

ANOTHER hand is beckoning us,
  Another call is given;
And glows once more with Angel-steps
  The path which reaches Heaven.

Our young and gentle friend whose smile
  Made brighter summer hours,
Amid the frosts of autumn time
  Has left us, with the flowers.

No paling of the cheek of bloom
  Forewarned us of decay;
No shadow from the Silent Land
  Fell around our sister's way.

The light of her young life went down,
  As sinks behind the hill
The glory of a setting star —
  Clear, suddenly, and still.

As pure and sweet, her fair brow seemed —
  Eternal as the sky;
And like the brook's low song, her voice —
  A sound which could not die.

And half we deemed she needed not
  The changing of her sphere,
To give to Heaven a Shining One,
  Who walked an Angel here.

The blessing of her quiet life
  Fell on us like the dew;
And good thoughts, where her footsteps pressed
  Like fairy blossoms grew.

Sweet promptings unto kindest deeds
  Were in her very look ;
We read her face, as one who reads
  A true and holy book :

The measure of a blessed hymn,
  To which our hearts could move ;
The breathing of an inward psalm ;
  A canticle of love.

We miss her in the place of prayer,
  And by the hearth-fire's light ;
We pause beside her door to hear
  Once more her sweet "Good night!"

There seems a shadow on the day,
  Her smile no longer cheers ;
A dimness on the stars of night,
  Like eyes that look through tears.

Alone unto our Father's will
  One thought hath reconciled ;
That He whose love exceedeth ours
  Hath taken home His child.

Fold her, oh Father! in thine arms,
  And let her henceforth be
A messenger of love between
  Our human hearts and Thee.

Still let her mild rebuking stand
  Between us and the wrong,
And her dear memory serve to make
  Our faith in Goodness strong.

And, grant that she who, trembling, here
  Distrusted all her powers,
May welcome to her holier home
  The well beloved of ours.

APPENDIX.

THE CURSE OF THE CHARTER-BREAKERS.

[THE rights and liberties affirmed by MAGNA CHARTA were deemed of such importance, in the 13th century, that the Bishops, twice a year, with tapers burning, and in their pontifical robes, pronounced, in the presence of the king and the representatives of the estates of England, the greater excommunication against the infringer of that instrument. The imposing ceremony took place in the great Hall of Westminster. A copy of the curse, as pronounced in 1253, declares that, "By the authority of Almighty God, and the blessed Apostles and Martyrs, and all the saints in heaven, all those who violate the English liberties, and secretly or openly, by deed, word, or counsel, do make statutes, *or observe them being made*, against said liberties, are accursed and sequestered from the company of heaven and the sacraments of the Holy Church."

WILLIAM PENN, in his admirable political pamphlet, "*England's Present Interest Considered*," alluding to the curse of the Charter-breakers, says:—"I am no Roman Catholic, and little value their other curses; yet I declare I would not for the world incur this curse, as every man deservedly doth, who offers violence to the fundamental freedom thereby repeated and confirmed."]

IN Westminster's royal halls,
Robed in their pontificals,
England's ancient prelates stood
For the people's right and good.

Closed around the waiting crowd,
Dark and still, like winter's cloud;
King and council, lord and knight,
Squire and yeoman, stood in sight—

Stood to hear the priest rehearse,
In God's name, the Church's curse,
By the tapers round them lit,
Slowly, sternly uttering it.

"Right of voice in framing laws,
Right of peers to try each cause;
Peasant homestead, mean and small,
Sacred as the monarch's hall —

"Whoso lays his hand on these,
England's ancient liberties —
Whoso breaks, by word or deed,
England's vow at Runnymede —

"Be he Prince or belted knight,
Whatsoe'er his rank or might,
If the highest, then the worst,
Let him live and die accursed.

"Thou, who to thy Church hast given
Keys alike, of hell and heaven,
Make our word and witness sure,
Let the curse we speak endure!"

Silent, while that curse was said,
Every bare and listening head
Bowed in reverent awe, and then
All the people said, Amen!

Seven times the bells have tolled,
For the centuries grey and old,
Since that stoled and mitred band
Cursed the tyrants of their land.

Since the priesthood, like a tower,
Stood between the poor and power;
And the wronged and trodden down
Blessed the abbot's shaven crown.

Gone, thank God, their wizard spell,
Lost, their keys of heaven and hell;
Yet I sigh for men as bold
As those bearded priests of old.

Now, too oft the priesthood wait
At the threshold of the state—
Waiting for the beck and nod
Of its power as law and God.

Fraud exults, while solemn words
Sanctify his stolen hoards;
Slavery laughs, while ghostly lips
Bless his manacles and whips.

Not on them the poor rely,
Not to them looks liberty,
Who with fawning falsehood cower
To the wrong, when clothed with power.

Oh! to see them meanly cling,
Round the master, round the king,
Sported with, and sold and bought—
Pitifuller sight is not!

Tell me not that this must be:
God's true priest is always free;
Free, the needed truth to speak,
Right the wronged, and raise the weak.

Not to fawn on wealth and state,
Leaving Lazarus at the gate—
Not to peddle creeds like wares—
Not to mutter hireling prayers—

Nor to paint the new life's bliss
On the sable ground of this—
Golden streets for idle knave,
Sabbath rest for weary slave!

Not for words and works like these,
Priest of God, thy mission is;
But to make earth's desert glad,
In its Eden greenness clad;

And to level manhood bring
Lord and peasant, serf and king;
And the Christ of God to find
In the humblest of thy kind!

Thine to work as well as pray
Clearing thorny wrongs away;
Plucking up the weeds of sin,
Letting heaven's warm sunshine in —

Watching on the hills of Faith;
Listening what the spirit saith,
Of the dimseen light afar,
Growing like a nearing star.

God's interpreter art thou,
To the waiting ones below;
'Twixt them and its light midway
Heralding the better day —

Catching gleams of temple spires,
Hearing notes of angel choirs,
Where, as yet unseen of them,
Comes the New Jerusalem!

Like the seer of Patmos gazing,
On the glory downward blazing;
Till upon Earth's grateful sod
Rests the City of our God!

THE SLAVES OF MARTINIQUE.

"Beams of noon like burning lances, through the tree-tops flash and glisten,
As she stands before her lover, with raised face to look and listen."

Page [illegible]

THE SLAVES OF MARTINIQUE.

[SUGGESTED BY A DAGUERREOTYPE FROM A FRENCH ENGRAVING.]

Beams of noon, like burning lances, through the tree-tops flash and glisten,
As she stands before her lover, with raised face to look and listen.

Dark, but comely, like the maiden in the ancient Jewish song:
Scarcely has the toil of task-fields done her graceful beauty wrong.

He, the strong one and the manly, with the vassal's garb and hue,
Holding still his spirit's birthright, to his higher nature true;

Hiding deep the strengthening purpose of a freeman in his heart,
As the greegree holds his Fetich from the white man's gaze apart.

Ever foremost of his comrades, when the drivers morning horn
Calls away to stifling mill-house, to the fields of cane and corn;

Fall the keen and burning lashes, never on his back or limb;
Scarce with look or word of censure, turns the driver unto him.

Yet, his brow is always thoughtful, and his eye is hard and stern;
Slavery's last and humblest lesson, he has never deigned to learn.

And, at evening, when his comrades dance before their master's door,
Folding arms and knitting forehead, stands he silent evermore.

God be praised for every instinct which rebels against a lot,
Where the brute survives the human, and man's upright form is not!

As the serpent-like bejuco winds his spiral fold on fold,
Round the tall and stately ceiba, till it withers in its hold;—

Slow decays the forrest monarch, closer girds the fell embrace,
Till the tree is seen no longer, and the vine is in his place—

So a base and bestial nature, round the vassal's manhood twines,
And the spirit wastes beneath it, like the ceiba choked with vines.

God is Love, saith the Evangel; and our world of woe and sin
Is made light and happy only, when a Love is shining in.

Ye whose lives are free as sunshine, finding wheresoe'er ye roam,
Smiles of welcome, looks of kindness, making all the world like home;

In the veins of whose affections, kindred blood is but a part,
Of one kindly current throbbing from the universal heart;

Can ye know the deeper meaning of a love in Slavery nursed,
Last flower of a lost Eden, blooming in that Soil accursed?

Love of Home, and Love of Woman!—dear to all, but doubly dear
To the heart whose pulses elsewhere measure only hate and fear.

All around the desert circles, underneath a brazen sky,
Only one green spot remaining where the dew is never dry!

From the horror of that desert, from its atmosphere of hell,
Turns the fainting spirit thither, as the diver seeks his bell.

'T is the fervid tropic noontime; faint and low the sea-waves beat;
Hazy rise the inland mountains through the glimmer of the heat, —

Where, through mingled leaves and blossoms arrowy sun-beams flash and glisten,
Speaks her lover to the slave girl, and she lifts her head to listen: —

"We shall live as slaves no longer! Freedom's hour is close at hand!
Rocks her bark upon the waters, rests the boat upon the strand!

"I have seen the Haytien Captain; I have seen his swarthy crew,
Haters of the pallid faces, to their race and color true.

"They have sworn to wait our coming till the night has passed its noon,
And the grey and darkening waters roll above the sunken moon!"

Oh! the blessed hope of freedom! how with joy and glad surprise,
For an instant throbs her bosom, for an instant beam her eyes!

But she looks across the valley, where her mother's hut is seen,
Through the snowy bloom of coffee, and the lemon leaves so green.

And she answers, sad and earnest: "It were wrong for thee to stay;
God hath heard thy prayer for freedom, and his finger points the way.

"Well I know with what endurance, for the sake of me and mine,
Thou hast borne too long a burden, never meant for souls like thine.

Go; and at the hour of midnight, when our last farewell is o'er,
Kneeling on our place of parting, I will bless thee from the shore.

But for me, my mother, lying on her sick bed all the day,
Lifts her weary head to watch me, coming through the twilight grey.

Should I leave her sick and helpless, even freedom, shared with thee,
Would be sadder far than bondage, lonely toil, and stripes to me.

For my heart would die within me, and my brain would soon be wild:
I should hear my mother calling through the twilight for her child!"

Blazing upward from the ocean, shines the sun of morning time,
Through the coffee trees in blossom, and green hedges of the lime.

Side by side, amidst the slave gang, toil the lover and the maid;
Wherefore looks he o'er the waters, leaning forward on his spade?

Sadly looks he, deeply sighs he: 't is the Haytien's sail he sees,
Like a white cloud of the mountains, driven seaward by the breeze!

But his arm a light hand presses, and he hears a low voice call:
Hate of Slavery, hope of Freedom, Love is mightier than all.

THE CRISIS.

[WRITTEN ON LEARNING THE TERMS OF THE TREATY WITH MEXICO.]

ACROSS the Stony Mountains, o'er the desert's drouth and sand,
The circles of our empire touch the Western Ocean's strand;
From slumberous Timpanogos, to Gila, wild and free,
Flowing down from Neuva Leon to California's sea;
And from the mountains of the East, to Santa Rosa's shore,
The eagles of Mexitli shall beat the air no more.

O Vale of Rio Bravo! Let thy simple children weep;
Close watch about their holy fire let maids of Pecos keep;
Let Taos send her cry across Sierra Madre's pines,
And Algodones toll her bells amidst her corn and vines;
For lo! the pale land-seekers come, with eager eyes of gain,
Wide scattering, like the bison herds on broad Salada's plain.

Let Sacramento's herdsmen heed what sound, the winds bring down,
Of footsteps on the crisping snow, from cold Neveda's crown!
Full hot and fast the Saxon rides, with rein of travel slack,
And, bending o'er his saddle, leaves the sunrise at his back;
By many a lonely river, and gorge of fire and pine,
On many a wintry hill-top, his nightly camp-fires shine.

O countrymen and brothers! that land of lake and plain,
Of salt wastes alternating with valleys fat with grain;
Of mountains white with winter, looking downward, cold, serene,
On their feet with spring-vines tangled and lapped in softest green;

Swift through whose black volcanic gates, o'er many a sunny vale,
Wind-like the Arapahoe sweeps the bison's dusty trail!

Great spaces yet untravelled, great lakes whose mystic shores
The Saxon rifle never heard, nor dip of Saxon oars;
Great herds that wander all unwatched, wild steeds that none have tamed,
Strange fish in unknown streams, and birds the Saxon never named;
Deep mines, dark mountain crucibles, where Nature's chemic powers
Work out the Great Designer's will: — all these ye say are ours!

Forever ours! for good or ill, on us the burden lies;
God's balance, watched by angels, is hung across the skies.
Shall Justice, Truth, and Freedom, turn the poised and trembling scale?
Or shall the Evil triumph, and robber Wrong prevail?
Shall the broad land o'er which our flag in starry splendor waves,
Forego through us its freedom, and bear the tread of slaves?

The day is breaking in the East, of which the prophets told,
And brightens up the sky of Time the Christian Age of Gold:
Old Might to Right is yielding, battle blade to clerkly pen,
Earth's monarchs are her peoples, and her serfs stand up as men;
The isles rejoice together, in a day are nations born,
And the slave walks free in Tunis, and by Stamboul's Golden Horn!

Is this, O countrymen of mine! a day for us to sow
The soil of new-gained empire with slavery's seeds of woe?
To feed with our fresh life-blood the old world's cast-off crime,
Dropped, like some monstrous early birth, from the tired lap of Time?
To run anew the evil race the old lost nations ran,
And die like them of unbelief of God, and wrong of man?

Great Heaven! Is this our mission? End in this the prayers and tears,
The toil, the strife, the watchings of our younger, better years?

Still, as the old world rolls in light, shall ours in shadow turn,
A beamless Chaos, cursed of God, through outer darkness borne?
Where the far nations looked for light, a blackness in the air?
Where for words of hope they listened, the long wail of despair?

The Crisis presses on us; face to face with us it stands,
With solemn lips of question, like the Sphinx in Egypt's sands!
This day we fashion Destiny, our web of Fate we spin;
This day for all hereafter choose we holiness or sin;
Even now from starry Gerizim, or Ebal's cloudy crown,
We call the dews of blessing or the bolts of cursing down!

By all for which the martyrs bore their agony and shame;
By all the warning words of truth with which the prophets came;
By the Future which awaits us; by all the hopes which cast
Their faint and trembling beams across the blackness of the Past;
And by the blessed thought of Him who for Earth's freedom died,
O, my people! O, my brothers! let us choose the righteous side.

So shall the Northern pioneer go joyful on his way,
To wed Penobscot's waters to San Francisco's bay;
To make the rugged places smooth, and sow the vales with grain;
And bear, with Liberty and Law, the Bible in his train:
The mighty West shall bless the East, and sea shall answer sea,
And mountain unto mountain call: PRAISE GOD, FOR WE ARE FREE!

THE KNIGHT OF ST. JOHN.

Ere down yon blue Carpathian hills
  The sun shall sink again!
Farewell to life and all its ills,
  Farewell to cell and chain.

These prison shades are dark and cold, —
  But, darker far than they,
The shadow of a sorrow old
  Is on my heart alway.

For since the day when Warkworth wood
  Closed o'er my steed and I,
An alien from my name and blood,
  A weed cast out to die, —

When, looking back in sunset light,
  I saw her turret gleam,
And from its casement, far and white,
  Her sign of farewell stream,

Like one who from some desert shore
  Doth home's green isles descry,
And, vainly longing, gazes o'er
  The waste of wave and sky;

So from the desert of my fate
  I gaze across the past;
Forever on life's dial-plate
  The shade is backward cast!

I 've wandered wide from shore to shore,
  I 've knelt at many a shrine;
And bowed me to the rocky floor
  Where Bethlehem's tapers shine;

And by the Holy Sepulchre
  I 've pledged my knightly sword
To Christ, his blessed Church, and her,
  The Mother of our Lord.

Oh, vain the vow, and vain the strife!
  How vain do all things seem!
My soul is in the past, and life
  To day is but a dream!

In vain the penance strange and long,
  And hard for flesh to bear;
The prayer, the fasting, and the thong,
  And sackcloth shirt of hair.

The eyes of memory will not sleep, —
  Its ears are open still;
And vigils with the past they keep
  Against my feeble will.

And still the loves and joys of old
  Do evermore uprise;
I see the flow of locks of gold,
  The shine of loving eyes!

Ah me! upon another's breast
  Those golden locks recline;
I see upon another rest
  The glance that once was mine!

"O faithless Priest! — O perjured knight!"
  I hear the Master cry;
"Shut out the vision from thy sight,
  Let Earth and Nature die!

"The Church of God is now thy spouse,
  And thou the bridegroom art;
Then let the burden of thy vows
  Crush down thy human heart!"

In vain! This heart its grief must know,
  Till life itself hath ceased,
And falls beneath the self-same blow,
  The lover and the priest!

O pitying Mother! souls of light,
  And saints, and martyrs old!
Pray for a weak and sinful knight,
  A suffering man uphold.

Then let the Paynim work his will,
  And death unbind my chain,
Ere down yon blue Carpathian hill
  The sun shall fall again.

THE HOLY LAND.

[FROM LAMARTINE.]

I HAVE not felt o'er seas of sand,
The rocking of the desert bark;
Nor laved at Hebron's fount my hand,
By Hebron's palm-trees cool and dark;
Nor pitched my tent at even-fall,
On dust where Job of old has lain,
Nor dreamed beneath its canvas wall,
The dream of Jacob o'er again.

One vast world-page remains unread;
How shine the stars in Chaldea's sky,
How sounds the reverent pilgrim's tread,
How beats the heart with God so nigh! —
How round gray arch and column lone
The spirit of the old time broods,
And sighs in all the winds that moan
Along the sandy solitudes!

In thy tall cedars, Lebanon,
I have not heard the nations' cries,
Nor seen thy eagles stooping down
Where buried Tyre in ruin lies.
The Christian's prayer I have not said,
In Tadmor's temples of decay,
Nor startled with my dreary tread,
The waste where Memnon's empire lay.

Nor have I, from thy hallowed tide,
  O, Jordan! heard the low lament,
Like that sad wail along thy side,
  Which Israel's mournful prophet sent!
Nor thrilled within that grotto lone,
  Where deep in night, the Bard of Kings
Felt hands of fire direct his own,
  And sweep for God the conscious strings.

I have not climbed to Olivet,
  Nor laid me where my Saviour lay,
And left his trace of tears as yet
  By angel eyes unwept away;
Nor watched at midnight's solemn time,
  The garden where His prayer and groan,
Wrung by His sorrow and our crime,
  Rose to One listening ear alone.

I have not kissed the rock-hewn grot,
  Where in His Mother's arms He lay,
Nor knelt upon the sacred spot
  Where last His footsteps pressed the clay;
Nor looked on that sad mountain head,
  Nor smote my sinful breast, where wide
His arms to fold the world He spread,
  And bowed His head to bless — and died!

www.ingramcontent.com/pod-product-compliance
Lightning Source LLC
LaVergne TN
LVHW020109110826
845151LV00001B/109
* 9 7 8 1 4 2 5 5 4 3 4 0 2 *